THE THOMAS JEFFERSON PAPERS

THE PAPERS OF THE FOUNDING FATHERS

THE
THOMAS JEFFERSON
PAPERS

SELECTED WITH COMMENTARY BY

FRANK DONOVAN

DODD, MEAD & COMPANY

NEW YORK

Printed in the United States of America

APOLLO EDITION

This book is
dedicated to
Nick, Muriel,
Kathy, Susan
and Chris

IN EXPLANATION AND
ACKNOWLEDGMENT

Before the days of Noah Webster's dictionary and the development
of rigid rules of punctuation, a writer was allowed more freedom
to express his personal idiosyncrasies in handling the language. If
Jefferson chose to write, in the Declaration of Independence, that
certain colonial rights were "unacknologed," that was his privilege;
and if he refrained from beginning a sentence with a capital letter—as he invariably did—that, too, was his right.

In reproducing the papers of the past, there are two schools of
thought as to what should be done about this. The purist says that
they should be printed exactly as written. The popularizer says that
spelling, capitalization and punctuation should be modernized for
easier readability so long as this does not change the sense of what
was written. The latter practice has been followed in this book—
although Jefferson's reference to the great state of "Techas" was
omitted with reluctance.

Many of the papers included here have been abridged, but a
sincere effort has been made not to quote out of context, so that
Jefferson's ideas and meanings are carefully preserved. Deletions
are indicated by an ellipses (. . .).

All of the research for this book was done in the great library
of Yale University, with the unfailing assistance of members of its
staff. It was not necessary to go back to original documents in the
Library of Congress and several other depositories. Many scholarly editors have done this for more than a century, and the modern
writer may proceed from their research. The first collected writings

of Jefferson were published by his grandson, Thomas Jefferson Randolph, in 1829, in four volumes under the title *Memoirs, Correspondence and Miscellaneous from the Papers of Thomas Jefferson*. Next came nine volumes of *The Writings of Thomas Jefferson* edited by Henry A. Washington in 1853. This was followed by another *Writings of Thomas Jefferson* in ten volumes edited by Paul Leicester Ford, published between 1892 and 1899, and reissued in twelve volumes in 1904. The most recent collection, bearing the same title, is the twenty-volume edition edited in 1903–1904 by A. A. Lipscomb and A. E. Bergh.

None of these works is complete. A full presentation of the papers of the great Virginian will have to await the completion of *The Papers of Thomas Jefferson* which are currently being edited by Julian Boyd at Princeton University. It is estimated that this work will comprise fifty-two volumes. Sixteen have appeared since publication was started in 1950. It may be almost a generation before this work is completed.

In the Library of Congress catalogue, under the subject of Jefferson, there are more than four hundred entries. These include many collections of writings and anthologies in special fields, as well as scores of biographies. Among the many worthy biographies that have appeared since George Tucker wrote the first in 1837 are books by James Parton (1874), John T. Morse (1883), David S. Muzzey (1919), Claude G. Bowers (1925), Albert J. Nock (1926), Francis W. Hirst (1926), Gilbert Chinard (1929), Saul Padover (1942) and Nathan Schachner (1951).

More recently, Marie Kimball had completed the first three volumes of a biography that takes Jefferson's life to 1789, and Dumas Malone has published the first three of five volumes, covering Jefferson's life to the beginning of his first term as President, entitled *Jefferson and His Time*. This will become the definitive biography of Jefferson when the final volumes are published. In the meantime, a word should be said for the three-volume biography written by Henry Randall in 1858. Modern writers are customarily contemptuous of most ante bellum nineteenth-century biographers, but Randall, at least, is an exception. Although the reader must accept a certain political bias, and an understandable partiality to his subject, Randall's work, after more than a century, remains the most complete and satisfactory narrative of Jefferson's life.

CONTENTS

᭙

CONTENTS

Extended quotations from Thomas Jefferson and others appear in the larger of the two sizes of type used for the text.

CHAPTER I

THE FIRST FOURTH

❦

At 6 A.M. on July 4, 1776, the temperature in Philadelphia was 68 degrees, according to an entry in Thomas Jefferson's account book. This is one of the few facts about that memorable day which has not been the subject of controversy. Even other aspects of the weather are disputed. Jefferson said "fine sunshine, pleasant morning wind S.E." Years later another member of the Congress wrote that it was raining.

Jefferson, invariably an early riser, was up with the sun in his lodgings "in the house of a Mr. Graaf, a new brick house three stories high of which," he wrote, "I rented the second floor consisting of a parlor and bedroom ready furnished." A few hours later he started, reluctantly, toward the State House, pausing en route to buy a thermometer—for which, according to his account book, he paid the surprisingly high price of three pounds, fifteen shillings—and seven pairs of gloves for Mrs. Jefferson.

The reluctance of the grave Virginian to take his seat in the small room off the entrance to what is now called Independence Hall was due to the fact that the Second Continental Congress there assembled would continue, as they had for two days past, to pick apart the announcement he had written to proclaim a very important congressional resolution.

In fact, Jefferson was somewhat reluctant to be in Philadelphia in July of 1776. The Virginia Convention was in session in Williamsburg and, a week after his arrival in Philadelphia on May 14, Jefferson had written to a fellow member of that body: "Should our Convention propose now to establish a form of government, perhaps it might be agreeable to recall for a short time their delegates [from the Continental Congress]. It is work of the most interesting nature and such as every individual would wish to have his voice in. . . . In the other colonies who have instituted government they recalled their delegates, leaving only one or two to give information to Congress of matters which relate to their country particularly." Jefferson's "country" was Virginia. He considered what was happening in Williamsburg more vital than what might happen in Philadelphia.

The story of the first Fourth starts on May 15, 1776, in Williamsburg, when the Virginia Convention voted to instruct its delegates to propose independence for the colonies to the Continental Congress. On June 7 the senior member of the Virginia delegation, Richard Henry Lee, offered a resolution:

THAT THESE UNITED COLONIES are, and of right ought to be free and independent states, that they are absolved from all allegiance to the British crown, and that all political connection between them and the state of Great Britain is, and ought to be totally dissolved.

That it is expedient forthwith to take the most effectual measures for forming foreign alliances.

That a plan of confederation be prepared and transmitted to the respective colonies for their consideration and approbation.

John Adams of Massachusetts seconded Lee's motion. Jefferson

picks up the tale in the "Notes" which are incorporated in his
autobiography.

THE HOUSE being obliged to attend at that time to some other
business, the proposition was referred to the next day when
the members were ordered to attend punctually at ten o'clock.

Saturday June 8. They proceeded to take it into consideration and referred it to a committee of the whole, into which
they immediately resolved themselves, and passed that day
and Monday, the tenth in debating on the subject.

It was argued by Wilson, Robert R. Livingston, E. Rutledge,
Dickinson and others:

That though they were friends to the measures themselves,
and saw the impossibility that we should ever again be united
with Great Britain, yet they were against adopting them at this
time:

That the conduct we had formerly observed was wise and
proper now, of deferring to take any capital step till the voice
of the people drove us into it: that they were our power, and
without them our declarations could not be carried into effect:

That the people of the middle colonies (Maryland, Delaware, Pennsylvania, the Jerseys and New York) were not yet
ripe for bidding adieu to British connection, but that they
were fast ripening, and in a short time would join in the general voice of America. . . .

That if such a declaration should now be agreed to, these
delegates must retire, and possibly their colonies might secede
from the Union:

That such a secession would weaken us more than could be
compensated by any foreign alliance:

That in the event of such a division, foreign powers would
either refuse to join themselves to our fortune, or having us
so much in their power as that desperate declaration would
place us, they would insist on terms proportionally more hard
and prejudicial:

That we had little reason to expect an alliance with those to whom alone as yet we had cast our eyes:

That France and Spain had reason to be jealous of that rising power which would one day certainly strip them of all their American possessions: . . .

That it was prudent to fix among ourselves the terms on which we would form alliance, before we declared we would form one at all events:

And that if these were agreed on, and our declaration of independence ready by the time our Ambassador should be prepared to sail, it would be as well as to go into that declaration at this day.

On the other side it was urged by J. Adams, [R. H.] Lee, Wythe and others:

That no gentleman had argued against the policy or the right of separation from Britain, nor had supposed it possible we should ever renew our connection: that they had only opposed its being now declared:

That the question was not whether, by a declaration of independence, we should make ourselves what we are not; but whether we should declare a fact which already exists:

That as to the people or Parliament of England, we had always been independent of them, their restraints on our trade deriving efficacy from our acquiescence only, and not from any rights they possessed of imposing them, and that so far our connection had been federal only and was now dissolved by the commencement of hostilities: . . .

That the people wait for us to lead the way: . . .

That it would be vain to wait either weeks or months for perfect unanimity, since it was impossible that all men should ever become of one sentiment on any question:

That the conduct of some colonies from the beginning of this contest had given reason to suspect it was their settled policy to keep in the rear of the confederacy, that their particular prospect might be better even in the worst event:

That therefore it was necessary for those colonies who had thrown themselves forward and hazarded all from the beginning, to come forward now also, and put all again to their own hazard: . . .

That a declaration of independence alone could render it consistent with European delicacy for European powers to treat with us, or even to receive an Ambassador from us: . . .

That though France and Spain may be jealous of our rising power, they must think it will be much more formidable with the addition of Great Britain, and will therefore see it their interest to prevent a coalition; but should they refuse, we shall be but where we are, whereas without trying we shall never know whether they will aid us or not:

That the present campaign may be unsuccessful, and therefore we had better propose an alliance while our affairs wear a hopeful aspect: . . .

That it would be idle to lose time in settling the terms of alliance, till we had first determined we would enter into alliance: . . .

It appearing in the course of these debates that the colonies of New York, New Jersey, Pennsylvania, Deleware, Maryland and South Carolina were not yet matured for falling from the parent stem, but that they were fast advancing to that state, it was thought most prudent to wait a while for them, and to postpone the final decision to July 1. But that this might occasion as little delay as possible a committee was appointed to prepare a declaration of independence. The committee were J. Adams, Dr. Franklin, Roger Sherman, Robert R. Livingston and myself. Committees were also appointed at the same time to prepare a plan of confederation for the colonies, and to state the terms proper to be proposed for foreign alliance. The committee for drawing the declaration of independence desired me to do it.

Much has been written speculating on why Jefferson, junior

member from Virginia, was selected for the committee instead of R. H. Lee, the senior member, who had proposed the resolution, and why Jefferson was selected by the committee to write the declaration. In his autobiography, written almost thirty years later, John Adams offered this explanation:

MR. JEFFERSON had been now about a year a member of Congress, but had attended his duty in the House a very small part of the time, and, when there, had never spoken in public. During the whole time I sat with him in Congress, I never heard him utter three sentences together. It will naturally be inquired how it happened that he was appointed on a committee of such importance. There were more reasons than one. Mr. Jefferson had the reputation of a masterly pen; he had been chosen a delegate in Virginia in consequence of a very handsome public paper which he had written for the House of Burgesses. . . . Another reason was, that Mr. Richard Henry Lee was not beloved by the most of his colleagues from Virginia, and Mr. Jefferson was set up to rival and supplant him. This could be done only by the pen, for Mr. Jefferson could stand no competition with him or anyone else in elocution and public debate.

In a later letter Adams wrote:

MR. JEFFERSON came into Congress in June, 1775, and brought with him a reputation for literature, science, and a happy talent of composition. Writings of his were handed about remarkable for the peculiar felicity of expression. Though a silent member in Congress, he was so prompt, frank, explicit and decisive upon committees and in conversation, not even Sam Adams was more so, that he soon seized upon my heart, and upon this occasion I gave him my vote and did all in my power to procure the votes of others. I think he had one more vote than any other, and that placed him at the head of the committee. I had the next highest number and that placed me the second.

There were political animosities within the Congress. Adams and Lee were of one faction; some of the other Virginia delegates were of the other. There is no indication that there was any discord between Lee and Jefferson. In a sense, Jefferson was a compromise candidate. As chairman of the committee, because he was selected by the greatest number of votes, Jefferson would presumably write its report. But Adams reports a sprightly discussion between himself and Jefferson on this subject in a letter written in 1822:

THE COMMITTEE MET, discussed the subjects, and then appointed Mr. Jefferson and me to make the draft; I suppose because we were the two highest on the list. The subcommittee met; Jefferson proposed to me to make the draft.

I said, "I will not; you shall do it."

"Oh no!"

"Why will you not?"

"You ought to do it."

"I will not."

"Why?"

"Reasons enough."

"What can be your reasons?"

"Reason first. You are a Virginian and Virginia ought to appear at the head of this business. Reason second. I am obnoxious, suspected and unpopular; you are very much otherwise. Reason third. You can write ten times better than I can."

"Well," said Jefferson, "if you are decided, I will do as well as I can."

When this letter became public in 1823, Jefferson wrote to James Madison contradicting his octogenarian friend:

MR. ADAMS' MEMORY has led him into unquestionable error. At the age of eighty-eight, and forty-seven years after the transactions of independence, this is not wonderful. Nor should I, at the age of eighty, on the small adventage of that difference only, venture to oppose my memory to his, were it not supported by written notes, taken by myself at the moment and on the spot. . . .

Now these details are quite incorrect. The committee of five met; no such thing as a subcommittee was proposed, but they unanimously pressed on myself alone to undertake the draft. I consented; I drew it; but before I reported it to the committee, I communicated it separately to Doctor Franklin and Mr. Adams, requesting their corrections, because they were the two members of whose judgments and amendments I wished most to have the benefit, before presenting it to the committee: and you have seen the original paper now in my hands, with the corrections of Doctor Franklin and Mr. Adams interlined in their own handwritings. Their alterations were two or three only, and merely verbal. I then wrote a fair copy, reported it to the committee, and from them, unaltered, to Congress.

A writer in *Life* magazine recently made this wistful comment on these two letters.

THE THOUGHT of these two magnificent old men, gently quibbling via the posts, lights history with a lovely warmth. One can imagine them: Jefferson fiercely proud of his authorship; and Adams, slightly jealous of the praise heaped on Jefferson at every Fourth of July celebration, letting it be known that *he* could have written the Declaration if he had wanted to.

Jefferson wrote the Declaration between June 11 and June 28 on a little portable writing desk which was then new. Forty-nine years later his granddaughter married a Joseph Coolidge and moved to Boston. Her luggage was lost at sea, including a writing desk containing some of her grandfather's letters. To compensate for the loss, Jefferson sent her husband another small desk, four-teen inches long, ten wide and three deep, to the underside of which he attached the replacement desk's pedigree:

TH. JEFFERSON gives this writing desk to Joseph Coolidge, Jr., as a memorial of affection. It was made from a drawing of his own, by Ben Randall, cabinetmaker of Philadelphia, with whom he first lodged on his arrival in that city in May, 1776, and is the identical one on which he wrote the Declaration of Independence. Politics, as well as religion, has its superstitions. These gaining strength with time may, one day, give imaginary value to this relic, for its association with the birth of the great charter of our independence.

The writing of the Declaration did not come easy. Jefferson was seeking literary perfection in this epochal announcement and labored long over words and phrases. The full extent of his labors has only recently been appreciated. Until less than twenty years ago the earliest known version of the Declaration was what Jefferson called the rough draft, which is now in the Library of Congress. Then a scrap of paper came to light, by chance, in the Library of Congress, which indicates that the so-called rough draft was actually a fair copy of previous drafts. On this scrap is written, in Jefferson's hand, an acceptance of the resignation which Brigadier General John Sullivan tendered to Congress on July 26, 1776. But below this is a fragment of the Declaration of Independence—obviously an earlier version than the rough draft. Of the 156 words in the fragment 43 had been changed or corrected, indicating the extent to which Jefferson worked over his composition before he prepared even a rough draft.

The rough draft underwent much revision before it reached Congress. There is no clear record of the progress of the document through the committee. There is evidence that Adams and Franklin each perused it. There are two changes on it in Adams' hand and five in Franklin's. There are sixteen additional changes and three added paragraphs in Jefferson's hand. It cannot be determined whether these changes originated with Jefferson or other members of the committee. The extent to which the so-called rough draft was labored over is evident from this sample of the first part of the second paragraph:

> We hold these truths to be ~~sacred & undeniable~~ self-evident; that all men are created equal ~~& independent~~; that ~~from~~ they are endowed by their creator with ~~equal rights some of which are~~ ~~that equal creation they derive in rights~~ inherent & inalienable rights; that among ~~which~~ these are ~~the preservation of~~ life, & liberty, & the pursuit of happiness.

Jefferson's "Notes" continue the story of the Declaration:

I REPORTED IT to the House on Friday the twenty-eighth of June, when it was read and ordered to lie on the table. On Monday the 1st of July the House resolved itself into a committee of the whole and resumed the consideration of the original motion made by the delegates of Virginia, which being again debated through the day, was carried in the affirmative by the votes of New Hampshire, Connecticut, Massachusetts, Rhode Island, New Jersey, Maryland, Virginia, North Carolina and Georgia. South Carolina and Pennsylvania voted against it. Delaware having but two members present, they were divided; the delegates for New York declared they were for it themselves and were assured their constituents were for it, but that their instructions having been drawn near a twelvemonth before, when reconciliation was still the general object, they were enjoined by them to do nothing which should impede that object. They therefore thought themselves not justifiable in voting on either side, and asked leave to withdraw from the question, which was given them. The committee rose and reported their resolution to the House. Mr. Edward Rutledge of South Carolina then requested the determination might be put off to the next day, as he believed his colleagues, though they disapproved of the resolution, would then join in it for the sake of unanimity. The ultimate question whether the House would agree to the resolution of the committee was accordingly postponed to the next day, when it was again moved, and South Carolina concurred in voting for it. In the meantime a third member had come post from the Delaware counties and turned the vote of that colony in favor of the resolution. Members of a different sentiment attending that morning from Pennsylvania also, their vote was changed, so that the whole twelve colonies, who were authorized to vote at all, gave their voices for it; and within a few days the convention of New York approved of it and thus supplied the void occasioned by the withdrawing of their delegates from the vote.

Congress proceeded the same day to consider the Declaration of Independence which had been reported and laid on the table Friday preceding and on Monday referred to a committee of the whole. The pusillanimous idea that we had friends in England worth keeping terms with still haunted the minds of many. For this reason those passages which conveyed censures on the people of England were struck out, lest they should give them offense. The clause, too, reprobating the enslaving the inhabitants of Africa was struck out in complaisance [to] South Carolina and Georgia, who had never attempted to restrain the importation of slaves, and who on the contrary still wished to continue it. Our Northern brethren also I believe felt a little tender under those censures; for though their people have very few slaves themselves yet they had been pretty considerable carriers of them to others. The debates having taken up the greater parts of the second, third, and fourth days of July were, in the evening of the last, closed the Declaration was reported by the committee, agreed to by the House and signed by every member present except Mr. Dickinson. As the sentiments of men are known not only by what they receive, but what they reject also, I will state the form of the Declaration as originally reported. The parts struck out by Congress shall be distinguished by a black line drawn under them; and those inserted by them shall be placed in the margin or in a concurrent column.

The manner in which Jefferson indicated the changes made by Congress, by underlining and putting added words in the margin, is difficult to follow on the printed page. In the following Declaration, taken from the "Notes," the unchanged portion is printed in roman type, deletions made by Congress are in italics and in parentheses, words added by Congress are in capitals.

A Declaration by the Representatives of the United States of American in General Congress Assembled.

When in the course of human events, it becomes necessary for one people to dissolve the political bands which have connected them with another, and to assume among the powers of the earth the separate and equal station to which the laws of nature and of nature's God entitle them, a decent respect to the opinions of mankind requires that they should declare the causes which impel them to the separation.

We hold these truths to be self-evident; that all men are created equal; that they are endowed by their Creator with CERTAIN (*inherent and*) inalienable ([1]) rights; that among these are life, liberty, and the pursuit of happiness; that to secure these rights, governments are instituted among men,

[1] In all copies in Jefferson's hand the word is "inalienable." In the printed copy, and all subsequent copies, including the parchment one with the signatures, the word is "unalienable." It is presumed that this is a mistake of the printer's, although there is a possibility that John Adams changed it deliberately before the document was printed. Adams was a member of the group which supervised the printing, and he habitually spelled the word this way.

deriving their just powers from the consent of the governed; that whenever any form of government becomes destructive of these ends, it is the right of the people to alter or to abolish it, and to institute new government, laying its foundation on such principles, and organizing its powers in such form, as to them shall seem most likely to effect their safety and happiness. Prudence indeed will dictate that governments long established should not be changed for light and transient causes; and accordingly all experience hath shown that mankind are more disposed to suffer while evils are sufferable, than to right themselves by abolishing the forms to which they are accustomed. But when a long train of abuses and usurpations (*begun at a distinguished period and*) pursuing invariably the same object, evinces a design to reduce them under absolute despotism, it is their right, it is their duty to throw off such government, and to provide new guards for their future security. Such has been the patient sufferance of these colonies; and such is now the necessity which constrains them to ALTER (*expunge*) their former systems of government. The history of the present king of Great Britain is a history of REPEATED (*unremitting*) injuries and usurpations, ALL HAVING (*among which appears no solitary fact to contradict the uniform tenor of the rest, but all have*) in direct object the establishment of an absolute tyranny over these states. To prove this, let facts be submitted to a candid world (*for the truth of which we pledge a faith yet unsullied by falsehood*).

He has refused his assent to laws the most wholesome and necessary for the public good.

He has forbidden his governors to pass laws of immediate and pressing importance, unless suspended in their operation till his assent should be obtained; and when so suspended, he has utterly neglected to attend to them.

He has refused to pass other laws for the accommodation of large districts of people, unless those people would relinquish the right of representation in the legislature, a right inestimable to them, and formidable to tyrants only.

He has called together legislative bodies at places unusual, uncomfortable, and distant from the depository of their public records, for the sole purpose of fatiguing them into compliance with his measures.

He has dissolved representative houses repeatedly (*and continually*) for opposing with manly firmness his invasions on the rights of the people.

He has refused for a long time after such dissolutions to cause others to be elected, whereby the legislative powers, incapable of annihilation, have returned to the people at large for their exercise, the state remaining in the meantime exposed to all the dangers of invasion from without and convulsions within.

He has endeavored to prevent the population of these states; for that purpose obstructing the laws for naturalization of foreigners, refusing to pass others to encourage their migrations hither, and raising the conditions of new appropriations of lands.

He has OBSTRUCTED (*suffered*) the administration of justice (*totally to cease in some of these states*) BY refusing his assent to laws for establishing judiciary powers.

He has made (*our*) judges dependent on his will alone, for the tenure of their offices, and the amount and payment of their salaries.

He has erected a multitude of new offices (*by a self-assumed power*) and sent hither swarms of new officers to harass our people and eat out their substance.

He has kept among us in times of peace standing armies (*and ships of war*) without the consent of our legislatures.

He has affected to render the military independent of, and superior to the civil power.

He has combined with others to subject us to a jurisdiction foreign to our constitutions and unacknowledged by our laws, giving his assent to their acts of pretended legislation for quartering large bodies of armed troops among us; for protecting them by a mock trial from punishment for any murders which they should commit on the inhabitants of these states; for cutting off our trade with all parts of the world; for imposing taxes on us without our consent; for depriving us IN MANY CASES of the benefits of trial by jury; for transporting us beyond seas to be tried for pretended offenses; for abolishing the free system of English laws in a neighboring province, establishing therein an arbitrary government, and enlarging its boundaries, so as to render it at once an example and fit instrument for introducing the same absolute rule into these COLONIES (*states*); for taking away our charters, abolishing our most valuable laws, and altering fundamentally the forms of our governments; for suspending our own legislatures, and declaring themselves invested with power to legislate for us in all cases whatsoever.

He has abdicated government here BY DECLARING US OUT OF HIS PROTECTION, AND WAGING WAR AGAINST US (*withdrawing his governors, and declaring us out of his allegiance and protection*).

He has plundered our seas, ravaged our coasts, burnt our towns, and destroyed the lives of our people.

He is at this time transporting large armies of foreign mercenaries to complete the works of death, desolation, and tyranny already begun with circumstances of cruelty and perfidy SCARCELY PARALLELED IN THE MOST BARBAROUS AGES, AND TOTALLY unworthy the head of a civilized nation.

He has constrained our fellow citizens taken captive on the high seas to bear arms against their country, to become the executioners of their friends and brethren, or to fall themselves by their hands.

He has EXCITED DOMESTIC INSURRECTIONS AMONG US, AND HAS endeavored to bring on the inhabitants of our frontiers the merciless Indian savages, whose known rule of warfare is an undistinguished destruction of all ages, sexes, and conditions (*of existence*).

(*He has incited treasonable insurrections of our fellow citizens, with the allurements of forfeiture and confiscation of our property.*)

(*He has waged cruel war against human nature itself, violating its most sacred rights of life and liberty in the persons of a distant people who never offended him, captivating and carrying them into slavery in another hemisphere, or to incur miserable death in their transportation thither. This piratical warfare, the opprobrium of infidel powers, is the warfare of the CHRISTIAN king of Great Britain. Determined to keep open a market where MEN should be bought and sold, he has prostituted his negative for suppressing every legislative attempt to prohibit or to restrain this execrable commerce. And that this assemblage of horrors might want no fact of distinguished die, he is now exciting those very people to rise in arms among us, and to purchase that liberty of which he has deprived them, by murdering the people on whom he also obtruded them: thus paying off former crimes committed against the liberties of one people with crimes which he urges them to commit against the lives of another.*)

In every stage of these oppressions we have petitioned for redress in the most humble terms: our repeated petitions have been answered only by repeated injuries.

A prince whose character is thus marked by every act which may define a tyrant is unfit to be a ruler of a FREE people (*who mean to be free. Future ages will scarcely believe that the hardiness of one man adventured, within the short compass of twelve years only, to lay a foundation so broad and so undisguised for tyranny over a people fostered and fixed in principles of freedom.*)

Nor have we been wanting in attentions to our British brethren. We have warned them from time to time of attempts

by their legislature to extend AN UNWARRANTABLE
(*a*)jurisdiction over US (*these our states*). We have reminded
them of the circumstances of our emigration and settlement
here, (*no one of which could warrant so strange a pretension:
that these were effected at the expense of our own blood and
treasure, unassisted by the wealth or the strength of Great
Britain; that in constituting indeed our several forms of government, we had adopted one common king, thereby laying a
foundation for perpetual league and amity with them: but that
submission to their parliament was no part of our constitution,
nor ever in idea, if history may be credited: and*) we HAVE
appealed to their native justice and magnanimity AND WE
HAVE CONJURED THEM BY (*as well as to*) the ties of
our common kindred to disavow these usurpations which
WOULD INEVITABLY (*were likely to*) interrupt our connection and correspondence. They too have been deaf to the
voice of justice and of consanguinity, (*and when occasions
have been given them, by the regular course of their laws, of
removing from their councils the disturbers of our harmony,
they have by their free election, re-established them in power.
At this very time too, they are permitting their chief magistrate
to send over not only soldiers of our common blood, but Scotch
and foreign mercenaries to invade and destroy us. These facts
have given the last stab to agonizing affection, and manly spirit
bids us to renounce forever these unfeeling brethren. We must
endeavor to forget our former love for them, and hold them as
we hold the rest of mankind, enemies in war, in peace friends.
We might have been a free and a great people together; but a
communication of grandeur and of freedom it seems is below
their dignity. Be it so, since they will have it. The road to happiness and to glory is open to us, too. We will tread it apart
from them, and*) WE MUST THEREFORE acquiesce in the
necessity which denounces our (*eternal*) separation AND
HOLD THEM AS WE HOLD THE REST OF MANKIND,
ENEMIES IN WAR, IN PEACE FRIENDS!

We, therefore, the representatives of the United States of America in General Congress assembled, appealing to the Supreme Judge of the world for the rectitude of our intentions, do in the name, and by the authority of the good people of these

(states reject and renounce all allegiance and subjection to the kings of Great Britain and all others who may hereafter claim by, through, or under them; we utterly dissolve all political connection which may heretofore have subsisted between us and the people or Parliament of Great Britain: and finally we do assert and declare these colonies to be free and independent states,) COLONIES SOLEMNLY PUBLISH AND DECLARE, THAT THESE UNITED COLONIES ARE, AND OF RIGHT OUGHT TO BE FREE AND INDEPENDENT STATES; THAT THEY ARE ABSOLVED FROM ALL ALLEGIANCE TO THE BRITISH CROWN, AND THAT ALL POLITICAL CONNECTION BETWEEN THEM AND THE STATE OF GREAT BRITAIN IS, AND OUGHT TO BE, TOTALLY DISSOLVED;

and that as free and independent states, they have full power to levy war, conclude peace, contract alliances, establish commerce, and to do all other acts and things which independent states may of right do.

And for the support of this declaration, WITH A FIRM RELIANCE ON THE PROTECTION OF DIVINE PROVIDENCE, we mutually pledge to each other our lives, our fortunes, and our sacred honor.

Jefferson's pride as an author was somewhat wounded by Congress' changes. He promptly made a copy of his rough draft and sent it, together with a printed copy of the Declaration as approved by Congress, to R. H. Lee, saying: "I enclose you a copy of the Declaration of Independence as agreed to by the House and also as originally framed. You will judge whether it is better or worse for the critics."

Apparently, he never did agree with some of the changes. In 1818 he wrote:

WHEN THE DECLARATION OF INDEPENDENCE was under the consideration of Congress, there were two or three unlucky expressions in it which gave offense to some members. The words 'Scotch and other foreign auxiliaries' excited the ire of a gentleman or two of that country. Severe strictures on the conduct of the Britsh King, in negativing our repeated repeals of the law which permitted the importation of slaves, were disapproved by some Southern gentlemen, whose reflections were not yet matured to the full abhorrence of that traffic. Although the offensive expressions were immediately yielded, these gentlemen continued their depredations on other parts of the instrument. I was sitting by Dr. Franklin, who perceived that I was not insensible to these mutilations.

In this letter he continued to describe how Franklin tried to console him by telling a story of the hatter who designed a sign reading "John Thompson, Hatter, makes and sells hats for ready money." When he showed this to a group of friends for their opinions, each of them took out one or more words as being unnecessary until he was left with a sign bearing only his name and a picture of a hat.

Actually, Jefferson was lucky in the caliber of his critics. Every writer who has submitted a piece of work to a group for approval knows that they almost invariably lengthen it—either by adding somebody's ideas or by "spelling something out" at greater length. Congress shortened the Declaration by more than 25 per cent. Most of their eighty-seven changes were in wording rather than

ideas and resulted, in most cases, in better phrasing and the elimi-
nation of nonessential words. Of the words in the Declaration as
adopted, approximately 90 per cent are Jefferson's (and the committee's) and 10 per cent are Congress'. Every student of the
Declaration agrees that virtually all the changes made by Congress
added to the literary merit of the document.

From the standpoint of content, Congress made two important
changes. They threw out altogether Jefferson's vitriolic condemnation of slavery and the slave traffic, which he blamed upon the
King. The New England colonies were doing a profitable business
in transporting slaves that were an economic necessity to the southern states. Congress eliminated Jefferson's condemnation of the
British people, who, he had written, "have by their free election
re-established . . . in power" the "disturbers of our harmony."
They also deleted his only reference to the British Parliament.
Congress wisely felt that the justification of the rebellion of the
colonies would be stronger if, instead of dissolving "all political
connection . . . between us and the people or Parliament of Great
Britain," they simply declared that the colonies were "absolved
from all allegiance to the British crown."

Congress also changed the title from Jefferson's "A Declaration
by the Representatives of the United States of America, in General
Congress assembled," to "The unanimous Declaration of the
thirteen United States of America." Officially, there is no such
thing as "The Declaration of Independence."

The purpose of the document was not to declare independence
—that had been done two days before it was adopted. Rather, it
was to proclaim and justify the act to the world. Jefferson expresses
this purpose in the strikingly beautiful and solemn first paragraph,
ending with the words: "a decent respect to the opinions of mankind requires that they should declare the causes which impel them
to the separation."

There was a twofold reason for having a momentous manifesto
to announce the act of independency. One was its emotional im-
pact on the people of the colonies. The other—and perhaps the

primary purpose in the minds of Congress—was its effect on prospective allies in Europe. This was the "candid world" to which Jefferson submitted facts concerning the tyranny of George III in a series of impressive paragraphs starting with the reiterative "He has."

Jefferson directed his charges at the King to prove that George III had deliberately, and with malice aforethought, tyrannized the colonies to an extent that they were justified in taking action to escape his despotism. Historically, Jefferson's point of view was not correct. There were instances to support every charge that he made, but they were not all attributable to George III. Many were the result of carelessness, stupidity or ignorance on the part of British colonial officials in America and abroad. But Jefferson was not concerned with writing history—he was making it.

It was hard to justify the right of rebellion against any monarch to the sovereigns of Europe, who believed that all kings ruled by divine right. Jefferson sought to do it by setting up, in the beginning of the second paragraph of the Declaration, a political philosophy under which a people have a right to overthrow their government when it seeks "to reduce them under absolute despotism" by suppressing their natural rights as free men. The theory of natural rights is the sole basis under which Jefferson sought to make this rebellion respectable. He did not present the charges against the King as justifications for rebellion, but to prove the malevolent purpose of George to suppress the inalienable rights of the colonists.

Finally, Jefferson sought to convince the world that the colonists had suffered patiently as martyrs under this oppression—they had "petitioned for redress in the most humble terms" until the situation became unbearable. Obviously, he did not mention the unpopular stamp officials who were tarred and fathered by Sons of Liberty, the tea that was dumped in Boston harbor, nor the rocks that were thrown at Lobsterbacks. His list of charges claimed that it was solely George's deliberate and purposeful tyranny which had brought the colonists to the point where they had to either throw off the yoke or submit to slavery. For free men there could be but one choice.

In 1823 Timothy Pickering, a staunch Federalist, sought to belittle Jefferson's contribution to independence and "to show how little was his merit in compiling" the Declaration. In a Fourth of July speech he quoted a letter from John Adams concerning the Declaration in which the latter said:

... THERE IS NOT AN IDEA in it, but what had been hackneyed in Congress for two years before. The substance of it is contained in the Declaration of Rights and the violation of those rights, in the *Journal of Congress* in 1774. Indeed, the essence of it is contained in a pamphlet, voted and printed by the Town of Boston before the first Congress met, composed by James Otis, as I suppose—in one of his lucid intervals, and pruned and polished by Sam Adams.

Jefferson commented on this in a letter to James Madison:

PICKERING'S OBSERVATIONS, and Mr. Adams' in addition, "that it contained no new ideas, that it is a commonplace compilation, its sentiments hackneyed in Congress for two years before, and its essence contained in Otis' pamphlet," may all be true. Of that I am not to be the judge. Rich. H. Lee charged it as copied from Locke's treatise in government. Otis' pamphlet I never saw, and whether I had gathered my ideas from reading or reflection I do not know. I know only that I turned to neither book or pamphlet while writing it. I did not consider it as any part of my charge to invent new ideas altogether.

Two years later Jefferson wrote to R. H. Lee that he was only trying to express the ideas of men who all agreed on the principles embodied in the Declaration. The important thing, wrote Jefferson, was:

NOT TO FIND OUT new principles, or new arguments, never before thought of; not merely to say things which had never been said before; but to place before mankind the common sense of the subject, [in] terms so plain and firm as to command their assent, and to justify ourselves in the independent stand we [were] impelled to take. Neither aiming at originality of principle or sentiment, nor yet copied from any particular and previous writing, it was intended to be an expression of the American mind. . . . All its authority rests then on the harmonizing sentiments of the day, whether expressed in conversation, in letters, printed essays, or the elementary books of public right, as Aristotle, Cicero, Locke, Sidney, etc.

The attempt to criticize Jefferson's creation on the grounds that the ideas on which it was based did not originate with him was patently ridiculous. He could not possibly have justified a rebellion based on principles which nobody had ever heard of. The philosophy of the natural rights of man had been expressed by Rousseau in France, by Locke in England—among others. It was an accepted theory among liberals throughout Europe as well as in the colonies. Only on such a recognized basis could the rebellion be justified.

But Jefferson's statement that he "turned to neither book or pamphlet" may be questioned by one who would split hairs. He certainly copied from a document which he had previously written, and probably leaned on another which was written by a fellow Virginian, George Mason, and published in the Philadelphia newspapers during June, 1776.

The previous document written by Jefferson was titled "Constitution of Virginia. First ideas of Th. J. communicated to a member of the Convention," which he sent to Williamsburg on June 13. This included most of the charges against George III. These were incorporated in the preamble of the Virginia Constitution. In several cases the wording of the charges sent to Virginia and those in the Declaration is identical. Jefferson later wrote:

THE FACT IS that the preamble was prior in composition to the Declaration, and both having the same object, of justifying our separation from Great Britain, they have used necessarily the same materials of justification: hence their similitude.

In the Virginia Constitution, immediately following the charges against the King, is George Mason's "Bill of Rights," which Jefferson had undoubtedly read in the Philadelphia papers within a few days before he started to write the Declaration. The ideas in the Virginia Bill of Rights did not originate with Mason any more than they did with Jefferson, but Jefferson's contribution to the acceptance of the theory of natural rights is evident from a comparison of the way the two men expressed the same idea. Mason's first paragraph read:

THAT ALL MEN are born equally free and independent and have certain inherent rights, of which they cannot, by any compact, deprive or divest their posterity; among which are the enjoyment of life and liberty, with the means of acquiring and possessing property, and pursuing and obtaining happiness and safety.

Jefferson expressed the same thought by writing:

WE HOLD THESE TRUTHS to be self-evident: that all men are created equal; that they are endowed by their Creator with inherent and inalienable rights; that among these are life, liberty, and the pursuit of happiness.

Mason's paragraph is a pedantic philosophical thesis—Jefferson's is singing prose.

What happened after the Declaration was adopted on the first Fourth involves one mystery and one major controversy. The mystery has to do with what might be called the "original copy" of the Declaration. The controversy has to do with who signed what—if anybody signed anything—on July 4.

It seems incredible that no record was kept, no letter was written, containing the details of that memorable evening—Jefferson said that the event culminated in the evening. But it must be remembered that the Declaration was, in a way, an anticlimax. The important event had taken place on the second of July, and there are numerous contemporary letters commenting on this. Also, the Congress was meeting as a committee of the whole during the debate on the Declaration, so that no minutes were kept.

In 1825 Jefferson wrote that the rough draft "is now in my possession, and a fair copy of this was reported to the committee and passed by them without amendment, and then reported to Congress; this paper should be among the records of the old Congress." No "fair copy" was with the papers of Congress, nor is there any referenc to such a copy except that made by Jefferson. There has been some speculation that there never was a fair copy; that Jefferson's memory was at fault. This does not seem likely for several reasons. The Secretary of the Congress, Charles Thomson, must have made the changes in some copy as they were ordered by Congress, yet the rough draft was apparently in Jefferson's hands. He made the changes on this either at the time they were ordered or later in conformity to some other copy. It is beyond reason that the rough draft, which, with its changes, cannot be read without a glass, would have been sent to the printer; yet the Declaration was printed from some copy on the night of July 4. The printed copies, which were delivered to Congress on the fifth, end with the words "Signed by order and in behalf of Congress, John Hancock, President. Attest, Charles Thomson, Secretary." The compositor must have had some copy to set this from, and the words are not on the rough draft.

If there was a fair copy—and it seems obvious that there was

—what happened to it? There is an opinion that it was destroyed after the fully signed parchment copy came into existence. Another possibility is that it never came back from the printer—some unknown compositor threw away the original of the Declaration of Independence.

The controversy regarding the signing started in 1817. Thomas McKean, a member of the Second Congress from Delaware, wrote in a letter:

Now THAT I am on this subject, I will tell you some truths, not generally known. In the printed public *Journal of Congress* for 1776, vol. 2, it would appear that the Declaration of Independence was signed on the fourth July by the members, whose names are there inserted, but the fact is not so, for no person signed it on that day nor for many days after. . . .

However, Jefferson's "Notes" say:

. . . THE DEBATES having taken up the greater part of the second, third, and fourth days of July were, in the evening of the last, closed the Declaration was reported by the committee, agreed to by the House and signed by every member present except Mr. Dickinson.

After this controversy started—forty-one years after the Declaration was adopted—Jefferson inserted a slip of paper into his original "Notes" on which is written, "I took notes in my place while these things were going on, and at their close wrote them out in form and correctness." It would seem that if Jefferson made a record at the time that the Declaration was signed on July 4 there should be no question about it. Yet most scholars who have studied all the evidence are of the opinion that the Declaration was not signed on that day.

They base this opinion on the following points. (1) There is no signed paper copy and it seems unreasonable that a signed copy would have been handled carelessly or destroyed. (2) Neither the rough Journal of Congress, the corrected Journal, nor the secret Journal mention the signing. (3) The printed copy has the names of Hancock and Thomson—if there were other signatures the printer would have reproduced them as well as these two. (4) On July 9, five days after the event, John Adams wrote: "As soon as an American seal is prepared I conjecture the Declaration will be subscribed by all the members." (5) On July 21 Elbridge Gerry, another member of the Congress, wrote: "Pray subscribe for me ye Declaration of Independence if ye same is to be signed as proposed"—his letter implies that he had not previously signed, although he had been present on the fourth. (6) The Journals of Congress note a resolution for the fourth that the Declaration should be "authenticated and printed"; the notation for the nineteenth states that it is to be "engrossed and signed."

The signed parchment copy of the Declaration which is now on view in the Library of Congress was ordered on July 19 by a resolution which said: "Resolved that the Declaration passed on the fourth be fairly engrossed on parchment with the title and style of 'The Unanimous Declaration of the Thirteen United States of America' and that the same be signed by every member of Congress." On August 2 the *Journal* states, "The Declaration of Independence being engrossed and compared at the table was signed."

Some of the August 2 signers were not members of Congress on July 4, and some members signed after August 2. One, Matthew Thornton, did not join Congress until November 4. Another argument against the July 4 signing is that the New York delegates could not have signed; their Convention did not give its approval until July 9.

The large majority of scholars who argue against a July 4 signing discount Jefferson's "Notes" on one of two grounds. There is evidence that he did not write his notes out "in form and correctness" immediately. He did it sometime later, possibly many years later. They reason that Jefferson took very sketchy notes at the time and filled them out much later from memory and the printed

Journal of Congress. This time lapse would account for an error.

The other explanation of the "Notes" is based on a reinterpretation of the sentence, "The debates having taken up the greater part of the second, third and fourth days of July were, in the evening of the last, closed the Declaration was reported by the committee, agreed to by the House and signed by every member present except Mr. Dickinson." There is punctuation missing in this sentence. There should be either a semicolon or a period after the word "closed." Since Jefferson habitually did not capitalize the first letter of a sentence, it might as well be the latter as the former. If this statement is broken into two sentences the words "in the evening of the last" may apply only to "the debates" and not to "signed by every member." Under this interpretation Jefferson's "Notes" might refer to the signing on August 2.

This seems to be a wealth of logical evidence, although it is all negative. On the other side, in addition to Jefferson's "Notes," there is a letter from Benjamin Franklin to his sister dated July 4, 1786, in which he wrote, "There is much rejoicing in town today, it being the anniversary of the Declaration of Independence, which we signed this day ten years, and thereby hazarded lives and fortunes." There is also a letter from John Adams in 1814, which says; "The final vote for independence, after the last debate, was passed on the second or third of July and the Declaration prepared and signed on the fourth. What are we to think of history when in less than forty years such diversities appear in the memories of living persons who were witnesses?" Finally, there is in existence a printed copy of the *Journal of Congress* for 1776 containing marginal notes in the handwriting of Thomson saying that the New York delegates signed on July 15.

It is very unlikely that this controversy will ever be resolved. Most informed opinion is on the side of no signing on July 4, explaining the contrary statements of Jefferson, Franklin and Adams by the fact that they were old men when they made them. It seems rather strange to ignore the evidence of men like these even if they were in their eighties.

A supposition that has not previously been advanced is that some members might have autographed the document informally on the evening of July 4. When Hancock banged his gavel to adjourn the session it seems possible that some members, who felt very strongly about the Declaration, might have walked to Thomson's table and written their names on the paper copy laying thereon, while others left the room. This would explain all of the "evidence" on both sides of the controversy except Jefferson's statement that it was signed "by every member present except Mr. Dickinson"—which could be accounted for by repunctuating the "Notes."

Jefferson's final comment on the Fourth of July was contained in the last letter that he wrote—fifty years after the first Fourth and ten days before his death. He had been invited to attend a fiftieth-anniversary celebration. In declining he wrote, of his country's national holiday:

I SHOULD, INDEED, with peculiar delight, have met and exchanged there congratulations personally with the small band, the remnant of that host of worthies, who joined with us on that day in the bold and doubtful election we were to make for our country, between submission or the sword; and to have enjoyed with them the consolatory fact, that our fellow citizens, after half a century of experience and prosperity, continue to approve the choice we made. May it be to the world, what I believe it will be (to some parts sooner, to others later, but finally to all) the signal of arousing men to burst the chains under which monkish ignorance and superstition had persuaded them to bind themselves, and to assume the blessings and security of self-government. That form which we have substituted restores the free right to the unbounded exercise of reason and freedom of opinion. All eyes are opened, or opening, to the rights of man. The general spread of the light of science has already laid open to every view the palpable truth; that the mass of mankind has not been born with saddles on their backs, nor a favored few booted and spurred, ready to ride them legitimately, by the grace of God. These are grounds of hope for others. For ourselves, let the annual return of this day forever refresh our recollections of these rights, and an undiminished devotion to them.

CHAPTER II

THE MAKING OF A VIRGINIAN

⟑

"As to myself, I wish that not only no act but no thought of mine shall be unknown." To effectuate this wish Thomas Jefferson wrote more than eighteen thousand letters in which his acts in many areas and his thoughts on countless subjects are recorded. Yet, paradoxically, nobody knows Thomas Jefferson. His voluminous writings, so potent with ideas on many subjects and replete with information on many things, give but a vague concept of the man in whom a great intellect was housed. In trying to learn to know him through his writings one must agree with historian Henry Adams who wrote, "Jefferson could be painted only touch by touch, with a fine pencil, and the perfection of the likeness depended upon the shifting and uncertain flicker of its semi-transparent shadows."

Jefferson wrote an autobiography. Like that of fellow Founding Father Franklin, it was unfinished. This is the only point of similarity between the two works. Franklin's is still one of the greatest autobiographies in the English language. Jefferson's, as an autobiography, is one of the most unsatisfactory documents in American history. He covers in two pages the history of his family, his boyhood, his education, his study of law and his admission to the state legislature—a period of twenty-six years. He then devotes nine pages to explaining the arguments advanced by various members of the Continental Congress in connection with the Articles of Confederation of the colonies. There are but terse referments to his wife and children. But the causes of the French Revolution are presented in great detail.

The reason for the lack of intimate knowledge of the great Virginian's feelings and emotions—as opposed to his thoughts and ideas—was his almost pathological passion for privacy in matters personal. There is ample evidence that he was a devoted family man with a deep affection for his wife and children and a passionate attachment to his home. Yet references to what went on behind the walls of Monticello are almost nonexistent in his writings. Scholars who have tried to describe Jefferson have used the adjectives "shy," "remote," "impenetrable," "sensitive to criticism." They have remarked that it was impossible for him to be familiar. Yet the same scholars have commented on his graciousness, his approachability, his easy manners—have used such phrases as "delightful of acquaintance," "good companionship." The qualities mentioned are, in many cases, opposites. This is part of the paradox of Jefferson.

For what it is worth, his autobiography describes the first twenty-four years of his life as follows:

January 6, 1821

AT THE AGE of seventy-seven, I begin to make some memoranda, and state some recollections of dates and facts concerning myself, for my own more ready reference, and for the information of my family.

The tradition in my father's family was that their ancestor came to this country from Wales, and from near the mountain of Snowdon, the highest in Great Britain. I noted once a case from Wales, in the law reports, where a person of our name was either plaintiff or defendant; and one of the same name was secretary to the Virginia Company. These are the only

instances in which I have met with the name in that country.
I have found it in our early records; but the first particular information I have of any ancestor was of my grandfather, who
lived at the place in Chesterfield called Ozborne's, and owned
the lands afterwards the glebe of the parish. He had three sons;
Thomas who died young, Field who settled on the waters of
Roanoke and left numerous descendants, and Peter, my father,
who settled on the lands I still own, called Shadwell, and joining my present residence. He was born February 29, 1707–8,
and intermarried 1739 with Jane Randolph, of the age of
nineteen, daughter of Isham Randolph, one of the seven sons
of that name and family, settled at Dungeoness in Goochland.
They trace their pedigree far back in England and Scotland,
to which let every one ascribe the faith and merit he chooses.

My father's education had been quite neglected; but being
of a strong mind, sound judgment, and eager after information,
he read much and improved himself, insomuch that he was
chosen, with Joshua Fry, professor of mathematics in William
and Mary college, to continue the boundary line between Virginia and North Carolina, which had been begun by Colonel
Byrd; and was afterwards employed, with the same Mr. Fry,
to make the first map of Virginia which had ever been made,
that of Captain Smith being merely a conjectural sketch. They
possessed excellent materials for so much of the country as is
below the Blue Ridge; little being then known beyond that
ridge. He was the third or fourth settler, about the year 1737,
of the part of the country in which I live. He died August 17,
1757, leaving my mother a widow, who lived till 1776, with
six daughters and two sons, myself the elder. To my younger
brother he left his estate on James River, called Snowdon,
after the supposed birthplace of the family; to myself, the lands
on which I was born and live.

He placed me at the English school at five years of age, and
at the Latin at nine, where I continued until his death. My
teacher, Mr. Douglas, a clergyman from Scotland, with the

rudiments of the Latin and Greek languages, taught me the French; and on the death of my father, I went to the Reverend Mr. Maury, a correct classical scholar, with whom I continued two years; and then, to wit, in the spring of 1760, went to William and Mary college, where I continued two years. It was my great good fortune, and what probably fixed the destinies of my life, that Dr. William Small of Scotland, was then professor of mathematics, a man profound in most of the useful branches of science, with a happy talent of communication, correct and gentlemanly manners and an enlarged and liberal mind. He, most happily for me, became soon attached to me, and made me his daily companion when not engaged in the school; and from his conversation I got my first views of the expansion of science, and of the system of things in which we are placed. Fortunately, the philosophical chair became vacant soon after my arrival at college, and he was appointed to fill it *per interim:* and he was the first who ever gave, in that college, regular lectures in ethics, rhetoric and belles-lettres. He returned to Europe in 1762, having previously filled up the measure of his goodness to me by procuring for me, from his most intimate friend, George Wythe, a reception as a student of law, under his direction, and introduced me to the acquaintance and familiar table of Governor Fauquier, the ablest man who had ever filled that office. With him, and at his table, Dr. Small and Mr. Wythe, his *amici omnium horarum* [friends of all hours], and myself, formed a *partie quarée* [party of four] and to the habitual conversations on these occasions I owed much instruction. Mr. Wythe continued to be my faithful and beloved mentor in youth, and my most affectionate friend through life. In 1767, he led me into the practice of the law at the bar of the General court, at which I continued until the Revolution shut up the courts of justice.

Something more than these bare facts is known. His birth date —one of the personal facts which he neglected to include in his autobiography—was April 2, 1743, by the calendar then in use; April 13 by the current calendar. He was born a gentleman. His mother, whose pedigree Jefferson brushes off so lightly in his autobiography, was from one of the first families of Virginia. His father was a planter of the second class—not a land baron like the Randolphs, the Byrds, the Fairfaxes or the Carters, but he left not an inconsiderable estate of about 7,500 acres. His son Thomas inherited approximately 2,650 of them.

Jefferson was not part of the log-cabin frontier, but he spent much of his boyhood near it. Albemarle County was in the second tier of counties behind the frontier, but its proximity to the wilderness is evident from the county records of the frequent bounties paid on wolves while Jefferson was growing up. The close proximity of the primeval to civilization as young Jefferson knew it is evident from a letter he wrote, in later life, to John Adams:

SO MUCH IN ANSWER to your inquiries concerning Indians, a people with whom, in the early part of my life, I was very familiar, and acquired impressions of attachment and commiseration for them which have never been obliterated. Before the Revolution, they were in the habit of coming often and in great numbers to the seat of government, where I was very much with them. I knew much of the great Ontassete, the warrior and orator of the Cherokees; he was always the guest of my father, on his journeys to and from Williamsburg. I was in his camp when he made his great farewell oration to his people, the evening before his departure for England. The moon was in full splendor, and to her he seemed to address himself in his prayers for his own safety on the voyage, and that of his people during his absence; his sounding voice, distinct articulation, animated action, and the solemn silence of his people at their several fires, filled me with awe and veneration, although I did not understand a word he uttered.

The first authoritative biography of Jefferson was written in

1858, when its writer, Henry Randall, could interview Jefferson's grandchildren. Historically the stories that they told of Jefferson's boyhood were in the nature of legends or family traditions. They describe a boy who was even then a study in contrasts—a violin-playing bookworm who was at home in the woods, was a good shot and an excellent horseman.

The first school that he mentions was conducted by a parson in a little outbuilding at the home of William Randolph, of whose estate Peter Jefferson was executor. The second and third schools, those of Mr. Douglas and Mr. Maury, were parsonages at which he boarded during the school term. The old account books show that Douglas was paid sixteen pounds sterling per annum for teaching and boarding the future founding father; Maury was paid twenty pounds. He finished this phase of his education at the age of seventeen, three years after his father's death. It was then that he wrote the first Jefferson "paper" of which there is any record—a letter to his guardian, John Harvie:

Shadwell, January 14, 1760

SIR, I was at Colonel Peter Randolph's about a fortnight ago, and my schooling falling into discourse, he said he thought it would be to my advantage to go to the college, and was desirous I should go, as indeed I am myself for several reasons. In the first place, as long as I stay at the mountains the loss of one fourth of my time is inevitable, by company's coming here and detaining me from school. And likewise my absence will in a great measure put a stop to so much company, and by that means lessen the expenses of the estate in housekeeping. And on the other hand by going to the college I shall get a more universal acquaintance, which may hereafter be serviceable to me; and I suppose I can pursue my studies in the Greek and Latin as well there as here, and likewise learn something of the mathematics. I shall be glad of your opinion.

When Jefferson came down from the hills to the College of

William and Mary in Williamsburg he was already a good classical scholar, reading Greek and Roman writers in the original, and speaking French, probably with a brogue as his early tutors were Scotsmen. He later wrote:

AMONG THE VALUES of a classical education, I estimate the luxury of reading the Greek and Roman authors in all the beauty of their originals. . . . I think myself more indebted to my father for this than for all the other luxuries his cares and affections have placed within my reach.

Physically, William and Mary did not make a favorable impression on its most famed student. He described its buildings as "rude, misshapen piles, which but that they had roofs, would be taken for brick kilns." Fortunately, Jefferson came under the close influence of the one oustanding member of the faculty. For almost the entire twenty-five months of his college career his sole professor was the Dr. William Small whom he lauds so highly in his autobiography. Small introduced him to physics and mathematics of which Jefferson later wrote:

HAVING TO CONDUCT my grandson through his course of mathematics, I have resumed that study with great avidity. It was ever my favorite one. We have no theories there, no uncertainties remain in the mind; all is demonstration and satisfaction.

If Jefferson wrote anything describing his life at college it has never come to light. Dr. Small introduced him to George Wythe who later taught him law and, still later, signed his Declaration of Independence. These two procured for him, wrote Jefferson,

. . . THE ATTENTIONS of Governor Fauquier, the ablest man who ever filled the chair of government there. They were inseparable friends, and at their frequent dinners with the Governor (after his family had returned to England), he admitted me always, to make it a *partie quarrae*. At these dinners I have heard more good sense, more rational and philosophical conversation, than in all my life besides. They were truly Attic societies. The Governor was musical also, and a good performer, and associated me with two or three other amateurs in his weekly concerts.

This *partie quarrae* was a strangely assorted foursome. The Governor, who had lost his fortune at cards, was in his middle fifties, Small probably in his mid-forties, and Wythe about thirty-five. Jefferson was entering his twenties when the association started. How well Jefferson played the violin in the concerts that he mentions is another subject of speculation. He once said that he practiced three hours a day in the years before the Revolution, and of music he wrote, "This is the favorite passion of my soul, and fortune has cast my lot in a country where it is a state of deplorable barbarism."

Jefferson is quoted as saying that he studied for fifteen hours a day. A schoolmate later wrote that "He used to be seen with his Greek grammar in his hand while his comrades were enjoying relaxation in the intervals of school hours." In later years he plagued his children, grandchildren and nephews with advice based on his cult of diligence: "It is while you are young that the cult of industry is formed," he wrote. "If not then it never is afterwards." And again, "Determine never to be idle." Or, "No person will have occasion to complain about the want of time who never loses any." His principal reference to this period was in a letter of advice to a grandson written in 1808:

YOUR SITUATION, thrown at such a distance from us, and alone, cannot but give us all great anxieties for you. As much has been secured for you, by your particular position and the acquaintance to which you have been recommended, as could be done towards shielding you from the dangers which surround you. But thrown on a wide world, among entire strangers, without a friend or guardian to advise, so young too and with so little experience of mankind, your dangers are great, and still your safety must rest on yourself. A determination never to do what is wrong, prudence and good humor, will go far towards securing to you the estimation of the world. When I recollect that, at fourteen years of age, the whole care and direction of myself was thrown on myself entirely, without a relation or friend qualified to advise or guide me, and recollect the various sorts of bad company with which I associated from time to time, I am astonished I did not turn off with some of them, and become as worthless to society as they were. I had the good fortune to become acquainted very early with some characters of very high standing, and to feel the incessant wish that I could ever become what they were. Under temptations and difficulties, I would ask myself what would Dr. Small, Mr. Wythe, Peyton Randolph do in this situation? What course in it will insure me their approbation? I am certain that this mode of deciding on my conduct tended more to its correctness than any reasoning powers I possessed. Knowing the even and dignified line they pursued, I could never doubt for a moment which of two courses would be in character for them. Whereas, seeking the same object through a process of moral reasoning, and with the jaundiced eye of youth, I should often have erred. From the circumstances of my position, I was often thrown into the society of horse racers, card players, fox hunters, scientific and professional men, and of dignified men; and many a time have I asked myself, in the enthusiastic moment of the death of a fox, the victory of a favorite horse, the issue of a question eloquently argued at the bar, or in the great council of the nation, well, which of these kinds of reputation should I prefer? That of a horse jockey—a fox hunter—an orator? Or the honest advocate of my country's rights? Be assured, my dear Jefferson, that these little returns into ourselves, this self-catechizing habit, is not trifling nor useless, but leads to the prudent selection and steady pursuit of what is right.

Jefferson's picture of himself as a deserted teen-ager in a cruel world, "without a relation or friend . . . to advise or guide me," is not quite accurate. He was a moderately wealthy and well-loved half orphan. In addition to his guardian, John Harvie, he had several capable, interested and influential distaff relatives. And there was his mother—although Jefferson never believed that any woman, even his mother, was qualified to "advise or guide."

There are several Jefferson letters extant, written when he was nineteen and twenty years old, that present a somewhat different picture of his life and interests in Williamsburg. Most of these were written to John Page—a boyhood friend and later Governor of Virginia. This one was sent from the home of a relative on Christmas Day, 1762. The "old Coke" to which he refers is a lawbook. The picture in the watch was of Rebecca Burwell, sister of a classmate.

Fairfield, December 25, 1762

DEAR PAGE, This very day, to others the day of greatest mirth and jollity, sees me overwhelmed with more and greater misfortunes than have befallen a descendant of Adam for these thousand years past, I am sure; and perhaps, after excepting Job, since the creation of the world. I think his misfortunes were somewhat greater than mine: for although we may be pretty nearly on a level in other respects, yet, I thank my God, I have the advantage of brother Job in this, that Satan has not as yet put forth his hand to load me with bodily afflictions. You must know, dear Page, that I am now in a house surrounded with enemies, who take counsel together against my soul; and when I lay me down to rest, they say among themselves, come let us destroy him. I am sure if there is such a thing as a Devil in this world, he must have been here last night and have had some hand in contriving what happened to me. Do you think the cursed rats (at his instigation, I suppose) did not eat up my pocketbook, which was in my pocket, within a foot of my head? And not contented with plenty for the present, they carried away my jemmy-worked silk garters, and half a dozen new minuets I had just got, to serve, I suppose, as provision for the winter. But of this I should not have accused the Devil, because, you know rats will be rats, and hunger, without the addition of his instigations, might have urged them to do this, if something worse, and from a different quarter, had not happened. You know it rained last night, or if you do not know it, I am sure I do. When I went to bed, I laid my watch in the usual place, and going to take her up after I arose this morning, I found her in the same place, it's true! but . . . all afloat in water, let in at a leak in the roof of the house, and as silent and still as the rats that had eaten my pocketbook. Now, you know, if chance had had anything to do in this matter, there were a thousand other spots where it might have chanced to leak as well as this one, which was perpendicularly over my watch. But I'll tell you: it's my opinion that the Devil came and bored the hole over it on purpose. Well, as I was saying, my poor watch had lost her speech. I should not have cared much for this, but something worse attended it; the subtle particles of the water with which the case was filled, had, by their penetration, so overcome the cohesion of the particles of the paper, of which my dear picture and watch paper were composed, that, in attempting to take them out to dry them . . . ! my cursed fingers gave them such a rent, as I fear I never shall get over. This, cried I, was the last stroke Satan had in reserve for me: he knew I cared not for anything else he could do to me, and was determined to try this last most fatal expedient. . . . I would have cried bitterly, but I thought it beneath the dignity of a man . . . However, whatever misfortunes may attend the picture . . . there is so lively an image of her imprinted in my mind, that I shall think of her too often, I fear, for my peace of mind; and too often,

I am sure, to get through old Coke this winter; for God knows I have not seen him since I packed him up in my trunk in Williamsburg. Well, Page, I do wish the Devil had old Coke, for I am sure I never was so tired of an old dull scoundrel in my life. . . . As brother Job says (who, by the bye, I think began to whine a little under his afflictions) "Are not my days few? Cease then, that I may take comfort a little before I go whence I shall not return, even to the land of darkness, and the shadow of death." But the old fellows say we must read to gain knowledge, and gain knowledge to make us happy and admired. *Mere jargon!* Is there any such thing as happiness in this world? No. And as for admiration, I am sure the man who powders most, perfumes most, embroiders most, and talks most nonsense, is most admired. Though to be candid, there are some who have too much good sense to esteem such monkeylike animals as these, in whose formation, as the saying is, the tailors and barbers go halves with God Almighty; and since these are the only persons whose esteem is worth a wish, I do not know but that, upon the whole, the advice of these old fellows may be worth following. . . .

Remember me affectionately to all the young ladies of my acquaintance, particularly the Miss Burwells, and Miss Potters, and tell them that though that heavy earthly part of me, my body, be absent, the better half of me, my soul, is ever with them; and that my best wishes shall ever attend them. . . . I would fain ask the favor of Miss Becca Burwell to give me another watch paper of her own cutting, which I should esteem much more, though it were a plain round one, than the nicest in the world cut by other hands—however, I am afraid she would think this presumption, after my suffering the other to get spoiled. If you think you can excuse me to her for this, I should be glad if you would ask her. Tell Miss Sukey Potter that I heard, just before I came out of town, that she was offended with me about something, what it is I do not know; but this I know, that I never was guilty of the least disrespect

to her in my life, either in word or deed; as far from it as it
has been possible for one to be. . . . Tell—tell—in short tell
them all ten thousand things more than either you or I can now
or ever shall think of as long as we live.

Of the thousands of Jefferson letters a few early epistles, written
during the first two years of his law studies, are the only ones in
which he cast reticence aside and bared his young emotions. The
romance with sixteen-year-old Rebecca Burwell came to naught.
He asked for Page's advice in his courtship. From Shadwell he
wrote; "Had I better stay here and do nothing, or go down and
do less? . . . Inclination tells me to go, receive my sentence, and
be no longer in suspense: but reason says, if you go, and your
attempt proves unsuccessful, you will be ten times more wretched
than ever." But, later in the same letter, he intimates that he would
not really be so wretched by writing:

HAVE YOU AN INCLINATION to travel, Page? Because if you
have, I shall be glad of your company. For you must know
that . . . I shall visit particularly England, Holland, France,
Spain, Italy (where I would buy me a good fiddle) and Egypt,
and return through the British provinces to the northward,
home. This to be sure, would take us two or three years, and
if we should not both be cured of love in that time, I think
the Devil would be in it.

He later suggested to Page that the latter sound out the young
lady as to whether she would like to wait until Jefferson finished
his travels, and finally he made a somewhat desultory proposal
which he described to Page:

IN THE MOST MELANCHOLY FIT that ever any poor soul was, I
sit down to write to you. Last night, as merry as agreeable
company and dancing with Belinda in the Apollo [a room in
the Raleigh Tavern] could make me, I never could have

thought the succeeding sun would have seen me so wretched as I now am! I was prepared to say a great deal: I had dressed up in my own own mind, such thoughts as occurred to me, in as moving language as I knew how, and expected to have performed in a tolerably creditable manner. But, good God! When I had an opportunity of venting them, a few broken sentences, uttered in great disorder, and interrupted with pauses of uncommon length, were the too visible marks of my strange confusion! The whole confab I will tell you, word for word, if I can, when I see you, which God send may be soon.

Rebecca was not interested in waiting while her suitor made the grand tour. Her marriage to another in 1764 started twenty-one-year-old Jefferson on a brief period of misogyny. After the "affair Burwell" the student settled down at Shadwell to read law with his customary diligence.

Perhaps the best example of the regime that Jefferson practiced —and there is no reason to doubt that he practiced what he preached—is contained in a letter of advice that he wrote to a law student shortly after he himself had been admitted to the bar. It outlines an almost incredible daily study program from dawn to long after dark, for Jefferson always burned much midnight oil. Apparently there was no violin playing during these years, nor any of the long walks that he later insisted were essential to physical fitness.

THE CARRYING ON several studies at a time is attended with advantage. Variety relieves the mind as well as the eye, palled with too long attention to a single object, but, with both, transitions from one object to another may be so frequent and transitory as to leave no impression. The mean is therefore to be steered, and a competent space of time allotted to each branch of study. Again, a great inequality is observable in the vigor of the mind at different periods of the day. Its powers at these periods should therefore be attended to in marshalling the business of the day. For these reasons I should recommend the following distribution of your time. Till eight o'clock in the morning, employ yourself in physical studies, ethics, religion, natural and sectarian, and natural law, reading . . . books [on] agriculture . . . chemistry . . . anatomy . . . zoology . . . botany . . . ethics and . . . religion. . . .

From eight to twelve read law. . . . In reading the Reporters, enter in a commonplace book every case of value, condensed into the narrowest compass possible, which will admit of presenting distinctly the principles of the case. This operation is doubly useful, insomuch as it obliges the student to seek out the pith of the case, and habituates him to a condensation of thought, and to an acquisition of the most valuable of all talents, that of never using two words where one will do. It fixes the case, too, more indelibly in the mind.

From twelve to one read politics . . . In the afternoon read history . . . ancient . . . modern . . . English . . . American. . . .

From dark to bedtime: belles-lettres; criticism; rhetoric; oratory, . . . Read the best of the poets, epic, didactic, dramatic, pastoral, lyric, etc.; but among these, Shakespeare must be singled out by one who wishes to learn the full powers of the English language. . . . This portion of time (borrowing some of the afternoon when the days are long and the nights short) is to be applied also to acquiring the art of writing and speaking correctly by the following exercises: Criticize the style of any book whatsoever, committing the criticism to writing. Translate into the different styles, *to wit,* the elevated, the middling, and the familiar. Orators and poets will furnish subjects of the first, historians of the second, and epistolary and comic writers of the third. Undertake, at first, short compositions as themes, letters, etc., paying great attention to the elegance and correctness of your language. Read the orations of Demosthenes and Cicero; analyze these orations, and examine the correctness of the disposition, language, figures, state of the cases, arguments, etc.; read good samples also of English eloquence . . . Exercise yourself afterwards in preparing orations on feigned cases.

Of this, and similar early papers Jefferson later said: "They were written at a time of life when I was bold in the pursuit of knowledge, never fearing to follow truth and reason to whatever results they led and bearding every authority which stood in their way." Actually, there was never a time in Jefferson's life when he was not "bold in the pursuit of knowledge."

As a lawyer Jefferson was thorough, well grounded, sincere and relatively inarticulate. He was not temperamentally capable of emotionally moving a jury, and his voice grew so husky as to be almost inaudible during a long speech.

Among Jefferson's papers are the digests of only two cases that he tried. In one he appeared for the plaintiff—in this case, the underdog. He said that the case

. . . WAS REFERRED TO THE DETERMINATION of the court, on the facts stated by the counsel for both parties, which were, that the plaintiff's grandmother was a mulatto, begotten of a white woman by a Negro man, after the year 1705, and bound by the church wardens, under the law of that date, to serve to the age of thirty-one. That after the year 1723, but during her servitude, she was delivered of the plaintiff's mother, who, during her servitude, to wit, in 1742, was delivered of the plaintiff, and he again was sold by the person to whom his grandmother was bound, to the defendant, who now claims his service till he shall be thirty-one years of age . . . I suppose it will not be pretended that the mother being a servant, the child would be a servant also under the law of nature, without any particular provision of the act. Under the law of nature all men are born free, everyone comes into the world with a right to his own person, which includes the liberty of moving and using it at his own will. This is what is called personal liberty, and is given him by the Author of nature, because necessary for his own sustenance. The reducing of the mother to servitude was a violation of the law of nature: surely then the same law cannot prescribe a continuance of the violation to her issue, and that too without end, for if it extends to any, it must be to every degree of descendants . . . so that the position at first laid down is now proven, that the act of 1705 makes servants of the first mulatto, that of 1723 extends it to her children, but that it remains for some future legislature, if any shall be found wicked enough, to extend it to the grandchildren and other issue more remote.

Jefferson lost the case to Wythe, who appeared for the defense. The courts of Virginia were not ready for an argument based on the premise that "all men are created equal."

There are no wonderful Lincolnesque anecdotes of a circuit-riding Jefferson. The Virginian was not the stuff of which anecdotes are made. An impression of his life in Williamsburg during this period may be gained from a few excerpts from his account book:

APRIL 11, paid for seeing an elk 7½ [pence]. April 18, paid at playhouse 5/. April 27, paid for play tickets 22/6[22 shillings, 6 pence]. April 29, paid at playhouse 10/. April 30, paid at concert 5/.

May 2, paid at playhouse 5/. May 5, paid at a concert 5/. May 6, paid at playhouse 5/. May 7, gave Jupiter [his body servant] to pay Bramer for candles 4/, Mayer for bread 7½, Burdet for candles 2/6. May 25, paid Dr. Pasteur for violin £5. May 30, paid for play tickets 15/. Paid Cary Wilkerson for books 26/. Paid at playhouse for punch 3/9.

June 1, paid T. Skinner for pineapples and oranges 12/6. June 17, paid Bailis for pomatum 1/3. June 18, gave in charity 20/. June 20, paid at concert for tickets 20/. August 20, paid at Read's for whisky 6/. Won at shooting 1/6. September 4, paid at Hornsby's for fiddlestrings 3/.

1769: —April 11, paid for seeing a hog weighing more than 1,050 pounds 1/. April 14, paid for seeing a puppet show 7/6. April 17, paid towards publishing a poem I never saw nor ever wish to see 2/6. Paid at Singleton's for punch 1/6. Paid for two tickets at puppet show 5/.

May 5, paid at Charlton's for arrack 5/. May 30, gave Mr. Maury to pay for books in England . . . £7–10. June 20, paid women at Staunton for singing 3d.3/4. June 21, lost at pitchers with T. Bowyer 7d.½. June 23, paid at Bowyer's for punch 2/. Paid T. Bowyer for entertainment 1–19. Lost with Mr. Madison at pitchers 7d.½. June 27, gave in charity 20/.

August 11, paid at race at Charlottesville 5/9. September 21, gave a woman to buy cakes 5/. September 30, lost shooting at Moon's muster 2/6. Paid at Moon's muster for brandy 12/6. October 17, paid Craig for mending microscope and perspective glass 2/6. October 23, paid legerdemain man 2/6. Paid at playhouse for punch 1/6. October 24, gave an Indian 3d.3/4. October 27, paid for seeing a tiger 1/3.

From the frequent reference to the playhouse, concerts, puppet shows and shooting matches, it is obvious that the young bachelor was not, at this time, studying fifteen hours a day. The entries relating to whisky, brandy and wagers are misleading. Among contemporary young Virginia gentlemen, gambling, heavy drinking and horse racing were the order of the day. Jefferson's gambling was limited to a rare small wager. His grandson said that he did not know one card from another. For most of his life his drinking was limited to light wines and beer. Part of his living was gained by growing and selling tobacco, but he did not smoke. And, although he always owned the finest horses, there is but a single recorded instance of his entering one in a race.

Shadwell, his mother's home, burned down in 1770, "and in it" wrote Jefferson, "every paper I had in the world and almost every book. On a reasonable estimate I calculate the cost of the books burned to have been two hundred pounds sterling. Would to God it had been the money, *then* had it never cost me a sigh. . . . If this conflagration, by which I was burned out of a home, had come before I had advanced so far in preparing another, I do not know but I might have cherished some treasonable thoughts of leaving these my native hills."

The other home which he mentioned was started in 1768. In his account book is an entry: "Work to be done at Hermitage. Plant raspberries—gooseberries—currants—strawberries—asparagus—artichokes—fill up trees—sow grass—hen house—cherry tree—lucerne—road—wagoning wood and sand." The word "Hermitage" is crossed out and the name "Monticello" written in. Another item in the account book reads: "May 15, agreed with Mr. Moore that he shall level 250 ft. square on the top of the mountain at the N.E. end by Christmas, for which I am to give 180 bushels of wheat, and 24 bushels of corn, 12 of which are not to be paid till corn comes in. If there should be any solid rock to dig we will leave to indifferent men to settle that part between us." Unlike most planters of the day, who built along the riverbanks, Jefferson selected a site on a mountain top overlooking Shadwell. Compared to the distant Blue Ridge which could be viewed from its crest it was a "little mountain"—in Italian, Monticello.

By February, 1771, he could write: "I have lately removed to the mountain from whence this is dated. . . . I have here but one room which, like the cobbler's, serves me for parlor, for kitchen and hall. I may add, for bedchamber and study, too. . . . I have hope, however, of getting more elbow room this summer." Family tradition has it that this one-room house is the home to which he brought Mrs. Jefferson, although his records indicate that much building was done during the remainder of 1771.

Where he brought his bride has to be legend because Jefferson's only mention of his marriage is this from his autobiography.

ON THE FIRST of January, 1772, I was married to Martha Skelton, widow of Bathurst Skelton, and daughter of John Wayles, then twenty-three years old. Mr. Wayles was a lawyer of much practice, to which he was introduced more by his great industry, punctuality and practical readiness, than by eminence in the science of his profession. He was a most agreeable companion, full of pleasantry and good humor, and welcomed in every society. He acquired a handsome fortune, and died in May, 1773, leaving three daughters: the portion which came on that event to Mrs. Jefferson, after the debts should be paid, which were very considerable, was about equal to my own patrimony, and consequently doubled the ease of our circumstances.

Jefferson's oldest daughter left an account of the marriage trip:

THEY LEFT THE FOREST after a fall of snow, light then, but increasing in depth as they advanced up the country. They were finally obliged to quit the carriage and proceed on horseback. Having stopped for a short time at Blenheim, where an overseer only resided, they left it at sunset to pursue their way through a mountain track rather than a road, in which the snow lay from eighteen inches to two feet deep, having eight miles to go before reaching Monticello. They arrived late at night, the fires all out and the servants retired to their own houses for the night. The horrible dreariness of such a house, at the end of such a journey, I have often heard both relate.

Except for Martha Jefferson's household accounts, indicating that she was a good and efficient housekeeper, and the records of the birth of six children, all but two of whom died in infancy, nothing more is positively known of Jefferson's married life.

Sometime before his marriage Jefferson had intimated what should be expected from a wife in a rather curious document which he either composed, or copied from an unknown source.

SWEETNESS OF TEMPER, affection to a husband and attention

to his interests constitute the duties of a wife and form the basis of matrimonial felicity.

The charms of beauty and the brilliancy of wit, though they may captivate in the mistress, will not long delight in the wife: they will shorten even their own transitory reign if, as I have often seen, they shine more for the attraction of everybody else than their husbands. . . .

Never consider as a trifle what may tend to please him. The great articles of duty he will set down as his own. . . .

But wedlock, even in its happiest lot, is not exempted from the common fate of all sublunary blessings. The rapture of extravagant love will evaporate and waste; the conduct of the wife must substitute in its room, other regards, as delicate and more lasting. . . .

The office of a wife includes the exertion of a friend. There are situations where it will not be enough to love, to cherish, to obey: she must teach her husband to be at peace with himself, to be reconciled to the world, etc., etc.

There are afflictions less easy to be endured. Those which a husband inflicts, and the best wives feel most severely. The fortitude that can resist can only cure. Complaints debase her who suffers, and harden him who aggrieves. Let not a woman always look for their cause in the injustice of her lord: They may proceed from many trifling errors in her own conduct. . . .

Above all, let a wife beware of communicating to others any want of duty or tenderness she may think she has perceived in her husband. This untwists, at once, those delicate cords which preserve the unity of the marriage engagements. Its sacredness is broken forever, if third parties are made witnesses of its failings.

I am astonished at the folly of many women who are still reproaching their husbands for leaving them alone, preferring this or that company to theirs, for treating them with this or the other mark of disregard or indifference, when to speak the truth, they have themselves in a great measure to blame, not

that I would justify the men in any thing wrong on their part;
but had you behaved to them with a more respectful observance, and a more equal tenderness, studying their humors,
overlooking their mistakes, submitting to their opinions in
matters indifferent, passing by little instances of unevenness,
caprice, or passion, giving soft answers for hasty words, complaining as seldom as possible and making your daily care to
relieve their anxieties. . . .

Although this paper is undated the handwriting indicates that it
was undoubtedly written in the 1760s, probably in the "post-Bur-
well" period. Although Mrs. Jefferson is a faint shadow in history,
there is no evidence that she was the pallid handmaiden that the
document describes—or that Jefferson so treated her. His deep
grief at her death, in 1782, is well authenticated. In his autobiography he merely said, of her death, "I . . . lost the cherished companion of my life, in whose affections, unabated on both sides, I
had lived the last ten years in uncheckered happiness." His daughter Martha, then ten years old, later wrote of her father's grief:

As A NURSE, no female ever had more tenderness or anxiety.
He nursed my poor mother in turn with Aunt Carr and her
own sister, sitting up with her and administering her medicines
and drink to the last. For four months that she lingered, he
was never out of calling; when not at her bedside, he was writing in a small room which opened immediately at the head of
her bed. A moment before the closing scene, he was led from
the room almost in a state of insensibility by his sister, Mrs.
Carr, who with great difficulty, got him into the library, where
he fainted, and remained so long insensible that they feared
he never would revive. The scene that followed I did not witness; but the violence of his emotion, when almost by stealth
I entered his room at night, to this day I dare not trust myself
to describe. He kept to his room three weeks, and I was never
a moment from his side. He walked almost incessantly night

and day, only lying down occasionally, when nature was completely exhausted, on a pallet that had been brought in during his long fainting fit. . . . When at last he left his room, he rode out, and from that time he was incessantly on horseback, rambling about the mountain, the least frequented roads, and just as often through the woods. In those melancholy rambles, I was his constant companion, a solitary witness to many a voilent burst of grief.

Jefferson's sole expression of his inconsolable loss was in a letter to his sister-in-law, principally concerned with the welfare of her nieces.

THE GIRLS BEING UNABLE to assure you themselves of their welfare, the duty devolves on me, and I undertake it the more willingly as it will lay you under the necessity of sometimes letting us hear from you. They are in perfect health and as happy as if they had no part in the unmeasurable loss we have sustained. Patsy rides with me five or six miles a day and presses for permission to accompany me on horseback to Elkhill whenever I shall go there. When that may be however I cannot tell; finding myself absolutely unable to attend to anything like business. This miserable kind of existence is really too burdensome to be borne, and were it not for the infidelity of deserting the sacred charge left me, I could not wish its continuance a moment. For what could it be wished? All my plans of comfort and happiness reversed by a single event and nothing answering in prospect before me but a gloom unbrightened with one cheerful expectation. The care and instruction of our children indeed affords some temporary abstractions from wretchedness and nourishes a soothing reflection that if there be beyond the grave any concern for the things of this world there is one angel at least who views these attentions with pleasure and wishes continuance of them while she must pity the miseries to which they confine me.

Perhaps the best relic of the deep love of Martha and Thomas Jefferson is a few lines from Laurence Sterne's *Tristram Shandy*. Within a few weeks, or perhaps days, of her impending death Mrs. Jefferson wrote these, apparently from memory, down to the words "everything presses on." The remainder of the quotation is in Thomas Jefferson's hand.

TIME WASTES too fast: every letter
I trace tells me with what rapidity
life follows my pen. The days and hours
of it are flying over our heads like
time I kiss thy hand to bid adieu, every absence which
clouds of windy day never to return—
more everything presses on—and every
follows it, are preludes to that eternal separation
which we are shortly to make!

CHAPTER III

THE PUBLIC MAN IN VIRGINIA

❦

"The whole of my life has been a war with my natural tastes, feelings and wishes. Domestic life and literary pursuits were my first and latest inclinations; circumstances and not my desire led me to the path I have trod." So said Jefferson when he eagerly "shook off the shackles of power" after forty years of public life.

The first thirteen of those years, embracing the entire period of the Revolution, were spent in the service of Virginia, except for brief excursions to the second Continental Congress. He was unique among the Founding Fathers in that he served the cause within his own colony rather than on the broader national or international scene. During the war he turned down all opportunities to enter the big picture—either in Congress or with Franklin in France. He pleaded the health of his family as an excuse, but personal preference may have entered into it. Although he advocated union for the colonies, Virginia, at that time, came first.

His first public office was membership in the House of Burgesses, to which he was elected in 1769 and which he described as "the most dignified body of men ever assembled to legislate." Jefferson was immediately drawn to the one member who did not lend dignity to the assembly—fiery Patrick Henry. In the early days these two united the tongue and the pen in the cause of liberty. Later their political views diverged. In 1812 Henry Wirt, Patrick Henry's biographer, asked Jefferson to set down his recollections of the orator. Jefferson replied with a long reminiscence which, in part, reflected the opinion of his later life.

MY ACQUAINTANCE with Mr. Henry commenced in the winter of 1759–60. On my way to college I passed the Christmas holidays at Colonel Dandridge's, in Hanover, to whom Mr. Henry was a near neighbor. During the festivity of the season I met him in society every day, and we became well acquainted, although I was much his junior, being then but in my seventeenth year and he a married man. The spring following he came to Williamsburg to obtain a license as a lawyer, and he called on me at college. He told me he had been reading law only six weeks. Two of the examiners, however, Peyton and John Randolph, men of great facility of temper, signed his license with as much reluctance as their dispositions would permit them to show. Mr. Wythe absolutely refused.

Mr. Henry began his career with very little property. He acted, as I have understood, as barkeeper in the tavern at Hanover courthouse for sometime. He married very young; settled, I believe, at a place called the Roundabout in Louisa, got credit for some little store of merchandise, but very soon failed. From this he turned his views to the law, for the acquisition or practice of which, however, he was too lazy. Whenever the courts were closed for the winter session he would make up a party of poor hunters of his neighborhood; would go off with them to the piny woods of Fluvanna and pass weeks in hunting deer, of which he was passionately fond; sleeping under a tent before a fire, wearing the same shirt the whole time and covering all the dirt of his dress with a hunting shirt. He never undertook to draw pleadings if he could avoid it, or to manage that part of a cause, and very unwillingly engaged, but as an assistant, to speak in the cause.

And the fee was an indispensable preliminary, observing to the applicant that he kept no accounts, never putting pen to paper, which was true. His powers over a jury were so irresistible that he received great fees for his services, and had the reputation of being insatiable in money. . . .

The . . . great occasion on which he signalized himself was that which may be considered as the dawn of the Revolution in March, 1764. The British Parliament had passed resolutions preparatory to the levying a revenue on the colonies by a stamp tax. The Virginia assembly, at their next session, prepared and sent to England very elaborate representations addressed in separate forms to the King, Lords and Commons, against the right to impose such taxes. The famous Stamp Act was, however, passed in January, 1765, and in the session of the Virginia assembly of May following, Mr. Henry introduced the celebrated resolutions of that date. . . . They were opposed by . . . all the old members whose influence in the house had till then been unbroken. . . . But torrents of sublime eloquence from Mr. Henry . . . prevailed. . . .

I came into the legislature . . . about nine years after Mr. Henry had entered on the stage of public life. The exact conformity of our political opinions strengthened our friendship. . . . In ordinary business he was a very inefficient member. He could not draw a bill on the most simple subject which would bear legal criticism, or even the ordinary criticism which looks to correctness of style and ideas, for indeed there was no accuracy of idea in his head. His imagination was copious, poetical, sublime, but vague also. He said the strongest things in the finest language, but without logic, without arrangement, desultorily.

Henry's Stamp Act speech, on that "great occasion" to which Jefferson referred as the "dawn of the Revolution," was described by Wirt:

IT WAS IN THE MIDST of this magnificent debate, while he [Henry] was descanting on the tyranny of the obnoxious act, that he exclaimed, in a voice of thunder, and with the look of a god, "Caesar had his Brutus, Charles the First his Cromwell, and George the Third"—("Treason!" cried the Speaker, "treason! treason!" echoed from every part of the House. It was one of those trying moments which is decisive of character. Henry faltered not an instant; but rising to a loftier attitude, and fixing on the Speaker an eye of the most determined fire, he finished his sentence with the firmest emphasis)—"*may profit by their example*. If *this* be treason, make the most of it."

Of this Jefferson wrote:

I WELL REMEMBER the cry of treason, the pause of Mr. Henry at the name of George the Third, and the presence of mind with which he closed his sentence, and baffled the charge vociferated. . . .

Mr. Henry took the lead out of the hands of those who had heretofore guided the proceedings of the House, that is to say, of Pendleton, Wythe, Bland, Randolph, Nicholas. These were honest and able men, . . . but with a moderation more adapted to their age and experience. Subsequent events favored the bolder spirits of Henry, the Lees, Pages, Mason, and company, with whom I went in all points. Sensible, however, of the importance of unanimity among our constituents, although we often wished to have gone faster, we slackened our pace, that our less ardent colleagues might keep up with us; and they, on their part, differing nothing from us in principle, quickened their gait somewhat beyond that which their prudence might of itself have advised, and thus consolidated the phalanx which breasted the power of Britain. By this harmony of the bold with the cautious, we advanced with our constituents in undivided mass, and with fewer examples of separation than, perhaps, existed in any other part of the Union.

It is difficult to conceive of two men who were so opposite in most things than the patrician Jefferson and the rustic Henry. Jefferson considered his friend lazy, ill-read and avaricious. Yet the "forest-born Demosthenes," as Lord Byron dubbed Henry, had a fascination for Jefferson, who said:

IT WAS TO HIM that we were indebted for the unanimity that prevailed among us. He would address the assemblages of the people at which he was present in such strains of native eloquence as Homer wrote in . . . where he got that torrent of language is inconceivable. I have frequently shut my eyes while he spoke, and when he was done asked myself what he had said, without being able to recollect a word of it. He was no logician. He was truly a great man, however, one of enlarged views.

Jefferson's first public paper was a set of polite, routine resolutions to be presented to the new Governor, Lord Botetourt. There was nothing unusual about them except in hindsight. Jefferson would not long be sending the King's emissary a "most humble and dutiful address," nor be concerned for "his Majesty's sacred person and government" or hope that "Providence, and the royal pleasure, may long continue his lordship the happy ruler of a free and happy people." The resolutions, said Jefferson, "were accepted by the House, and Pendleton, Nicholas, myself and some others, were appointed a committee to prepare an address. The committee desired me to do it, but when presented it was thought to pursue too strictly the diction of the resolutions, and that their subjects were not sufficiently amplified. Mr. Nicholas chiefly objected to it, and was desired by the committee to draw one more at large, which he did with amplification enough, and it was accepted. Being a young man as well as a young member, it made on me an impression proportioned to the sensibility of that time of life."

After this first failure he wrote no public paper of any consequence for almost five years. There was some excitement in the

first session of the Burgesses after Jefferson was elected, which he
describes in his autobiography:

To THAT MEETING became known the joint resolutions and
address of the Lords and Commons, of 1768-9, on the proceedings in Massachusetts. Counter-resolutions, and an address to the King by the House of Burgesses, were agreed to
with little opposition, and a spirit manifestly displayed itself
of considering the cause of Massachusetts as a common one.
The Governor dissolved us, but we met the next day in the
Apollo of the Raleigh tavern, formed ourselves into a voluntary convention, drew up articles of association against the
use of any merchandise imported from Great Britain, signed
and recommended them to the people, repaired to our several
counties, and were re-elected without any other exception
than of the very few who had declined assent to our proceedings.

Nothing of particular excitement occurring for a considerable time, our countrymen seemed to fall into a state of insensibility to our situation.

This lull before the storm was certainly the happiest four or five
years of Jefferson's life, embracing as it did his marriage, the start
of his family and the establishment of Monticello—a time of
"philosophic evenings and rural days."

Jefferson kept records and made observations in three different
books during this period; his account books, his Garden Book, and
what he called his "Commonplace" Book. The first two tell the
story of the formative years of Monticello. In 1769, "four good
fellows, a lad and two girls about sixteen each in eight and one-half
hours dug in my cellar of mountain clay"; "in digging my well, at
a depth of fourteen feet, I observe one digger, one filler, one
drawer at the windlass to . . . gave one another full employment."
This note continued to say that, but for some "hard stones as large
as a man's head or larger" the digger would have had time to

spare. An orchard was laid out, "One row of pears two and a half feet apart twelve in a row . . . two rows of cherries . . . one of New York apples . . . one of peach . . . ditto apricots." And, says the account book for July 16, "Memorandum: George Dudley began on Friday fourteenth instant about my bricks. I am to give him three per thousand for molding and burning and four a week for diet."

The Garden Book was started in 1766. It was kept sporadically. In some years there is page after page of planting and harvesting records interspersed with odd facts such as "a coach and six will turn in eighty feet," or "Mrs. Wythe puts one-tenth very fine malmsey to a dry Madeira and makes a fine wine." In other years —1770 and 1776—there are no entries. Typical of the book are these items for the first seven months of 1772.

JANUARY 26, the deepest snow we have ever seen. In Albemarle it was about three feet deep. March 30, sowed a patch of later peas. July 15, cucumbers came to table. Planted out celery. Sowed a patch of peas for the fall. Planted snap beans. July 31, had Irish potatoes from the garden. Julius Shard fills the two-wheeled barrow in three minutes, and carries it thirty yards in one and a half minutes more. Now this is four loads of the common barrow with one wheel. . . . September 1, to enclose the top of mountain, the garden and fruitery, will take one thousand four hundred and fifty yards of paling. October 8, gathered two plum-peaches at Monticello. November 12, in making the Roundabout walk, three hands would make eighty yards in a day in the old field, but in the woods where they had stumps to clear, not more than forty, and sometimes twenty-five yards.

The account books contained, principally, records of expenses, but, since Jefferson carried them with him, he sometimes used them as memorandum books. The account book for 1771 contains a lengthy description of his proposed cemetery at Monticello:

CHOOSE OUT FOR a burying place some unfrequented vale in the park, where is "no sound to break the stillness but a brook, that bubbling winds among the weeds; no mark of any human shape that had been there, unless the skeleton of some poor wretch, who sought that place out to despair and die in." Let it be among ancient and venerable oaks; intersperse some gloomy evergreens . . . in the center of it erect a small Gothic temple of antique appearance. Appropriate one half to the use of my own family, the other of strangers, servants, etc. Erect pedestals with urns, etc., and proper inscriptions. . . . On the grave of a favorite and faithful servant might be a pyramid erected of the rough rock stone; the pedestal made plain to receive an inscription. Let the exit . . . look on a small and distant part of the blue mountains. In the middle of the temple an altar, the sides of turf, the top of plain stone. Very little light, perhaps none at all, save only the feeble ray of a half-extinguished lamp.

Although Jefferson wrote no public papers during the early 1770s, his admission to the house of Burgesses obviously directed his thinking into new channels. His account book for 1769 lists an order for fourteen books, all dealing with the theory of government, instead of his usual assortment of books on literature, law and other subjects over which his fertile mind ranged. In English there were a *History of Parliament,* Locke's *On Government, Determinations of the House of Commons, Civil Society, Political Economy,* Ellis' *Tracts on Liberty;* in French there were Burlamaqui's *Le Droit Naturel* and *Oeuvres de Montesquieu;* in Latin, *Modus Tenendi Parliamentum.*

Entries in the Commonplace Book indicate his trend of thought at this time. This book contains 905 numbered items, all except the last few of which were obviously written before 1776. The first 749 items relate solely to law. But then Jefferson started to copy down opinions relating to government from many sources— all of them liberal. The whole pattern of these notes shows that

Jefferson, lawyerlike, was seeking precedent for the ideas of the relation of the government to the governed that were forming in his mind. He seemed to be seeking proof that the oldest forms of government known to the primitive peoples of Europe were based on popular sovereignty. For instance,

717. STANYAN SAYS that the first kings of Greece were elected by the free consent of the people. They were considered chiefly as the leaders of their armies. Thucydides therefore observes that under Cerops and the other ancient kings of Attica till the time of Theseus the king was not consulted but in time of danger; for that each city had its own magistrates and courts, by which they carried on the ordinary course of government, and were a sort of commonwealth within themselves. The kings however from their credit and good conduct found means to enlarge their powers, to extend them to the civil administration, and to become absolute. But coming in process of time to abuse their trust, the people, as opportunity offered, resumed the power in their own hands; and this gave rise to so many different forms of government in Greece.

In the Commonplace Book he also noted precedents for colonies asserting their independence:

718. CORINTH PLANTED its two famous colonies of Syracuse and Corcyra. . . . These colonies were at first subject to Corinth their metropolis, and were governed much after the same manner, but as they increased in power, they renounced their obedience; Stanyan speaks of the inhabitants of Mycenae throwing off their dependence on Argos. Question what was that dependence, and whether they were a colony of Argos?

Most of the comments of this character in the Commonplace Book related to the theory of natural rights as expressed by others, rather than to facts of history. The most interesting is item 832, which says:

THOSE WHO ALLEGE that the Parliament of Great Britain have power to make laws binding the American colonies reason in the following manner: "that there is and must be in every state a supreme, irresistible, absolute, uncontrolled authority in which the *jura summi imperii,* or the rights of sovereignty reside. *Blackstone 48, 49.* That this supreme power, is, by the constitution of Great Britain, vested in the King, Lords and Commons. *Blackstone 50, 51.* That therefore the acts of the King, Lords, and Commons, or in other words, acts of Parliament, have by the British constitution a binding force on the American colonies, they composing a part of the British empire." I admit that the principle on which this argument is founded is of great importance; its importance however is derived from its tendency to promote the ultimate end of all government, but if the application of it would in *any* instance, destroy, instead of promoting, that end it ought in *that* instance to be rejected: for to admit it would be to sacrifice the end to the means, which are valuable only so far as they would advance it. —Will it then ensure and increase the happiness of the American colonies, that the Parliament of Great Britain should possess a supreme, irresistible, uncontrolled authority over them? *Wilson's Considerations on the Nature and Extent of the Legislative Authority of the British Parliament.*

Wilson's "Considerations" to which he refers in the last sentence was written in America, probably in 1770. Jefferson's article 832, except for the legal references to Blackstone, is a copy of Wilson's first two paragraphs—but, strangely, he did not copy Wilson's third paragraph which expressed the essence of the Declaration of Independence:

(C) ALL MEN ARE, by nature, equal and free: No one has a

right to any authority over another without his consent: All lawful government is founded on the consent of those who are subject to it: Such consent was given with a view to ensure and to increase the happiness of the governed above what they could enjoy in an independent and unconnected state of nature. The consequence is, that the happiness of the society is the first law of every government.

There has been much scholarly discussion as to whom Jefferson leaned on in connection with these ideas. There can be no unanimity of opinion, because he obviously leaned on no one man. As he said, he "turned to no written book or pamphlet," but he had thoroughly studied all opinion in this area before he wrote anything on it.

His first public paper in which he expressed these ideas was titled by Jefferson merely *Instructions*, but it is generally known as *A Summary View of the Rights of British America*, a title which it was given when it was printed. He outlined the background for this paper in his autobiography:

THE LEGISLATURE OF VIRGINIA happened to be in session in Williamsburg when news was received of the passage, by the British Parliament, of the Boston Port Bill, which was to take effect on the first day of June then ensuing. The House of Burgesses thereupon passed a resolution, recommending to their fellow citizens that that day should be set apart for fasting and prayer to the Supreme Being, imploring him to avert the calamities then threatening us, and to give us one heart and one mind to oppose every invasion of our liberties. The next day, May the twentieth, 1774, the Governor dissolved us. We immediately repaired to a room in the Raleigh tavern, about one hundred paces distant from the Capitol, formed ourselves into a meeting, Peyton Randolph in the chair, and came to resolutions, declaring that an attack on one colony to enforce arbitrary acts ought to be considered as an attack on all and to be opposed by the united wisdom of all. We therefore appointed a committee of correspondence to address letters to the Speakers of the several Houses of Representatives of the colonies, proposing the appointment of deputies from each to meet annually in a General Congress to deliberate on their common interests and on the measures to be pursued in common. The members then separated to their several homes, except those of the committee, who met the next day, prepared letters according to instructions and dispatched them by messengers express to their several destinations. It had been agreed, also, by the meeting that the Burgesses, who should be elected under the writs then issuing, should be requested to meet in convention on a certain day in August to learn the results of these letters and to appoint delegates to a Congress, should that measure be approved by the other colonies. At the election the people re-elected every man of the former Assembly as a proof of their approbation of what they had done.

Before I left home to attend the convention I prepared what I thought might be given, in instruction, to the delegates who should be appointed to attend the General Congress proposed. They were drawn in haste, with a number of blanks, with some uncertainties and inaccuracies of historical facts, which I neglected at the moment, knowing they could be readily corrected at the meeting.

A Summary View started by suggesting that the Virginia delegates to the first Continental Congress propose a petition to the King, "penned in the language of truth, and divested of those expressions of servility which would persuade his Majesty that we are asking favors, and not rights." The petition should start by reminding the King that:

OUR ANCESTORS, before their emigration to America, were the free inhabitants of the British dominions in Europe, and possessed a right, which nature has given to all men, of departing from the country in which chance, not choice, has placed them, of going in quest of new habitations and of there establishing new societies, under such laws and regulations as, to them, shall seem most likely to promote public happiness. That their Saxon ancestors had, under this universal law, in like manner, left their native wilds and woods in the north of Europe, had possessed themselves of the island of Britain, then less charged with inhabitants, and had established there that system of laws which has so long been the glory and protection of that country. Nor was ever any claim of superiority or dependence asserted over them, by that mother country from which they had migrated: and were such a claim made, it is believed his Majesty's subjects in Great Britain have too firm a feeling of the rights derived to them from their ancestors, to bow down the sovereignty of their state before such visionary pretensions. And it is thought that no circumstance has occurred to distinguish, materially, the British from the Saxon emigration.

It is interesting that Benjamin Franklin had already made this point of the Germanic origin of the English in his *Edict of the King of Prussia,* a hoax that he published in the British press in which he caused Frederick of Prussia to place the same restrictions on his "colonists" in England as Britain had placed on the American colonists. Franklin used this as a piece of humorous propaganda to arouse public sympathy in England. Jefferson, a more thorough student of history, apparently thought it was a valid argument. *A Summary View* continued:

AMERICA WAS CONQUERED, and her settlements made and firmly established, at the expense of individuals, and not of the British public. Their own blood was split in acquiring lands for their settlement, their own fortunes expended in making that settlement effectual. For themselves they fought, for themselves they conquered, and for themselves alone they have right to hold. . . . That settlement having been thus effected in the wilds of America, the emigrants thought proper to adopt that system of laws under which they had hitherto lived in the mother country, and to continue their union with her by submitting themselves to the same common sovereign, who was thereby made the central link connecting the several parts of the empire thus newly multiplied.

Jefferson then outlined acts of Parliament to which he objected, during reigns preceding that of George III, ending with the statement:

BUT . . . WE DO NOT point out to his Majesty the injustice of these acts with intent to rest on that principle the cause of their nullity; but to show that experience confirms the propriety of those political principles which exempt us from the jurisdiction of the British Parliament. The true ground on which we declare these acts void is that the British Parliament has no right to exercise authority over us.

In claiming that Parliament had no authority over the colonies Jefferson went much farther than anyone else had yet gone publicly. Others were merely questioning Parliament's right to impose certain taxes—although a few years earlier Franklin had taken much the same position as Jefferson in a letter to his son. Also, Jefferson's premise that the allegiance of the colonies to the King was voluntary was a new thought. Jefferson continued by saying:

THUS HAVE WE HASTENED through the reigns which preceded his Majesty's, during which the violation of our rights was less alarming because repeated at more distant intervals than that rapid and bold succession of injuries which is likely to distinguish the present from all other periods of American story [history]. Scarcely have our minds been able to emerge from the astonishment into which one stroke of parliamentary thunder has involved us, before another more heavy and more alarming is fallen on us. Single acts of tyranny may be ascribed to the accidental opinion of the day; but a series of oppressions, begun at a distinguished period, and pursued unalterably through every change of ministers, too plainly prove a deliberate, systematical plan of reducing us to slavery.

Then followed a list of the abuses during George III's reign— an act passed in the fifth year of his reign, entitled "an act for granting and applying certain stamp duties." In the sixth year, "an act for securing better dependence . . . upon the crown and Parliament of Great Britain." In the seventh year, "an act for granting duties on paper, tea, etc." and "an act for suspending the legislature of New York." The closing of the port of Boston as a result of the Boston Tea Party Jefferson blamed on:

THE PARTIAL representations of a few worthless ministerial dependants whose constant office it has been to keep that government embroiled, and who, by their treacheries, hope to obtain the dignity of British knighthood without calling for a party accused, without asking a proof, without attempting a distinction between the guilty and the innocent. The whole of that ancient and wealthy town is in a moment reduced from opulence to beggary.

In condemning the act which required a murderer in the colonies to be sent to England for trial Jefferson again flamed into words that might well have come from Patrick Henry's lips:

THE COWARDS who would suffer a countryman to be torn from the bowels of their society in order to be thus offered a sacrifice to parliamentary tyranny would merit that everlasting infamy now fixed on the authors of the act!

These are the acts of power, assumed by a body of men foreign to our constitutions and unacknowledged by our laws.

. . . We next proceed to the conduct of his Majesty, as holding the executive powers of the laws of these states, and mark out his deviation from the line of duty.

There followed a list of the "wanton exercise" of executive authority that is partially parallel to the list of charges in the Declaration of Independence and, to an extent, somewhat in the same diction. For instance, "For the most trifling reasons, and sometimes for no conceivable reasons at all, his Majesty has rejected laws of the most salutary tendency." He concluded *A Summary View* by saying:

THESE ARE OUR GRIEVANCES, which we have thus laid before his Majesty, with that freedom of language and sentiment which becomes a free people, claiming their rights as derived from the laws of nature, and not as the gift of their Chief Magistrate. Let those flatter who fear: it is not an American art. To give praise where it is not due might be well from the venal, but would ill beseem those who are asserting the rights of human nature. They know and will, therefore, say, that kings are the servants, not the proprietors of the people. Open your breast, sire, to liberal and expanded thought. Let not the name of George the Third be a blot on the page of history. You are surrounded by British counsellors, but remember that they are parties. You have no ministers for American affairs because you have none taken from among us, nor amenable to the laws on which they are to give you advice. It behooves you, therefore, to think and to act for yourself and your people. The great principles of right and wrong are legible to every reader; to pursue them requires not the aid of many counsellors. The whole art of government consists in the art of being honest. Only aim to do your duty and mankind will give you credit where you fail. No longer persevere in sacrificing the rights of one part of the empire to the inordinate desires of another; but deal out to all equal and impartial right. Let no act be passed by any one legislature which may infringe on the rights and liberties of another. This is the important post in which fortune has placed you, holding the balance of a great, if a well-poised empire. This, sire, is the advice of your great American council, on the observance of which may perhaps depend your felicity and future fame, and the preservation of that harmony which alone can continue, both to Great Britain and America, the reciprocal advantages of their connection. It is neither our wish nor our interest to separate from her. We are willing, on our part, to sacrifice everything which reason can ask, to the restoration of that tranquillity for which all must wish. On their part, let them be ready to establish union and a generous plan. . . . The God who gave us life, gave us liberty at the same time; the hand of force may destroy, but cannot disjoin them. This, sire, is our last, our determined resolution. And that you will be pleased to interpose, with that efficacy which your earnest endeavors may insure, to procure redress of these our great grievances, to quiet the minds of your subjects in British America against any apprehensions of future encroachment, to establish fraternal love and harmony through the whole empire, and that that may continue to the latest ages of time, is the fervent prayer of all British America.

A *Summary View* does not have that "felicity of prose" which marks the Declaration. Jefferson said it was "written in haste." But, as a Jefferson paper, it is in some ways more interesting than the Declaration. It was the first public document that expresses his full commitment to the theory of natural rights as applied to government. It was written two years before the Declaration and exclusively by Jefferson, without the help of a committee or Congress. It deserves immortality if only for the sentence, "The God who gave us life gave us liberty at the same time: the hand of force may destroy, but cannot disjoin them."

After writing his proposed instructions to the Virginia congressional delegates Jefferson says, in his autobiography,

I SET OUT FOR WILLIAMSBURG some days before that appointed for our meeting, but was taken ill of a dysentery on the road and was unable to proceed. I sent on, therefore, to Williamsburg, two copies of my draft, the one under cover to Peyton Randolph, who I knew would be in the chair of the convention, the other to Patrick Henry. Whether Mr. Henry disapproved the ground taken or was too lazy to read it (for he was the laziest man in reading I ever knew) I never learned: but he communicated it to nobody. Peyton Randolph informed the convention he had received such a paper from a member, prevented by sickness from offering it in his place, and he laid it on the table for perusal. It was read generally by the members, approved by many, though thought too bold for the present state of things; but they printed it in pamphlet form, under the title of *A Summary View of the Rights of British America.*

In the 1775 session of the Burgesses Jefferson sat quietly and listened to Henry ringingly proclaim, "Give me liberty or give me death." Then, without dramatics, he drafted Virginia's answer to Lord North's "conciliatory proposals," which provided that the colonies should be assessed, rather than taxed, by Parliament for a share of the expenses of the empire. This answer was "the very handsome public paper" to which John Adams referred as one reason for Jefferson being chosen as the draftsman of the Declaration. It was the first public document that expresses his full sympathy in the theory which was later embodied in *A Summary View.* You do not have that "felicity of pen" which marks the Declaration. Jefferson said it was "written in haste." But the "handsome public paper" was more interesting than the Declaration. It was the first public document that expresses his full sympathy in the theory which was later embodied in

Although Virginia wished "nothing so sincerely as the perpetual continuance of that brotherly love which we bear our fellow subjects of Great Britain," said Jefferson, she must reject Lord North's proposal because "it only changes the form of the oppression without lightening its burden." But it was not a matter solely for Virginia.

FINAL DETERMINATION we leave to the General Congress, now sitting. . . . To them, also, we refer the discovery of that proper method of representing our well-founded grievances. . . . For ourselves, we have exhausted every mode of application which our invention could suggest as proper and promising. We have decently remonstrated with Parliament, they have added new injuries to the old; we have wearied our King with supplications, he has not deigned to answer us; we have appealed to the native honor and justice of the British nation, their efforts in our favor have hitherto been ineffectual. What then remains to be done? That we commit our injuries to the evenhanded justice of that Being who doth no wrong; earnestly beseeching him to illuminate the councils and prosper the endeavors of those to whom America hath confided her hopes; that, through their wise direction, we may again see, reunited, the blessing of liberty and property, and the most permanent harmony with Great Britain.

Jefferson was not yet a thorough nationalist—he would not say, with Henry, "I am not a Virginian, but an American." But he was a strong unionist. He said that the weakness of the Continental Congress was that the individual colony would "conform to such resolutions only of the Congress as our deputies assent to: which totally destroys that union of conduct in the several colonies which was the very purpose of calling a Congress."

In May, 1775, Jefferson left for Philadelphia to replace the ailing Peyton Randolph in the Congress, traveling in style with four horses, a postilion and a body servant. In the spring and fall sessions of that year his pen was busy with much routine: with the Congress' reply to Lord North, and with a first draft of *A Declaration on the Necessity of Taking Up Arms.* Jefferson's version of this was too strong for the Congress, and it was watered down in a revision by Dickinson. After Congress adjourned Jefferson expressed his opinion on the impossibility of reconciliation to his loyalist friend John Randolph:

WE ARE TOLD, and everything proves it true, that he [the King] is the bitterest enemy we have. . . . To undo his empire, he has but one truth more to learn: that, after colonies have drawn the sword, there is but one step more they can take. That step is now pressed upon us by the measures adopted, as if they were afraid we would not take it.

Believe me, dear sir, there is not in the British empire a man who more cordially loves a union with Great Britain than I do. But by the God that made me, I will cease to exist before I yield to a connection on such terms as the British Parliament propose; and in this, I think I speak the sentiments of America.

We want neither inducement nor power to declare and assert a separation. It is will, alone, that is wanting, and that is growing apace under the fostering hand of our King. One bloody campaign will probably decide, everlastingly, our future course; and I am sorry to find a bloody campaign is decided on.

In the 1776 Congress Jefferson, after he wrote the Declaration, was involved only in tedious business, except on one committee in which he joined with Franklin and Adams to design a great seal for a new nation, and which adopted two famous mottoes. One of these, "Rebellion to tyrants is obedience to God," was suggested by Franklin, and so well expressed Jefferson's creed that he adopted it for his own. The other, "E pluribus unum," was suggested by a Swiss artist whom the committee consulted. He copied it from the masthead of a London publication, the *Gentlemen's Magazine,* which used it to indicate that this one magazine was made up from many newspapers.

To Jefferson, in the summer of 1776, more important things were happening in Williamsburg than in Philadelphia. He resigned from Congress and returned to his native state for the duration of the war. Virginia was in the throes of establishing a state government. This, said Jefferson, "is the whole object of the present controversy; for should a bad government be instituted for us in the future it had been as well to have accepted at first the bad one offered us from beyond the water without the risk and expense of contest." Jefferson's mind was already ranging ahead to consider, after independence—what? Independence in itself was meaningless unless it brought forth a form of government that corrected not only the specific abuses of King and Parliament, but the basic offenses against the rights of man that were inherent in the old system. And, said Jefferson, now was the time to do it:

IT CAN NEVER BE too often repeated, that the time for fixing every essential right on a legal basis is while our rulers are honest, and ourselves united. From the conclusion of this war we shall be going downhill. It will not then be necessary to resort every moment to the people for support. They will be forgotten therefore, and their rights disregarded. They will forget themselves, but in the sole faculty of making money, and will never think of uniting to effect a due respect for their rights. The shackles, therefore, which shall not be knocked off at the conclusion of this war, will remain on us long, will be made heavier and heavier, till our rights shall revive or expire in convulsion.

He said, "Our Revolution . . . presented us an album on which we were free to write what we pleased." During the next three years he wrote resolutions for the Virginia legislature designed to establish the foundation for a government which would protect the inalienable rights of the individual—his "life, liberty, and pursuit of happiness." It was at this time that he started to make effective the purpose to which he had dedicated himself, and which he later expressed by saying, "I have sworn upon the altar of God eternal hostility against every form of tyranny over the mind of man."

His attack on the old laws was on three broad fronts involving the ownership of land, religion and education. Of the first he wrote:

IN THE EARLIER TIMES of the colony when lands were to be obtained for little or nothing, some provident individuals procured large grants; and, desirous of founding great families for themselves, settled them on their descendants in fee tail [i.e. to remain in the family of the original owner]. The transmission of this property from generation to generation, in the same name, raised up a distinct set of families who, being privileged by law in the perpetuation of their wealth, were thus formed into a patrician order, distinguished by the splendor and luxury of their establishments. From this order, too, the king habitually selected his counsellors of state; the hope of which distinction devoted the whole corps to the interests and will of the crown.

"To annul this privilege and, instead of an aristocracy of wealth of more harm and danger than benefit to society, to make an opening for the aristocracy of virtue and talent, which nature has wisely provided for the direction of the interests of society and scattered with equal hand through all its conditions, was deemed essential to a well-ordered republic. To effect it no violence was necessary, no deprivation of natural right, but rather an enlargement of it by a repeal of the law.

This was indeed a radical view for the ruling class of landed aristocracy of Virginia, of which Jefferson was himself a member. But, he later wrote John Adams, "At the first session of our legislature after the Declaration of Independence, we passed a law abolishing entails. And this was followed by one abolishing the privilege of primogeniture, and dividing the lands of intestates equally among all their children, or other representatives. These laws, drawn by myself, laid the ax to the foot of pseudo-aristocracy."

The bill for which Jefferson fought hardest and which, next to the Declaration of Independence, he considered the crowning achievement of his career, came to be known as the *Statute of Virginia for Religious Freedom*. He described the situation at the time as follows:

THE FIRST SETTLERS in this country were emigrants from England, of the English Church, just at a point of time when it was flushed with complete victory over the religious of all other persuasions. Possessed, as they became, of the powers of making, administering, and executing the laws, they showed equal intolerance in this country with their Presbyterian brethren, who had emigrated to the northern government. . . . The Anglicans retained full possession of the country about a century. Other opinions began then to creep in, and the great care of the government to support their own church having begotten an equal degree of indolence in its clergy, two-thirds of the people had become dissenters at the commencement of the present Revolution.

Jefferson was appalled at the concept that government should control "the operations of the mind as well as the acts of the body." To correct this most flagrant violation of the rights of man he proposed a bill which provided, in part:

WE THE GENERAL ASSEMBLY of Virginia do enact that no man shall be compelled to frequent or support any religious worship, place or ministry whatsoever, nor shall be enforced, restrained, molested or burdened in his body or goods, or shall otherwise suffer, on account of his religious opinions or belief; but that all men shall be free to profess, and by argument to maintain, their opinions in matters of religion, and that the same shall in no wise diminish, enlarge or affect their civil capacities.

It was 1785 before James Madison could write to Jefferson in France to tell him that his bill on religion had been passed and that, in Virginia, "the ambitious hope of making laws for the human mind" had terminated. To which Jefferson replied:

IT IS COMFORTABLE to see the standard of reason at length

erected, after so many ages during which the human mind has been held in vassalage by kings, priests and nobles: and it is honorable for us to have produced the first legislature who had the courage to declare that the reason of man may be trusted with the formation of his own opinions."

His third bill, on education, caused Jefferson to be regarded as the father of public education in America. On this subject he wrote to his old law tutor, George Wythe:

I THINK BY FAR the most important bill in our whole code is that for the diffusion of knowledge among the people. No other sure foundation can be devised for the preservation of freedom and happiness. . . . Preach, my dear sir, a crusade against ignorance; establish and improve the law for educating the common people. Let our countrymen know . . . that the tax which will be paid for this purpose is not more than the thousandth part of what will be paid to kings, priests and nobles who will rise up among us if we leave the people in ignorance.

In summarizing his years as a lawmaker in Virginia Jefferson said:

I CONSIDERED . . . THESE BILLS . . . as forming a system by which every fiber would be eradicated of ancient or future aristocracy and a foundation laid for a government truly republican. The repeal of the laws of entail would prevent the accumulation and perpetuation of wealth in select families. . . . The restoration of the rights of conscience relieved the people from taxation for the support of a religion not theirs; for the establishment was truly of the religion of the rich, the dissenting sects being entirely composed of the less wealthy people; and these, by a bill for a general education, would be qualified to understand their rights, to maintain them and to exercise with intelligence their parts in any government; and all this would be effected without free violation of a single natural right of any one individual citizen.

Meanwhile the shooting war was far away to the north, and Monticello was expanding to cover the hilltop. Jefferson recorded that 90,000 brick had been made and that 14,120 were laid in one summer month. He had 4,000 new neighbors after January, 1779 —the "Convention army" of prisoners which Burgoyne had surrendered at Saratoga. British William Phillips rented nearby Blenheim, and the Hessian commander, General Baron von Riedesel, took the nearer residence of Colle. The amenities of war permitted social intercourse with these cultured gentlemen, and such invitations as this were exchanged between Blenheim and Monticello:

MAJOR GENERAL PHILLIPS sends his compliments to Mr. and Mrs. Jefferson, requests the favor of their company at dinner on Thursday next at two o'clock to meet General and Madame de Riedesel. Major General Phillips hopes Miss Jefferson will be permitted to be of the party to meet the young ladies from Colle.

Jefferson toyed with the idea of having a private orchestra and wrote to a friend in Italy:

THE BOUNDS of an American fortune will not admit the indulgence of a domestic band of musicians, yet I have thought that a passion for music might be reconciled with that economy which we are obliged to observe.

I retain among my domestic servants a gardener, a weaver, a cabinetmaker and a stonecutter, to which I would add a vigneron. In a country where, like [Italy], music is cultivated and practiced by every class of men, I suppose there might be found persons of these trades who could perform on the French horn, clarinet, or hautboy, and bassoon, so that one might have a band of two French horns, two clarinets, two

hautboys, and a bassoon without enlarging their domestic expenses. A certainty of employment for half a dozen years, and
at the end of that time to find them, if they choose, a convey-
ance to their own country, might induce them to come here on
reasonable wages. . . . Sobriety and good nature would be
desirable parts of their characters.

In 1779 Jefferson was elected Governor of Virginia to succeed
Patrick Henry. He did not seek the post but, he said, "In a virtuous
government . . . public offices are . . . burdens to those appointed
to them which it would be wrong to decline, though foreseen to
bring with them intense labor and great private loss." His two
terms as Governor brought not only labor and loss but libel which
plagued him for the remainder of his public career.

Jefferson was not well suited for the post of chief executive of
his state. The authority of the Governor was poorly defined in the
Virginia Constitution. He could recommend to the Assembly, but
he had no authority to compel action nor to veto. The times called
for a more aggressive man in the Governor's chair, one not so
sensitive as Jefferson to the niceties of constitutional authority. But
it is doubtful that, under the conditions of his second term, anybody could have done much better than Jefferson.

The situation in Virginia started to deteriorate when the war
moved south and Charleston, South Carolina, fell to the British in
May, 1780. Almost all the Virginia troops in the Continental army
were captured. Then Benedict Arnold sailed up the James River
to raid Richmond and drive the state government from the new
capital. The Assembly was supposed to reassemble at Charlottesville but, for all practical purposes, there was no government during
the spring of 1781. Cornwallis moved north to join Arnold and
detached Tarleton and his dragoons to make a dash to Charlottesville to capture members of the Assembly and to nearby Monticello
to capture the Governor. Jefferson and most of the few assemblymen who were at Charlottesville were saved only by the midnight
ride of a young man named Jack Jouett—a ride that was far more

dramatic than Paul Revere's. Jouett galloped along little-known paths through the woods to reach Charlottesville ahead of the dragoons. Legend has it that his face was so slashed by branches that he bore the scars for the rest of his life.

Jefferson, in his account of the incident, made no effort to dramatize his narrow escape from Tarleton's green-coated troopers. He merely wrote:

I NOW SENT OFF my family to secure them from danger, and was myself still at Monticello, making arrangements for my own departure, when Lt. Christopher Hudson arrived there at half speed and informed me the enemy were ascending the hill of Monticello. I departed immediately, and knowing that I should be pursued if I followed the public road, in which, too, my family would be found, I took my course through the woods along the mountains and overtook my family at Colonel Cole's, dined there, and carried them on to Rockfish after dinner, and the next day to Colonel Hugh Rose's in Amherst.

Virginia was virtually defenseless. Von Steuben, commanding what troops there were in the eastern part of the state, wanted to use stern measures, regardless of their legality, to impress men and horses. He proposed to use militia or slaves to dig fortifications. To this Jefferson replied, "The executives have not by the laws of this state any power to call a freeman to labor even for the public without his consent, nor a slave without that of his master." To the Prussian drillmaster this was ridiculous. He wrote to Washington, "The Governor has it not in his power to procure me forty Negroes to work at Hood's."

As the end of his second term as Governor neared Jefferson could see but one solution to the military situation. He wrote to Washington:

WE ARE TOO FAR REMOVED from the other scenes of war, to say whether the main force of the enemy be within this state, but I suppose they cannot anywhere spare so great an army for the operations of the field. Were it possible for this circumstance to justify in Your Excellency a determination to lend us your personal aid, it is evident from the universal voice that the presence of their beloved countryman, whose talents have been so long successfully employed in establishing the freedom of kindred states; to whose person they have still flattered themselves they retained some right; and have ever looked upon as their *dernier* resort in distress, that your appearance among them I say would restore full confidence of salvation, and would render them equal to whatever is not impossible. I cannot undertake to foresee and obviate the difficulties which stand in the way of such a resolution: the whole subject is before you of which I see only detached parts, and your judgment will be formed on view of the whole. Should the danger of this state and its consequence to the Union be such as to render it best for the whole that you should repair to its assistance, the difficulty would then be how to keep men out of the field. . . . A few days will bring to me that period of relief which the Constitution has prepared for those oppressed with the labors of my office, and a long declared resolution of relinquishing it to abler hands has prepared my way for retirement to a private station: still, however, as an individual citizen I should feel the comfortable effects of your presence.

Washington did not arrive until Jefferson was out of office. Had he served for a third term he would undoubtedly have received a share of the credit for the victory at Yorktown instead of the full, though unmerited, blame for the failure to check the British invasion of Virginia sooner. His term expired on June 3, the day before his near capture at Monticello. He therefore did not follow the fleeing assembly beyond the Blue Ridge to Staunton. Technically, he was no longer Governor. On June 12 enough assemblymen got together to elect Thomas Nelson as his successor and to adopt a resolution "That at the next session of Assembly an inquiry be made into the conduct of the executive of this state for the last twelve months."

The proposed inquiry deeply distressed Jefferson. Congress had appointed him as a member of a peace commission in France. He refused, saying; "I have retired to my farm, my family and books from which I think nothing will evermore separate me. A desire to leave public office with a reputation not more blotted than it deserves will oblige me to emerge at the next session of our Assembly and perhaps to accept a seat in it, but as I go with but a single object, I shall withdraw when that shall be accomplished."

The inquiry came to naught. The only charge against Jefferson that might have held water was that he did not call out the militia soon enough when Arnold's fleet was sighted off the mouth of the James. He thought it might be a French fleet and, as a result of a two-day delay until it was positively identified as hostile, there were only two hundred men under arms to defend Richmond when Arnold landed. Jefferson, being Jefferson, was more concerned with the "rights" of the militiamen than he was with the exigency of the military situation.

By the time the Assembly named a committee to investigate the charges against Jefferson, Cornwallis had surrendered. The committee reported that nobody had appeared to offer any specific charges and that, in its opinion, the whole thing was based on groundless rumor. The Assembly promptly and unanimously resolved:

THAT THE SINCERE THANKS of the General Assembly be given to our former Governor, Thomas Jefferson, Esq., for his impartial, upright and attentive administration while in office. The Assembly wish, in the strongest manner, to declare the high opinion which they entertain of Mr. Jefferson's ability, rectitude and integrity, as Chief Magistrate of this Commonwealth; and mean by thus publicly avowing their opinion, to obviate and remove all unmerited censure.

Jefferson was entirely vindicated, but the incident left a scar on his sensitive soul and would return to haunt him during later vicious political campaigns. At the time he felt so deeply about it that he was sure that he would never again accept public office. In declining a seat in the Assembly he wrote to James Monroe:

I CONSIDERED that I had been thirteen years engaged in public service: that during that time I had so totally abandoned all attention to my private affairs as to permit them to run into great disorder and ruin: . . . that by a constant sacrifice of time, labor, loss, parental and friendly duties I had been so far from gaining the affection of my countrymen which was the only reward I ever asked or could have felt, that I had even lost the small estimation I before possessed: that however I might have comforted myself under the disapprobation of the well-meaning but uninformed people . . . that of their representatives was a shock on which I had not calculated: that this indeed had been followed by an exculpatory declaration, but in the meantime I had been suspected and suspended in the eyes of the world without the least hint then or afterwards made public which might restrain them from supposing I stood arraigned for treasons of the heart and not mere weaknesses of the head. And I felt that these injuries, for such they have been since acknowledged, had inflicted a wound on my spirit which will only be cured by the all-healing grave.

In the spring of 1782, a few months before Mrs. Jefferson died, the Marquis de Chastelleux visited Monticello. When he returned to France he described the Jefferson whom he met in words that seem to be the obituary of a public man:

LET ME DESCRIBE to you a man, not yet forty, tall and with a mild and pleasant countenance, but whose mind and understanding are ample substitutes for every exterior grace. An American, who without ever having quitted his own country, is at once a musician, skilled in drawing, a geometrician, an astronomer, a natural philosopher, legislator and statesman. A senator of America who sat for two years in the famous Congress which brought about the Revolution . . . in voluntary retirement from the world and public business, because he loves the world inasmuch only as he can flatter himself with being useful to mankind. . . . A mild and amiable wife, charming children of whose education he himself takes charge, a house to embellish, great provisions to improve, and the arts and sciences to cultivate: these are what remain to Mr. Jefferson after having played a principal character in the theater of the New World.

Jefferson again served briefly in Congress during 1783–4, a session during which his most important contribution was the *Ordinance of 1784,* basis of the *Northwest Ordinance of 1787.* Virginia had ceded her western lands beyond the Ohio to Congress. Jefferson's bill provided for the division of new land into fourteen states and stated that "whenever any of the said states shall have, of free inhabitants, as many as shall then be in any one the least numerous of the thirteen original states, such state shall be admitted by its delegates into the Congress of the United States on an equal footing with the said original states: provided nine states agree to such admission." This admission of new states was the first concrete proposal for the pattern of the development of the United States beyond the original colonies.

Jefferson made five conditions for statehood:

(1) THAT THEY SHALL forever remain a part of this confederacy of the United States of America. (2) That in their persons, property and territory they shall be subject to the government of the United States in Congress assembled . . . (3) That they shall be subject to pay a part of the federal debts contracted or to be contracted, to be apportioned on them by Congress . . . (4) That their respective governments shall be

in republican forms and shall admit no person to be a citizen who holds any hereditary title. (5) That after the year 1800 of the Christian era, there shall be neither slavery nor involuntary servitude in any of the said states, otherwise than in punishment of crimes whereof the party shall have been convicted to have been personally guilty.

From his first condition it is obvious that Jefferson did not, at this time, recognize the right of secession. His fifth condition would have prohibited slavery not only in the territory already ceded but in lands subsequently to be ceded south of the river; in short, prevented its spread beyond the original states. Congress amended this, in the later ordinance, to apply only north of the river.

The sketch map that accompanied the proposal indicated the states as squares or rectangles except where they bordered rivers or lakes. His boundaries bear little relation to those of the states which ultimately were carved from this territory, except in the case of Ohio. And, fortunately for children who have trouble spelling Mississippi, most of the names he proposed for the states were ignored. Cherronesus, Assenisipia, Pelisipia, Metropotamia and Polypotamia never became states; Michigania became Michigan and his Illinois became Illinois.

To this same session of Congress Jefferson presented his *Notes on the Establishment of a Money Unit and of a Coinage for the United States*. In this he strongly advocated the Spanish dollar rather than the English pound as the money unit and insisted on multiples and divisions of the unit by the decimal system:

THE MOST easy ratio of multiplication and division is that by ten. Everyone knows the facility of Decimal Arithmetic. Every one remembers, that, when learning Money Arithmetic, he used to be puzzled with adding the farthings, taking out the fours and carrying them on; adding the pence, taking out the twelves and carrying them on; adding the shillings, taking out the twenties and carrying them on; but when he came to the

pounds, where he had only tens to carry forward, it was easy
and free from error. The bulk of mankind are schoolboys
through life. These little perplexities are always great to them.

He clinched his argument with comparative examples of money
arithmetic in British currency and his proposed system.

Addition

£	s.	d.	qrs.	Dollars
8	13	11	1-2	= 38.65
4	12	8	3-4	= 20.61
13	6	8	1-4	59.26

As coins he proposed almost exactly the units that were adopted:
a copper hundredth, a five-copper piece, a silver tenth, a "double
tenth" (instead of the quarter), a half dollar and a dollar.

CHAPTER IV

AMERICAN IN PARIS

☙

"Behold me at length on the vaunted scene of Europe." So wrote Jefferson in September, 1785, after he had been in Paris for a year. At long last he was embarked on the travels which he had proposed to John Page twenty-one years before. Congress had appointed him to join Benjamin Franklin and John Adams in France to negotiate treaties of commerce in Europe.

In the summer of the previous year he had made a swift and smooth crossing from Boston to Portsmouth with his twelve-year-old daughter Martha—called, in the family, "Patsy." The child left a more interesting account of their first days in the Old World than her father. Of the Channel crossing to Havre she said:

THE CABIN WAS NOT MORE than three feet wide and about four feet long. There was no other furniture than an old bench. . . . The door by which we came in at was so little that one was obliged to enter on all fours. There were two little doors on the side of the cabin, the way to our beds, which were composed of two boxes and a couple of blankets without either bed or mattress, so that I was obliged to sleep in my clothes. There being no window in the cabin, we were obliged to stay in the dark for fear of the rains coming in if we opened the door.

At Havre, continued Martha:

I FEAR we should have fared as badly at the arrival, for Papa spoke very little French and I not a word, if an Irish gentleman . . . seeing our embarrassment, had not been so good as to conduct us to a house. . . . It is amazing to see how they cheat the strangers. It cost Papa as much to have the baggage brought from the shore to the house, which was about half a square, as the bringing it from Philadelphia to Boston. From there we should have had a very agreeable voyage to Paris, for Havre-de-Grâce is built at the mouth of the Seine, and we followed the river all the way through the most beautiful country I ever saw in my life—it is a perfect garden—if the singularity of our carriage had not attracted the attention of all we met and whenever we stopped we were surrounded by beggars. One day I counted no less than nine where we stopped to change horses. . . .

I wish you could have been with us when we arrived. I am sure you would have laughed for we were obliged to send immediately for the staymaker, the mantuamaker, the milliner and even a shoemaker before I could go out. I have never had the *friseur* but once, but I soon got rid of him and turned down my hair in spite of all they could say, and I defer it now as much as possible for I think it always too soon to suffer.

Jefferson, too, needed a new outfit immediately upon his arrival in Paris, for experienced traveler John Adams had told him: "The first thing to be done in Paris is always to send for a tailor, a perukemaker and shoemaker, for this nation has established such a domination over the fashion that neither clothes, wigs nor shoes made in any other place will do in Paris."

This, plus the cost of refurnishing the house which he rented, caused him to complain to James Monroe, back in Congress, of the high cost of being a foreign minister:

ALL THE MINISTERS who came to Europe before me, came at a time when all expenses were paid and a sum allowed in addition for their time. Of course they all had their outfit. Afterwards they were put on fixed salaries, but still these were liberal [two thousand five hundred guineas]. Congress in the moment of my appointment struck off five hundred guineas of the salary, and made no other provision for the outfit but allowing me to call for two quarters' salary in advance. The outfit has cost me near a thousand guineas; for which I am in debt and which, were I to stay here seven years, I could never make good by savings out of my salary; for be assured we are the lowest and most obscure of the whole diplomatic tribe. . . .

I keep a hired carriage and two horses. A riding horse I cannot afford to keep. This . . . absorbs the whole allowance. . . . I mention these circumstances to you that if you should think the allowance reasonable and any opportunity should occur while you are in Congress wherein it can be decently obtained, you would be so good as to think of it.

Jefferson immediately called on old Dr. Franklin at his house in suburban Passy, and they were shortly joined by John Adams. Franklin had already negotiated a treaty with Sweden, and Congress naively supposed that all of Europe would welcome the opportunity to do business with the newly independent states. But Jefferson soon learned that there was a great deal of politics involved in commercial treaty making. Of their early efforts he said:

WITHOUT URGING, we sounded the ministers of the several European nations at the court of Versailles on their dispositions towards mutual commerce, and the expediency of encouraging it by the protection of a treaty. Old Frederick of Prussia met us cordially, and without hesitation. . . . Denmark and Tuscany entered also into negotiations with us. Other powers appearing indifferent, we did not think it proper to press them. They seemed, in fact, to know little about us but as rebels who had been successful in throwing off the yoke of the mother country. They were ignorant of our commerce, which had been always monopolized by England. . . . They were inclined, therefore, to stand aloof until they could see better what relations might be usefully instituted with us.

The treaty makers were no more successful in dealing with the vexing problem of the Barbary pirates. They reported to Congress:

TREATIES WITH THESE POWERS are formed under very peculiar circumstances . . . great presents and an annual tribute are requisite with some of them. The contributions under which they thus lay the powers of Europe are as heavy as they are degrading. . . . Presents or war is their usual alternative.

Jefferson was aghast at paying "a tribute for the forbearance of their piracies. When this idea comes across my mind my facilities are absolutely suspended between indignation and impotence." At the thought of such injustice the normally pacifistic Virginian proposed war:

I DO EXPECT that they would tax us at one, two, or perhaps three hundred thousand dollars a year. Surely our people will not give this. Would it not be better to offer them an equal treaty; if they refuse, why not go to war with them? . . . We ought to begin a naval power if we mean to carry on our own commerce. Can we begin it on a more honorable occasion, or with a weaker foe? I am of opinion Paul Jones with half a dozen frigates would totally destroy their commerce.

Before the end of 1785 Adams was appointed to the Court of St. James and moved to London. Franklin returned to America, leav-

ing Jefferson alone in Paris as "Minister Plenipotentiary to the
Court of His Most Christian Majesty," a position of which the
duties were hardly appealing to a man of Jefferson's tastes and interests. They were, he said:

CONFINED TO A FEW OBJECTS: the receipt of our whale oils,
salted fish and salted meats on favorable terms; the admission
of our rice on equal terms with that of Piedmont, Egypt and
the Levant; a mitigation of the monopolies of our tobacco by
the farmers-general, and a free admission of our productions
into their islands, were the principal commercial objects which
required attention. . . . In justice, I must . . . say, that I found
the government entirely disposed to befriend us on all occasions, and to yield us every indulgence not absolutely injurious
to themselves.

After a year in Paris Jefferson had what might be termed a
typical American tourist's conception of Europe—it did not measure up to the "good old U.S.A." He wrote to a professor at William
and Mary:

YOU ARE, PERHAPS, curious to know how this new scheme has
struck a savage of the mountains of America. Not advanta-
geously, I assure you. I find the general fate of humanity here
most deplorable. The truth of Voltaire's observation offers itself perpetually, that every man here must be either the ham-
mer or the anvil. It is a true picture of that country to which
they say we shall pass hereafter, and where we are to see God
and his angels in splendor, and crowds of the damned trampled
under their feet. While the great mass of the people are thus
suffering under physical and moral oppression, I have endeavored to examine more nearly the condition of the great to
appreciate the true value of the circumstances in their situation, which dazzle the bulk of spectators, and, especially to
compare it with that degree of happiness which is enjoyed in

America by every class of people. Intrigues of love occupy the younger, and those of ambition the elder, part of the great. Conjugal love having no existence among them, domestic happiness, of which that is the basis, is utterly unknown. In lieu of this are substituted pursuits which nourish and invigorate all our bad passions, and which offer only moments of ecstasy amidst days and months of restlessness and torment. Much, very much, inferior this, to the tranquil, permanent felicity with which domestic society in America blesses most of its inhabitants. . . .

In science, the mass of the people is two centuries behind ours; their literati, half a dozen years before us. . . . With respect to what are termed polite manners . . . I would wish my countrymen to adopt . . . much of European politeness. . . . Here it seems that a man might pass his life without encountering a single rudeness. In the pleasures of the table they are far before us, because with good taste they unite temperance. They do not terminate the most sociable meals by transforming themselves into brutes. I have never yet seen a man drunk in France, even among the lowest of the people.

Female *Parisians* of the upper class were particular objects of scorn to the man who strongly believed that "woman's place is in the home." He described a day in the life of *madame* as follows:

AT ELEVEN O'CLOCK it is day, *chez madame.* The curtains are drawn. Propped on bolsters and pillows, and her head scratched into a little order, the bulletins of the sick are read, and the billets of the well. She writes to some of her acquaintance, and receives the visits of others. If the morning is not very thronged she is able to get out and hobble round the cage of the Palais Royal; but she must hobble quickly, for the coiffeur's turn is come, and a tremendous turn it is! Happy if he does not make her arrive when dinner is half over! The torpitude of digestion a little past, she flutters half an hour through the streets by way of paying visits, and then to the spectacles. . . . After supper, cards; and after cards, bed; to rise at noon the next day and to tread, like a mill horse, the same trodden circle over again.

For American youth Europe had special pitfalls. He advised a young man who queried him on a foreign education:

LET US VIEW the disadvantages of sending a youth to Europe. . . . I will select a few. . . . He learns drinking, horse racing, and boxing. . . . He acquires a fondness for European luxury and dissipation and a contempt for the simplicity of his own country . . . he is led by the strongest of all the human passions into a spirit for female intrigue, destructive of his own and others' happiness . . . and . . . learns to consider fidelity to the marriage bed as an ungentlemanly practice and inconsistent with happiness. . . . It appears to me, then, that an American coming to Europe for education loses in his knowledge, in his morals, in his health, in his habits, and in his happiness.

All of this was written during his first year in Europe when, like so many American tourists since, he had formed his opinion of all of Europe from his experience in one capital city. Later, after he had moved around the hinterland of France, he developed a strong and lasting affection for the French people. When Abigail Adams wrote him praising London he replied:

I WOULD NOT GIVE the polite, self-denying, feeling, hospitable, good-humored people of this country, and their amiability in every point of view, for ten such races of rich, proud, hectoring, swearing, squibbing, carnivorous animals as those among whom you are. . . . I do love this *people* with all my heart, and think that with a better religion, a better form of government and their present governors, their condition and country would be most enviable.

It may be said that the French were more tolerant of Jefferson than Jefferson was, initially, of the French. Before he arrived the French Minister to the United States had sent a dossier on him to Vergennes, the French Foreign Minister, which said:

HE IS FULL OF HONOR and sincerity and loves his country greatly, but is too philosophic and tranquil to hate or love any other nation unless it is for the interest of the United States to do so. He has a principle that it is for the happiness and welfare of the United States to hold itself as much aloof from England as a peaceful state of affairs permits, that as a consequence of this system it becomes them to attach themselves particularly to France, even that Congress ought as quickly as possible to direct the affection of the people toward us in order to balance the penchant and numerous causes continually attracting them to England.

The French attitude toward Benjamin Franklin made Jefferson's work easier and his personal life far more pleasant. All of France, high and low, knew and idolized the old sage. To Frenchmen at all levels he was "Mr. America." He sponsored his younger successor not only with the politicians at court but among the literati, the economists and the scientists whose company was the breath of life to Jefferson. In some ways this was embarrassing. Jefferson said:

THE SUCCESSION TO DR. FRANKLIN at the court of France was an excellent school of humility. On being presented to anyone as the minister of America, the commonplace question used in such cases was *"C'est vous, Monsieur, qui remplace le Docteur Franklin?"*—"It is you, sir, who replace Dr. Franklin?" I generally answered, "No one can replace him, sir; I am only his successor."

To Jefferson, Franklin was the greatest American save only Washington. Upon Franklin's death a few years later Jefferson proposed to Washington that the Cabinet, in which he was then Secretary of State, should go into mourning. Washington demurred on the grounds that it would set an undesirable precedent. "I told him," said Jefferson, "the world had drawn so broad a line between himself and Dr. Franklin, on the one side, and the residue of mankind, on the other, that we might wear mourning for them, and the question still remain new and undecided as to all others."

Franklin introduced Jefferson into the small group of intellectual liberals who had inherited the mantles of Voltaire and Rousseau. They included, among others, the Duc de la Rochefoucauld and his mother, the Duchesse d'Anville, the Marquis de Condorcet, the Abbé Morellet, the writer Marmontel, Du Pont de Nemours, and, as a junior member, Lafayette. The older man also opened to Jefferson the doors of the famous salons of the day, where the best talk and ideas were exchanged. He was not received at Sannois, the suburban seat of the brilliant and ugly Madame d'Houdetot, as Franklin had been, with a paean of praise in a specially composed poem. Jefferson's record of his second visit merely states; "lost at lotto at Sannois, eighteen." But he did become part of the group here as well as at the salons of Madame Necker, wife of France's Minister of Finance, her daughter, Madame de Staël, and Madame Helvétius, to whom Franklin had proposed marriage.

Here was the fountainhead of that society which Jefferson described by saying:

POLITICS BECAME THE THEME of all societies, male and female, and a very extensive and zealous party was formed which acquired the appellation of the Patriotic party, who, sensible of the abusive government under which they live, sighed for occasions of reforming it. This party comprehended all the honesty of the kingdom sufficiently at leisure to think, the men of letters, the easy bourgeois, the young nobility.

Jefferson also inherited from Franklin the role of an American information service in Europe. There was great curiosity about the new nation. After a few months in Paris Jefferson decided to publish his *Notes on the State of Virginia*. In 1780 the Marquis de Barbe-Marbois, Secretary of the French Legation in America, had endeavored to compile information about America by sending questionnaires to each state. Virginia's had come to Governor Jefferson. When he retired as Governor he answered Marbois' queries by writing a book. It was a labor of love, for, he said:

I HAD ALWAYS made it a practice, whenever an opportunity occurred of obtaining any information of our country which might be of use to me in any station, public or private, to commit it to writing. These memoranda were on loose papers, bundled up without order, and difficult of recurrence when I had occasion for a particular one. I thought this a good occasion to embody their substance, which I did in the order of Mr. Marbois' queries, so as to answer his wish and to arrange them for my own use.

Notes went far beyond the twenty-three questions that Marbois had asked—and far beyond Virginia. It was, except for his unfinished autobiography, the only book that Jefferson ever wrote and, in the words of Charles Thomson, Secretary of Congress, it was "a most excellent natural history not merely of Virginia but of North America and possibly equal if not superior to that of any country yet published."

It started with geographical information—boundaries, rivers, mountains, seaports. But in every section Jefferson's enthusiasm for his native land carried him far beyond the original scope of the work. Of rivers he discussed not only Virginia's York, James and Chickahominy, but the distant Mississippi, Missouri and Ohio. He even dragged in the Hudson by predicting that, some day, the Potomac would carry the commerce of the west rather than the Hudson because the short portage from the waters of the Ohio, and the freedom from winter ice, made the southern river the logical channel. He did not envision the Erie Canal—although he did forecast that "the Mississippi will be one of the principal channels of future commerce for the country west of the Alleghany."

Notes told everything there was to tell about climate, population, laws, religion, manners, manufacturers and much else, but, though he started by giving facts, he interjected thoughts and ideas which reflected his philosophy of the new country. The book was Jefferson's greatest contribution to natural science.

Notes was strongly pro-American. In it Jefferson refuted a statement of Abbé Raynal, "America has not yet produced one good poet." Said Jefferson, "when we shall have existed as a people as long as the Greeks did before they produced a Homer, the Romans a Vergil, the French a Racine and Voltaire, the English a Shakespeare and Milton, should this reproach still be true, we will inquire from what unfriendly causes it has proceeded."

And to Raynal's charge that America had not produced "one able mathematician, one man of genius in a single art or a single science," Jefferson replied:

IN WAR WE HAVE PRODUCED a Washington, whose memory will be adored while liberty shall have votaries, whose name shall triumph over time, and will in future ages assume its just station among the most celebrated worthies of the world. . . . In physics we have produced a Franklin, than whom no one of the present age has made more important discoveries, nor has enriched philosophy with more or more ingenious solutions of the phenomena of nature. We have supposed Mr. Rittenhouse second to no astronomer living; that in genius he must be the first, because he is self-taught. As an artist he has exhibited as great a proof of mechanical genius as the world has ever produced. . . . As in philosophy and war, so in government, in oratory, in painting, in the plastic art, we might show that America, though but a child of yesterday, has already given hopeful proofs of genius. . . . We therefore suppose that this

reproach is as unjust as it is unkind; and that of the geniuses
which adorn the present age, America contributes its full
share. . . . The United States contains three millions of inhabitants; France twenty millions; and the British Islands ten. We
produce a Washington, a Franklin, a Rittenhouse. France then
should have half a dozen in each of these lines, and Great
Britain half that number, equally eminent. It may be true that
France has; we are just becoming acquainted with her. . . .
The present war having so long cut off all communication with
Great Britain, we are not able to make a fair estimate of the
state of science in that country. The spirit in which she wages
war is the only sample before our eyes, and that does not seem
the legitimate offspring either of science or of civilization. The
sun of her glory is fast descending to the horizon. Her philosophy has crossed the Channel, her freedom the Atlantic, and
herself seems passing to that awful dissolution whose issue is
not given human foresight to scan.

Having put Raynal in his place, Jefferson proceeded to the "remaining articles comprehended under the present query" and listed
over one hundred birds found in Virginia; "and doubtless many
others which have not yet been described and classed."

Marbois had asked about population. Jefferson gave him census
figures, starting with the year 1607. Then he philosophized on
population increase and the question of encouraging immigration.
On this he expressed ideas which he would change before the end
of the century:

IT IS FOR THE HAPPINESS of those united in society to harmo-
nize as much as possible in matters which they must of necessity transact together. Civil government being the sole object
of forming societies, its administration must be conducted by
common consent. Every species of government has its specific
principles. Ours perhaps are more peculiar than those of any
other in the universe. It is a composition of the freest principles

of the English constitution, with others derived from natural right and natural reason. To these nothing can be more opposed than the maxims of absolute monarchies. Yet from such we are to expect the greatest number of emigrants. They will bring with them the principles of the governments they leave, imbibed in their early youth. . . . In proportion to their numbers, they will share with us the legislation. They will infuse into it their spirit, warp and bias its directions and render it a heterogeneous, incoherent, distracted mass. . . . Is it not safer to wait with patience . . . for the attainment of any degree of population desired or expected? May not our government be more homogeneous, more peaceable, more durable?

In reply to Marbois' query on Virginia's system of government Jefferson wrote at length on the weaknesses of its Constitution— ideas which foreshadowed many of the doubts and difficulties of the later convention which produced the United States Constitution. The state Constitution, he said, "was formed when we were new and unexperienced in the science of government. It was the first, too, which was formed in the whole United States. No wonder then that time and trial have discovered very capital defects in it. The majority of the men in the state, who pay and fight for its support, are unrepresented in the legislature, the roll of freeholders entitled to vote not including generally the half of those on the roll of the militia, or of the taxgatherers." Also, the representation was disproportionate as to counties—the conservative Tidewater counties had greater representation in relation to their population than the more democratic western counties. Thus he touched on a subject that is still a controversy in many states.

But, wrote Jefferson, still smarting from the frustrations of his terms as Governor dominated by an Assembly, the greatest weakness was:

ALL THE POWERS of government, legislative, executive and judiciary, result to the legislative body. The concentrating these in the same hands is precisely the definition of despotic government. It will be no alleviation that these powers will be exercised by a plurality of hands, and not by a single one. One hundred and seventy-three despots would surely be as oppressive as one. . . . As little will it avail us that they are chosen by ourselves. An elective despotism was not the government we fought for, but one which should not only be founded on free principles, but in which the powers of government should be so divided and balanced among several bodies of magistracy, as that no one could transcend their legal limits, without being effectually checked and restrained by the others.

This, said Jefferson, would not last long:

THEY SHOULD LOOK FORWARD to a time, and that not a distant one, when a corruption in this, as in the country from which we derive our origin, will have seized the heads of government, and be spread by them through the body of the people; when they will purchase the voices of the people, and make them pay the price. Human nature is the same on every side of the Atlantic, and will be alike influenced by the same causes. The time to guard against corruption and tyranny is before they shall have gotten hold of us. It is better to keep the wolf out of the fold than to trust to drawing his teeth and talons after he shall have entered.

In 1786 Jefferson made a brief trip to London, at the request of Adams, to assist the latter in treaty making. It served only to intensify Jefferson's distrust of the English and confirm his hatred of their King. He said that it was "impossible for anything to be more ungracious" than the attitude of the King when he was presented and, as for the English generally, "They required to be kicked into common good manners."

With his return to Paris there started a romantic interlude of which history has made much smoke—although there apparently was very little fire. Artist John Trumbull had come to Paris in connection with his project to paint memorable scenes from the Revolution—a project to which we owe the famous painting of the signing of the Declaraton of Independence. He was staying with Jefferson and introduced him to the monkey-faced, foppish English miniaturist Richard Cosway and his young wife—Maria Louisa Catherine Cecilia. A contemporary described Maria as "a golden-haired, languishing Anglo-Italian, graceful to affectation and highly accomplished, especially in music."

Jefferson was immediately smitten with the obviously coquettish young Maria. He brushed business aside so that he could spend the remainder of that day sightseeing with the Cosways and Trumbull, sending "lying messengers" abroad to cancel his appointments. For more than a month he spent part of almost every day with the girl, seeing or hearing something beautiful. Toward the end he fell and broke his right wrist while with her and, for some time, wrote with his left hand.

It is not clear whether Jefferson's main interest was in the lady's charms or in her accomplishments and her sensitivity to beauty. Everything that he wrote on the subject would indicate the latter. In recalling to her their time together he described:

THE DAY WE WENT to St. Germain's. How beautiful was every object! the Port de Neuilly, the hills along the Seine, the rainbows of the machine of Marly, the terrace of St. Germain's, the château, the gardens, the statues of Marly, the *pavillon* of Lucienne. Recollect, too, *Madrid, Bagatelle,* the King's garden, the *Dessert.* How grand the idea excited by the remains of such a column! The spiral staircase too was beautiful. Every moment was filled with something agreeable. The wheels of time moved on with a rapidity of which those of our carriage gave but a faint idea. And yet in the evening when one took a retrospect of the day, what a mass of happiness had we traveled over! Retrace all those scenes to me, my good companion.

When the Cosways left London Jefferson wrote Maria a long letter couched in terms of a supposed dialogue between his Head and his Heart. This is the principal letter that Jefferson wrote, other than the boyhood ones to Page and on the death of his wife, which exposes a degree of personal feelings or emotion:

MY DEAR MADAM,

Having performed the last sad office of handing you into your carriage, at the Pavillon de St. Denis, and seen the wheels get actually in motion, I turned on my heel and walked, more dead than alive, to the opposite door, where my own was awaiting me. . . . I was carried home. Seated by my fireside, solitary and sad, the following dialogue took place between my Head and my Heart.

Head. Well, friend, you seem to be in a pretty trim.

Heart. I am indeed the most wretched of all earthly beings. Overwhelmed with grief, every fiber of my frame distended beyond its natural powers to bear, I would willingly meet whatever catastrophe should leave me no more to feel or to fear.

Head. These are the eternal consequences of your warmth and precipitation. This is one of the scrapes into which you are ever leading us. You confess your follies, indeed, but still you hug and cherish them, and no reformation can be hoped where there is no repentence.

Heart. Oh! My friend! This is no moment to upbraid my foibles. I am rent into fragments by the force of my grief! If you have any balm, pour it into my wounds; if none, do not harrow them by new torments. Spare me in this awful moment! At any other I will attend with patience to your admonitions.

Head. On the contrary, I never found that the moment of triumph with you was the moment of attention to my admonitions. While suffering under your follies you may perhaps be made sensible of them, but, the paroxysm over, you fancy it can never return. Harsh therefore as the medicine may be, it is my office to administer it. You will be pleased to remember, that when our friend Trumbull used to be telling us of the merits and talents of these good people, I never ceased whispering to you that we had no occasion for new acquaintances; that the greater their merits and talents, the more dangerous their friendship to our tranquillity, because the regret at parting would be greater.

Heart. . . . Sir, this acquaintance was not the consequence of my doings. It was one of your projects, which threw us in the way of it.

Heart went on to remind Head that they had met the Cosways at a firm of architects where they had gone, at Head's behest, to study the dome of a Paris market to consider its adaptation for a like edifice in Richmond. Head then pointed out the folly of becoming involved with these new friends because, said Head:

. . . I OFTEN TOLD YOU during the course that you were imprudently engaging your affections under circumstances that must cost you a great deal of pain; that the persons indeed were of the greatest merit, possessing good sense, good humor, honest hearts, honest manners, and eminence in a lovely art; that the lady had moreover qualities and accomplishments belonging to her sex, which might form a chapter apart for her, such as music, modesty, beauty, and that softness of disposition which is the ornament of her sex and charm of ours. But that all these considerations would increase the pang of separation; that their stay here was to be short; that you rack our whole system when you are parted from those you love, complaining that such a separation is worse than death.

Heart replied that they had promised to come back or, perhaps, they might come to America. There followed a plea for Maria to cross the ocean, starting with a description of the natural beauties of America—and Monticello—that would appeal to her as an artist. This was followed by a fervent portrait of the fine political system in America, a subject that Jefferson could not ignore even in a love letter—if this was such. Then, in a lengthy dialogue, Head and Heart presented a picture of Jefferson's innermost feelings that show him as, basically, a pathetically lonely man.

HEAD. . . . This is not a world to live at random in as you do. To avoid those eternal distresses to which you are forever exposing us, you must learn to look forward before you take a step which may interest our peace. Everything in this world is a matter of calculation. Advance then with caution, the balance in your hand. Put into one scale the pleasures which any object may offer; but put fairly into the other the pains which are to follow, and see which preponderates. . . . Do not bite at the bait of pleasure till you know there is no hook beneath it. The art of life is the art of avoiding pain, and he is the best pilot who steers clearest of the rocks and shoals with which it is beset. Pleasure is always before us, but misfortune is at our side; while running after that, this arrests us. The most effectual means of being secure against pain is to retire within ourselves, and to suffice for our own happiness. Those which depend on ourselves are the only pleasures a wise man will count on; for nothing is ours, which another may deprive us of. Hence the inestimable value of intellectual pleasures. Ever in our power, always leading us to something new, never cloying, we ride, serene and sublime above the concerns of this mortal world, contemplating truth and nature, matter and motion. . . . Let this be our employ. Leave the bustle and tumult of society to those who have not talents to occupy themselves without them. Friendship is but another name for an alliance with the follies and the misfortunes of others. Our own share of miseries is sufficient; why enter then as volunteers into those of another? Is there so little gall poured into our own cup that we must need help to drink that of our neighbor?

Heart. And what more sublime delight than to mingle tears with one whom the hand of heaven hath smitten! . . . When heaven has taken from us some object of our love, how sweet it is to have a bosom whereon to recline our heads, and into which we may pour the torrent of our tears! Grief, with such a comfort, is almost a luxury! In a life where we are perpetually exposed to want and accident, yours is a wonderful proposition, to insulate ourselves, to retire from all aid, and to wrap ourselves in the mantle of self-sufficiency! . . . Let the gloomy monk, sequestered from the world, seek unsocial pleasures in the bottom of his cell! Let the sublimated philosopher grasp visionary happiness while pursuing phantoms dressed in the garb of truth! Their supreme wisdom is supreme folly and they mistake for happiness the mere absence of pain. Had they ever felt the solid pleasure of one generous spasm of the heart, they would exchange for it all the frigid speculations of their lives. . . . When nature assigned us the same habitation, she gave us over it a divided empire. To you she allotted the field of science, to me that of morals. When the circle is to be squared, or the orbit of a comet to be traced; when the arch of greatest strength, or the solid of least resistance is to be investigated, take you the problem, it is yours; nature has given me no cognizance of it. In like manner in denying to you the feelings of sympathy, of benevolence, of gratitude, of justice, of love, of friendship, she has excluded you from their control. To these she has adapted the mechanism of the heart. Morals were too essential to the happiness of man to be risked on the uncertain combinations of the head. She laid their foundation therefore in sentiment, not in science. . . .

If our country, when pressed with wrongs at the point of the bayonet, had been governed by its heads instead of its hearts, where should we have been now? Hanging on a gallows as high as Haman's. You began to calculate and to compare wealth and numbers; we threw up a few pulsations of our warmest blood; we supplied enthusiasm against wealth and numbers: we put our existence to the hazard, when the hazard seemed against us, and we saved our country.

When Maria returned to Paris—without her husband—Head had apparently convinced Heart that the infatuation for the young lady must be subdued. Jefferson was "too busy" to see her frequently, although he sent her, with his pen, "breathings of pure affection." They continued to correspond for thirty-five years. By the 1820s Maria, a widow and a baroness, had founded and headed a girl's college in Italy. Jefferson, at the same time, was organizing the University of Virginia. Shortly before his death Maria wrote:

I WISH MUCH to hear from you, how you go on with your fine Seminary. I have had my great saloon painted, with the representation of the four parts of the world, and the most distinguished objects in them. I am at a loss for America, as I found very few small prints—however, Washington town is marked, and I have left a hill barren, as I would place Monticello and the Seminary: if you favor me with some description, that I might have it introduced, you would oblige me much.

Jefferson never answered. A later visitor to Maria's college described the painting in the *salon*. The hill on which Monticello was to be displayed was still bare.

After Maria's first visit to Paris Jefferson's broken wrist refused to heal. Doctors suggested treatment by the waters of Aix, in Provence. Jefferson had no more faith in the waters than he had in physicians, but their advice was an excuse for a trip through the south of France and Italy which was one of the most congenial episodes of his sojourn in France. He went alone, accompanied only by his ubiquitous account book, in which he recorded meticulous notes on French husbandry and architecture; and, as always, his thoughts on man and his rights. He described his procedure to Lafayette:

IN THE GREAT CITIES I go to see what travelers think alone worthy of being seen; but I make a job of it, and generally gulp it down in a day. On the other hand, I am never satiated with rambling through the fields and farms, examining the culture and cultivators with a degree of curiosity which makes some take me for a fool and others to be much wiser than I am. . . . I think you have not made this journey. It will be a great comfort to you to know from your own inspection the condition of all the provinces of your own country. This is perhaps the only moment of your life in which you can acquire that knowledge. And to do it most effectually you must be absolutely incognito, you must ferret the people out of their hovels as I have done, look into their kettles, eat their bread, loll on their beds under pretense of resting yourself, but in fact to find if they are soft. You will feel a sublime pleasure in the course of this investigation, and a sublimer one hereafter when you shall be able to apply your knowledge to the softening of their beds or the throwing a morsel of meat into their kettles of vegetables.

His travel observations led him to write to George Wythe:

IF ANYBODY THINKS that kings, nobles or priests are good conservators of the public happiness, send him here. It is the best school in the universe to cure him of that folly. . . . The omnipotence of their effect cannot be better proved than in this country particularly, where, notwithstanding the finest soil upon earth, the finest climate under heaven, and a people of the most benevolent, the most gay and amiable character of which the human form is susceptible; where such a people, I say, surrounded by so many blessings from nature, are loaded with misery by kings, nobles and priests, and by them alone.

When Jefferson returned to Paris he found news from home of Shays's rebellion, the uprising of debt-ridden farmers in Massachusetts that was suppressed by force. Jefferson, alone among the

American leaders, was not disturbed by the rebellion—perhaps because he was far enough away to view it objectively. He was upset by the use of force to control it, and wrote several letters which contained statements that were later used to label him a rabid and bloody revolutionist. In one letter he said:

I AM PERSUADED MYSELF that the good sense of the people will always be found to be the best army. They may be led astray for a moment, but will soon correct themselves. The people are the only censors of their governors: and even their errors will tend to keep these to the true principles of their institution. To punish these errors too severely would be to suppress the only safeguard of the public liberty. The way to prevent these irregular interpositions of the people is to give them full information of their affairs through the channel of the public papers, and to contrive that those papers should penetrate the whole mass of the people. The basis of our governments being the opinion of the people, the very first object should be to keep that right; and were it left to me to decide whether we should have a government without newspapers or newspapers without a government, I should not hesitate a moment to prefer the latter. . . . Do not be too severe upon their errors, but reclaim them by enlightening them. If once they become inattentive to the public affairs, you and I, and Congress and assemblies, judges and governors shall all become wolves. It seems to be the law of our general nature . . . that man is the only animal which devours his own kind, for I can apply no milder term to the governments of Europe, and to the general prey of the rich on the poor.

To Abigail Adams he wrote:

THE SPIRIT OF RESISTANCE to government is so valuable on certain occasions, that I wish it to be always kept alive. It will often be exercised when wrong, but better so than not to be exercised at all. I like a little rebellion now and then. It is like a storm in the atmosphere.

And he summed up his creed of liberty vs. lethargy by writing, still of Shays's Rebellion:

CAN HISTORY PRODUCE an instance of rebellion so honorably conducted? I say nothing of its motives. They were founded in ignorance, not wickedness. God forbid we should ever be twenty years without such a rebellion. The people cannot be all, and always, well informed. The part which is wrong will be discontented in proportion to the importance of the facts they misconceive. If they remain quiet under such misconceptions it is a lethargy, the forerunner of death to the public liberty. . . . What country can preserve its liberties if their rulers are not warned from time to time that their people preserve the spirit of resistance? Let them take arms. The remedy is to set them right as to facts, pardon and pacify them. What signify a few lives lost in a century or two? The tree of liberty must be refreshed from time to time with the blood of patriots and tyrants. It is its natural manure.

Shortly, there was more portentous news from home. A Convention had assembled to draft a Constitution to replace the Articles of Confederation under which the United States had been governed since the war years. It is ironic that Jefferson, probably the best legislative draftsman of the age, was absent on the two occasions when his brain and pen could have contributed so much. In 1776 he was in Philadelphia when his state formed a constitution. Now, he was in Paris when Philadelphia was the scene of action.

He was fully conscious of the basic weaknesses of the government under the Articles of Confederation. He later wrote:

OUR FIRST ESSAY, in America, to establish a federative government had fallen, on trial, very short of its object. During the War of Independence, while the pressure of an external enemy hooped us together, and their enterprises kept us necessarily on the alert, the spirit of the people, excited by danger, was a supplement to the Confederation, and urged them to zealous exertions, whether claimed by that instrument or not; but, when peace and safety were restored, and every man became engaged in useful and profitable occupation, less attention was paid to the calls of Congress. The fundamental defect of the Confederation was that Congress was not authorized to act immediately on the people, and by its own officers. Their power was only requisitory, and these requisitions were addressed to the several legislatures, to be by them carried into execution, without other coercion than the moral principle of duty. This allowed, in fact, a negative to every legislature, on every measure proposed by Congress; a negative so frequently exercised in practice as to benumb the action of the federal government and to render it inefficient in its general objects, and more especially in pecuniary and foreign concerns. The want, too, of a separation of the legislative, executive and judiciary functions worked disadvantageously in practice.

This concentration of all powers in a legislature and the absence of the chief executive had, he said, "been the source of more evil than we have experienced from any other cause." He had little respect for the ability of Congress to get things done. Of the Continental Congress he had said:

OUR BODY WAS little numerous, but very contentious. Day after day was wasted on the most unimportant questions. . . . If the present Congress errs in too much talking, how can it be otherwise, in a body to which the people send one hundred and fifty lawyers, whose trade it is to question everything, yield nothing, and talk by the hour? That one hundred and fifty lawyers should do business together ought not to be expected. [Still,] with all the imperfections of our present government it is without comparison the best existing or that ever did exist.

In Philadelphia James Madison was leading the crusade for a Constitution—and Madison could be relied on to fight for the ideals which both Virginians shared. Jefferson had been sending him books from Paris dealing with liberal thought and ancient and modern representative government. The younger man would surely make good use of them. Yet, when Jefferson received the proposed Constitution he was disappointed. He wrote to John Adams, isolated in London: "I confess there are things in it which stagger all my dispositions to subscribe to what such an assembly has proposed." He wrote Madison more fully as to what he liked and what he did not like in the proposed document:

I LIKE MUCH the general idea of framing a government which should go on of itself peaceably, without needing continual recurrence to the state legislatures. I like the organization of the government into legislative, judiciary and executive. I like the power given the legislature to levy taxes, and for that reason solely approve of the greater house being chosen by the people directly. For though I think a house chosen by them will be very illy qualified to legislate for the Union, for foreign nations, etc., yet this evil does not weigh against the good of preserving inviolate the fundamental principle that the people are not to be taxed but by representatives chosen immediately by themselves. I am captivated by the compromise of the opposite claims of the great and little states, of the latter to equal, and the former to proportional influence. I am much pleased too with the substitution of the method of voting by persons, instead of that of voting by states and I like the negative [veto power] given to the executive. . . . There are other good things of less moment. I will now add what I do not like. First the omission of a bill of rights providing clearly and without the aid of sophisms for freedom of religion, freedom of the press, protection against standing armies, restriction against monopolies, the eternal and unremitting force of the habeas corpus laws, and trials by jury. . . . The second feature I dislike, and greatly dislike, is the abandonment in every instance of the necessity of rotation in office, and most particularly in the case of the President. Experience concurs with reason in concluding that the first magistrate will always be re-elected if the Constitution permits it. He is then an officer for life. . . .

I do not pretend to decide what would be the best method of procuring the establishment of the manifold good things in this Constitution, and of getting rid of the bad. Whether by adopting it in hopes of future amendment, or, after it has been duly weighed and canvassed by the people, after seeing the parts they generally dislike, and those they generally approve, to say to them "We see now what you wish. Send together your deputies again, let them frame a Constitution for you omitting what you have condemned, and establishing the powers you approve. Even these will be a great addition to the energy of your government!"—At all events I hope you will not be discouraged from other trials, if the present one should fail of its full effect. . . .

I own I am not a friend to a very energetic government. It is always oppressive . . . it is my principle that the will of the majority should always prevail. If they approve the proposed Convention in all its parts, I shall concur in it cheerfully, in hopes that they will amend it whenever they shall find it work wrong. I think our governments will remain virtuous for many centuries, as long as they are chiefly agricultural; and this will be as long as there shall be vacant lands in any part of America. When they get piled upon one another in large cities, as in Europe, they will become corrupt as in Europe. Above all things I hope the education of the common people will be attended to; convinced that on their good sense we may rely with the most security for the preservation of a due degree of liberty.

He later reiterated to Madison: "A bill of rights is what the people are entitled to against every government on earth, general or particular [that is, federal or state], and what no just government should refuse, or rest on inferences." He soon got his bill of rights in the first ten amendments, but his other big objection, a self-perpetuating President, was not guarded against until the twenty-second amendment became effective in 1951.

Jefferson saw little difference between a lifetime President and a King. England had a congress and a judiciary—but they also had George III and here lay all the evil in Jefferson's mind. He was, he said:

. . . MUCH AN ENEMY to monarchy before I came to Europe. I am ten thousand times more so since I have seen what they are. There is scarcely an evil known in these countries which may not be traced to their king as its source, nor a good which is not derived from the small fibers of republicanism among them. I can further say with safety there is not a crowned head in Europe whose talents or merit would entitle him to be elected vestryman by the people of any parish in America.

Jefferson's sojourn in Paris continued for another two years. Six-year-old daughter Marie—called Polly—joined him and went to the convent school with her older sister until they were both yanked out when Martha announced her intention of becoming a nun. He followed John Adams to Amsterdam to save the credit of the United States by refinancing, without congressional permission, a loan from Dutch bankers. He returned via Italy, where he again studied agriculture and architecture. He moved into a more pretentious—and more expensive—house where he could entertain and bought pictures and plaster busts for this and Monticello. He maintained his pleasant association with intellectual liberals and listened, as had Franklin, to the French physiocrats. He continued to be a pleasant, cultured gentleman with a mind and a curiosity that inquired into every subject, and a ready pen that reported on his interests. But there is something somewhat pathetic in the frequent entries in his account book which record the Ambassador to France buying a single ticket to go alone to the opera or a concert, and in the apartment to which he frequently retired at a hermitage conducted by lay brothers on Mont Calvaire, where guests could speak only at dinner. He longed for home and wrote:

I AM AS HAPPY NOWHERE ELSE and in no other society, and all my wishes end, where I hope my days will end, at Monticello. Too many scenes of happiness mingle themselves with all the recollections of my native woods and fields to suffer them to be supplanted in my affection by any other. I consider myself here as a traveler only, and not a resident.

In France, the crisis was fast approaching, and Jefferson's pen reported the early stages of the French Revolution from 1787 to 1789. For the most part he was a spectator and, in this as in all else relating to the ultimate triumph of liberal ideas, an optimist. As late as March, 1789, less than four months before blood started to flow, he wrote:

A COMPLETE REVOLUTION in this government has, within the space of two years . . . been effected merely by the force of public opinion, aided indeed by the want of money, which the dissipations of the court had brought on. And this revolution has not cost a single life. . . . The assembly of the States General begins the twenty-seventh of April. The representation of the people will be perfect. But they will be alloyed by an equal number of nobility and clergy. The first great question they will have to decide will be whether they shall vote by orders or persons. . . . And I have hopes that the majority of the nobles are already disposed to join the Tiers État [the people], in de-

ciding that the vote shall be by persons. This is the opinion
à la mode at present, and mode has acted a wonderful part in
the present instance. All the handsome young women, for example, are for the Tiers État, and this is an army more powerful in France than the two hundred thousand men of the King.

He was strongly in favor of a revolution that would bring republican government to France, from which, he hoped, it might spread
throughout Europe. "Republicanism," he said, "is the only form of
government which is not eternally at open or secret war with the
rights of mankind," and he believed it "the catholic principle of republicanism . . . that every people may establish what form of
government they please and change it as they please, the will of
the nation being the only thing essential." But he wanted the revolution to be moderate. Repeatedly, he cautioned Lafayette on this.
He was sure that, if the people were firm but patient, the King
would grant all that they needed for liberty and happiness.

When, in June, 1789, a month before the storming of the Bastille, the cause of moderation seemed to have reached an impasse,
Jefferson briefly ceased to be a spectator and took an official hand
in French politics. He had spent the day at Versailles with Lafayette and deputy Rabautde St. Étienne. That night he sent to each
of them a copy of a proposed charter which he had written and
which, he told Lafayette, contained "all the good in which all
parties agree." He proposed that the King present this at a *séance
royale* and sign it publicly together with the representatives of the
nobles, the clergy and the Third Estate—the people. Everybody
was then to go home and let things quiet down. The charter provided for retaining the King as an executive but placed taxing and
lawmaking powers in the hands of the States General. Jefferson
apologized for his presumption in presenting the charter, saying
that he had no excuse except "an unmeasurable love of your nation
and a painful anxiety lest despotism . . . should seize you again
with tenfold fury."

Jefferson came close to being the traditional innocent bystander in the outbreak of hostilities in Paris on July 12. He described the incident in his autobiography:

IN THE AFTERNOON a body of about one hundred German cavalry were advanced and drawn up in the Place Louis XV and about two hundred Swiss posted at a little distance in their rear. This drew people to the spot, who thus accidentally found themselves in front of the troops, merely at first as spectators; but as their numbers increased, their indignation rose. They retired a few steps and posted themselves on and behind large piles of stones, large and small, collected in that place for a bridge which was to be built adjacent to it. In this position, happening to be in my carriage on a visit, I passed through the lane they had formed, without interruption. But the moment after I had passed, the people attacked the cavalry with stones. They charged, but the advantageous position of the people and the showers of stones obliged the horse to retire, and quit the field altogether, leaving one of their number on the ground, and the Swiss in their rear not moving to their aid. This was the signal for universal insurrection, and this body of cavalry, to avoid being massacred, retired towards Versailles.

By the time that the revolution degenerated into a blood bath Jefferson was back in America. Later, he blamed the "crimes and cruelties" and " the evils which have flowed from them" entirely on poor, pretty, shallow Marie Antionette. This was in accord with his lifelong opposition to a mixture of women and politics, but history can hardly endorse his view. he wrote:

THE KING WAS NOW BECOME a passive machine in the hands of the National Assembly, and had he been left to himself, he would have willingly acquiesced in whatever they should devise as best for the nation. A wise constitution would have been formed, hereditary in his line, himself placed at its head, with powers so large as to enable him to do all the good of his station, and so limited as to restrain him from its abuse. This he would have faithfully administered, and more than this I do not believe he ever wished. But he had a Queen of absolute sway over his weak mind and timid virtue; and of a character the reverse of his in all points. This angel . . . was proud, disdainful of restraint, indignant at all obstacles to her will, eager in the pursuit of pleasure and firm enough to hold to her desires, or perish in their wreck. Her inordinate gambling and dissipations, . . . had been a sensible item in the exhaustion of the treasury, which called into action the reforming hand of the nation; and her opposition to it, her inflexible perverseness and dauntless spirit, led herself to the guillotine, and drew the King on with her, and plunged the world into crimes and calamities which will forever stain the pages of modern history. I have ever believed that had there been no Queen, there would have been no revolution.

Jefferson had requested a leave of absence from his Paris post. The day after it was granted he wrote to Madison, making one of his perennial announcements of retirement, "You ask me if I would accept any appointment on that side of the water? You know the circumstances which led me from retirement, step by step, and from one nomination to another up to the present. My object is a return to the same retirement. Whenever therefore I quit the present, it will not be to engage in any other office, and most especially any one which would require a constant residence from home." When he left Paris on September 26, 1789, he expected to be back in about three months to finish his stint as Ambassador before retiring. On that same day, unknown to him, Congress confirmed his appointment as Secretary of State in Washington's Cabinet, the start of the political era of his career.

His position in party politics at the time had been expressed a few months earlier in a letter to Francis Hopkinson:

YOU SAY that I have been dished up to you as an Antifederalist, and ask me if it be just. My opinion was never worthy enough of notice to merit citing; but since you ask it I will tell it you. I am not a Federalist, because I never submitted the whole system of my opinions to the creed of any party of men whatever in religion, in philosophy, in politics or in anything else where I was capable of thinking for myself. Such an addiction is the last degradation of a free and moral agent. If I could not go to heaven but with a party, I would not go there at all. Therefore I protest to you I am not of the party of Federalists. But I am much farther from that of the Antifederalists.

This was a position which, sadly, he could not long maintain.

CHAPTER V

THE FIRST CABINET

ॐ

ON MY WAY HOME . . . I received a letter from the President, General Washington, by express, covering an appointment to be Secretary of State. I received it with real regret. My wish had been to return to Paris . . . and to see the end of the revolution, which I then thought would be certainly and happily closed in less than a year. I then meant to return home, to withdraw from political life, into which I had been impressed by the circumstances of the times, to sink into the bosom of my family and friends, and to devote myself to studies more congenial to my mind. . . . I expressed these dispositions candidly to the President . . . but assured him that . . . I would sacrifice my own inclinations without hesitation. . . . This I left to his decision. I arrived at Monticello on the twenty-third of December, where I received a second letter from the President, expressing his continued wish that I should take my station there. . . . This silenced my reluctance, and I accepted the new appointment.

So Jefferson described, in his autobiography, his reluctant acceptance of a post in Washington's Cabinet in 1789. He must have realized that he was the only logical choice. Franklin was dying. Adams was Vice-President. John Jay, who had held the equivalent post under the confederacy, had moved over to the more congenial position of Chief Justice. That left Jefferson as the most experienced man in foreign affairs.

But the job was not limited to foreign affairs. There were five departments in the executive branch of the government. The post office was isolated, its head not of Cabinet rank. The Attorney General, Jefferson's second cousin Edmund Randolph, was a legal adviser to the government rather than an administrative officer. The Secretary of War, Henry Knox, administered military and Indian affairs. The Secretary of the Treasury, Alexander Hamilton, was supposed to be concerned solely with financial affairs, although Hamilton did not confine his interests, nor his interference, to this area. All other domestic concerns were lumped, together with foreign affairs, in the Department of State, which Jefferson was to administer with a staff of four, a part-time translator and an annual budget of eight thousand dollars which included his salary of three thousand five hundred dollars.

Most of the domestic chores were drudgery—correspondence with governors, marshals, judges and like work. Some of it he enjoyed. His first important paper after taking office was a proposal for a decimal system of weights and measures, "thus bringing the calculations of the principal affairs of life within the arithmetic of every man who can multiply and divide plain numbers." Although Congress had accepted his decimal system of money they unfortunately did not accept his radical system for weights and measures—possibly because the advanced mathematics and physics in his proposal were beyond their collective comprehension. For instance, for an invariable standard of length he proposed, "Let the standard of measure, then, be a uniform cylindrical rod of iron of such length as, in latitude 45° in the level of the ocean and in a cellar, or other place, the temperature of which does not vary through the year, shall perform its vibrations in small and equal arcs in one second of mean time."

As to linear measures, he suggested; "Let the foot be divided into ten inches; the inch into ten lines; the line into ten points. Let ten feet make a decad; ten decads one rood; ten roods a furlong; ten furlongs a mile." Under this system the foot would have been slightly shorter than the present foot, the inch somewhat longer and the mile almost twice as long; and there would have been nothing so illogical as a sixteenth of an inch.

As to weights and cubic measures, he proposed a cubic foot as a base unit, to be called a bushel. This would be divided or multiplied by tens for other units. The smallest unit, which he called a meter, would be a cubic inch. The unit of weight was to be the ancient English avoirdupois ounce, which was to be "the weight of a cube of rain water, of one tenth of a foot; or, rather, that it be the thousandth part of the weight of a cubic foot of rain water, weighed in the standard temperature." There would be ten ounces to the pound.

The supervision of patents was another of his more congenial duties which permitted him to pore over drawings and, on occasion, have inventors make experiments in his office, as he did with a man who claimed to have a process for getting fresh water from the sea. One patent request was from Eli Whitney, to whom he wrote:

YOUR DRAWING of the cotton gin was received. . . . As the state of Virginia, of which I am, carries on household manufactures of cotton to a great extent, as I also do myself, and one of our great embarrassments is the clearing the cotton of the seed, I feel a considerable interest in the success of your invention for family use. Permit me therefore to ask information from you on these points. Has the machine been thoroughly tried in the ginning of cotton, or is it yet but a machine of theory? What quantity of cotton has it cleaned on an average of several days, and worked by hand, and how many hands? What will be the cost of one of them made to be worked by hand? Favorable answers to these questions would induce me to engage one of them.

But these duties were merely side lines. His main mission, as it developed, was in the political arena, fighting for a government which would defend the human rights which he held sacred. Before leaving France he had said that he was not an Antifederalist, that he did not belong to a party. In New York he soon learned that he *was* an Antifederalist and would not only have to belong to a party, but head it. He was never a party leader as the term is understood today. He was, rather, the embodiment of the ideals of the party— its symbol, its idealist. He was a political philosopher rather than a politician. Years later he defined the basic need for a two-party system:

MEN BY THEIR CONSTITUTIONS are naturally divided into two parties: (1) Those who fear and distrust the people, and wish to draw all powers from them, into the hands of the higher classes. (2) Those who identify themselves with the people, have confidence in them, cherish and consider them as the most honest and safe, although not the most wise depositary of the public interests. In every country these two parties exist, and in every one where they are free to think, speak and write, they will declare themselves. Call them, therefore, Liberals and Serviles, Jacobins and Ultras, Whigs and Tories, Republicans and Federalists, Aristocrats and Democrats, or by whatever name you please, they are the same parties still, and pursue the same object. . . .

In every free and deliberating society, there must, from the nature of man, be opposite parties, and violent dissensions and discords; and one of these, for the most part, must prevail over the other for a longer or shorter time.

Wherever there are men, there will be parties, and wherever there are free men they will make themselves heard. Those of firm health and spirits are unwilling to cede more of their liberty than is necessary to preserve order; those of feeble constitutions will wish to see one strong arm able to protect them from the many. These are the Whigs and Tories of nature.

These mutual jealousies produce mutual security; and while the laws shall be obeyed, all will be safe. He alone is your enemy who disobeys them.

In New York he was appalled at a situation in which he saw a threat of the return of monarchical government.

HERE, . . . I found a state of things which, of all I had ever contemplated, I the least expected. I had left France in the first year of her revolution, in the fervor of natural rights and zeal for reformation. My conscientious devotion to these rights could not be heightened, but it had been aroused and excited by daily exercise. The President received me cordially, and my colleagues and the circle of principal citizens apparently with welcome. The courtesies of dinner parties given me, as a stranger newly arrived among them, placed me at once in their familiar society. But I cannot describe the wonder and mortification with which the table conversations filled me.

Politics were the chief topic, and a preference of kingly over republican government was evidently the favorite sentiment. An apostate I could not be, nor yet a hypocrite; and I found myself for the most part the only advocate on the republican side of the question, unless among the guests there chanced to be some member of that party from the legislative houses.

Whether there was ever any real threat of a monarchical government has long been disputed. Jefferson was firmly convinced that there was, and that duty compelled him to combat it, no matter how distasteful the controversy to his sensitive nature. He took more seriously than most the fight in Congress over Washington's title. The Senate, over which Adams presided, had proposed to designate the Chief Executive as "His Highness the President of the United States and Protector of Their Liberties." Although Jefferson was, at that time, a good friend of Adams, he quoted in this connection Franklin's description of the Vice-President as being "always an honest man, often a wise one, but sometimes, and in some things, absolutely out of his senses."

The outward forms of the government distressed Jefferson: "the levees, birthdays, pompous cavalcade to the statehouse on the meeting of Congress, the formal speech from the throne, the procession of Congress in a body to re-echo the speech in answer, etc., etc., etc." Washington was holding court—unwillingly, perhaps, but it reminded his fellow Virginian of the sycophants surrounding George III and Louis XVI. Years later he recorded his first impression of the new capital:

WHEN, on my return from Europe, I joined the government in March, 1790, at New York, I was much astonished, indeed, at the mimicry I found established of royal forms and ceremonies, and more alarmed . . . by the monarchical sentiments I heard expressed and openly maintained in every company, and among others by the high members of the government, executive and judiciary (General Washington alone excepted). . . . I took occasion, at various times, of expressing to General Washington my disappointment at these symptoms of a change of principle, and that I thought them encouraged by the forms and ceremonies which I found prevailing, not at all in character with the simplicity of republican government, and looking as if wishfully to those of European courts.

Before Jefferson's arrival the schism had started to develop within the government that would lead to the two-party political system, and the nuclei of these parties were beginning to form in the Federalists and the Antifederalists. Jefferson would become the leader of the latter, who became known as Republicans. It is rather confusing that today's Democrats hold Jefferson Day dinners to honor the leader of what was then called the Republican party. The Virginian had no desire for party leadership. He was literally forced into it by his fellow Cabinet-member Alexander Hamilton.

It is almost impossible to imagine two men who were more opposite in every respect than Jefferson and Hamilton. Jefferson was tall, slender, loose jointed and sometimes referred to as "gangling." Hamilton, fourteen years younger, was short and neatly compact, moving with an erect military bearing. Jefferson was born a gentleman. Hamilton was born in the West Indies under what was then politely termed the "bar sinister." John Adams vulgarly called him "the bastard brat of a Scots peddler." He had come to New York at the age of fifteen, gained an education—and considerable facility with the pen—at what is now Columbia University. He had been admitted to the bar, served as Washington's aide and secretary during the war, entered Congress and was a member of the Constitutional Convention.

Jefferson longed for the peace and isolation of Monticello. Hamilton had a Napoleonic urge for power and place. Jefferson was mild and modest. Hamilton was dogmatic and aggressive. Yet, when a hallowed principle was involved, Jefferson could be more stubborn and tenacious than Hamilton. Both were personally honest, tremendously able. It is safe to say that no subsequent Cabinet has ever held, at the same time, two more outstanding intellects.

There was an irreconcilable difference between the men on every basic idea, ideal and method, principally in the area of human rights, self-government, and the freedom of the individual. To Jefferson these things were sacred. To Hamilton the people were "a great beast" who must be checked and controlled by a government headed by the "rich and wellborn"—the only ones capable of governing. Hamilton had great respect for the English form of government, with its permanent executive and upper legislative house. He said that "nothing but a permanent body can check the imprudence of democracy." In Jefferson's words he was "chained by native partialities to everything English." Jefferson was an Anglophobe and a Francophile. In Hamilton's words he had "a womanish attachment to France and a womanish resentment against Great Britain."

Jefferson penned many comments on the man who became his

arch political opponent. Perhaps the kindest is, "Hamilton was, indeed, a singular character. Of acute understanding, disinterested, honest, and honorable in all private transactions, amiable in society, and duly valuing virtue in private life, yet so bewitched and perverted by the British example as to be under thorough conviction that corruption was essential to the government of a nation." A less kindly remark was, "Hamilton was not only a monarchist but for a monarchy bottomed in corruption."

Perhaps the best vignette of the difference between the two men was Jefferson's description of an incident at a dinner which both attended. "The room being hung around with a collection of the portraits of remarkable men, among them were those of Bacon, Newton and Locke, Hamilton asked me who they were. I told him they were my trinity of the three greatest men the world had ever produced, naming them. He paused for some time: 'The greatest man,' said he, 'that ever lived was Julius Caesar.' "

Hamilton's first problem as Secretary of the Treasury was to take care of funding the war debts and establishing the national credit. He did this by putting through Congress bills to redeem the depreciated certificates of debt of the Continental Congress at face value, to assume the debts of the individual states which had been incurred in the national interest, and to establish a national bank.

Jefferson wrote his opinion of Hamilton's financial system in what he called his *Ana;* a word he apparently created from the Latin suffix *"ana,"* which, when terminating a proper name, denotes anecdotes or sayings of the person bearing that name, for instance, "Jeffersoniana." Jefferson used it to title a collection of writings which he later described by saying:

VERY OFTEN . . . I made memoranda on loose scraps of paper, taken out of my pocket in the moment, and laid by to be copied fair at leisure, which, however, they hardly ever were. These scraps, therefore, ragged, rubbed and scribbled as they were, I had bound with the others by a binder who came into my cabinet, did it under my own eye, and without the opportunity of reading a single paper. At this day, after the lapse of twenty-five years, or more, from their dates, I have given to the whole a calm revisal, when the passions of the time are passed away, and the reasons of the transactions act alone on the judgment.

Much of the *Ana* is directed against Hamilton and contains not only records of private and semiofficial conversations, but second- and thirdhand hearsay reports. Jefferson detractors have claimed that his editing of it in 1818, obviously for posthumous publication, was a dishonorable act, in that it could serve no purpose other than to defame the departed. It is not clear whether the following is part of his original writing or subsequent editing. At the time, before the political rift with Hamilton started, he did not so violently condemn the financial measures. In contemporary letters he seemed to consider them necessary evils. He came on the scene after the Congress had passed the bill to redeem the Continental certificates:

HAMILTON'S FINANCIAL SYSTEM had then passed. It had two objects: first, as a puzzle, to exclude popular understanding and inquiry; second, as a machine for the corruption of the legislature, for he avowed the opinion that man could be governed by one of two motives only, force or interest; force, he observed, in this country was out of the question, and the interests, therefore, of the members must be laid hold of to keep the legislative in unison with the executive. And with grief and shame it must be acknowledged that his machine was not without effect; that even in this, the birth of our government, some members were found sordid enough to bend their duty to their interests, and to look after personal rather than public good.

It is well known that during the war the greatest difficulty we encountered was the want of money or means to pay our soldiers who fought, or our farmers, manufacturers and merchants who furnished the necessary supplies of food and clothing for them. After the expedient of paper money had exhausted itself, certificates of debt were given to the individual creditors, with assurance of payment so soon as the United States should be able. But the distresses of these people often obliged them to part with these for the half, the fifth, and even a tenth of their value; and speculators had made a trade of cozening them from the holders by the most fraudulent practices, and persuasions that they would never be paid. In the bill for funding and paying these, Hamilton made no difference between the original holders and the fraudulent purchasers of this paper. Great and just repugnance arose at putting these two classes of creditors on the same footing, and great exertions were used to pay the former the full value, and to the latter, the price only which they had paid, with interest. But this would have prevented the game which was to be played, and for which the minds of greedy members were already tutored and prepared.

When the trial of strength on these several efforts had indicated the form in which the bill would finally pass, this being known within doors sooner than without, and especially than to those who were in distant parts of the Union, the base scramble began. Couriers and relay horses by land, and swift-sailing pilot boats by sea, were flying in all directions. Active partners and agents were associated and employed in every state, town and country neighborhood, and this paper was brought up at five shillings, and even as low as two shillings in the pound, before the holder knew that Congress had already provided for its redemption at par. . . . Men thus enriched by the dexterity of a leader would follow of course the chief who was leading them to fortune, and become the zealous instruments of all his enterprises.

This game was over, and another was on the carpet at the moment of my arrival; and to this I was most ignorantly and innocently made to hold the candle. This fiscal maneuver is well known by the name of the assumption. Independently of

the debts of Congress, the states had during the war contracted separate and heavy debts . . . and the more debt Hamilton could rake up, the more plunder for his mercenaries. . . .
And so another scramble was set on foot among the several
states, and some got much, some little, some nothing. But the
main object was obtained, the phalanx of the Treasury was
reinforced by additional recruits. This measure produced the
most bitter and angry contest ever known in Congress, before
or since the union of the states. I arrived in the midst of it.
But a stranger to the ground, a stranger to the actors on it, so
long absent as to have lost all familiarity with the subject, and
as yet unaware of its object, I took no concern in it.

The great and trying question, however, was lost in the
House of Representatives. So high were the feuds excited by
this subject that on its rejection business was suspended. . . .
The eastern [New England] members, particularly, who . . .
were the principal gamblers in these scenes, threatened a secession and dissolution. Hamilton was in despair. As I was
going to the President's one day, I met him in the street. He
walked me backwards and forwards before the President's
door for half an hour. He painted pathetically the temper into
which the legislature had been wrought; the disgust of those
who were called the creditor states; the danger of the secession
of their members, and the separation of the states. He observed that the members of the administration ought to act in
concert; that though this question was not of my department,
yet a common duty should make it a common concern; that
. . . it was probable that an appeal from me to the judgment
and discretion of some of my friends might effect a change in
the vote, and the machine of government, now suspended,
might be again set into motion.

I told him that I was really a stranger to the whole subject;
that not having yet informed myself of the system of finances
adopted, I knew not how far this was a necessary sequence;
that undoubtedly if its rejection endangered a dissolution of

our Union at this incipient stage, I should deem that the most unfortunate of all consequences, to avert which all partial and temporary evils should be yielded. I proposed to him, however, to dine with me the next day, and I would invite another friend or two, bring them into conference together, and I thought it impossible that reasonable men, consulting together coolly, could fail, by some mutual sacrifices of opinion, to form a compromise which was to save the Union.

The discussion took place. . . . It was finally agreed that . . . the preservation of the Union and of concord among the states was more important, and that therefore it would be better that the vote of rejection should be rescinded, to effect which some members should change their votes. But it was observed that this pill would be peculiarly bitter to the southern states, and that some concomitant measure should be adopted to sweeten it a little to them. There had before been propositions to fix the seat of government either at Philadelphia, or at Georgetown of the Potomac; and it was thought that by giving it to Philadelphia for ten years, and to Georgetown permanently afterwards, this might, as an anodyne, calm in some degree the ferment which might be excited by the other measure alone.

So two of the Potomac members . . . agreed to change their votes, and Hamilton undertook to carry the other point. . . . And so the assumption was passed, and twenty millions of stock divided among favored states, and thrown in as a pabulum to the stockjobbing herd. This added to the number of votaries to the Treasury, and made its chief the master of every vote in the legislature which might give to the government the direction suited to his political views.

I know well, and so must be understood, that nothing like a majority in Congress had yielded to this corruption. Far from it. But a division, not very unequal, had already taken place in the honest part of that body between the parties styled Republican and Federal. The latter being monarchists in principle adhered to Hamilton of course as their leader in that principle, and this mercenary phalanx added to them, insured him always a majority in both houses; so that the whole action of legislature was now under the direction of the Treasury. Still the machine was not complete. The effect of the funding system and of the assumption would be temporary; it would be lost with the loss of the individual members whom it had enriched, and some engine of influence more permanent must be contrived while these myrmidons were yet in place to carry it through all opposition. This engine was the Bank of the United States. . . .

This condemnation of Hamilton's fiscal plan should be considered as a partisan rather than an objective criticism. From a financial and economic standpoint, as opposed to a purely political view, there was much to be said for Hamilton's program. Jefferson never had an objective attitude toward government financing. He was an ardent proponent of "soak the rich," saying that "taxes should be proportioned to what may annually be spared by the individual." And, in connection with a tariff bill the burden of which "will fall principally on the rich, it is a general desire to make them contribute the whole money we want, if possible."

Jefferson expressed a unique opinion on fiscal matters shortly before leaving France in a letter to Madison, in which he presented the "self-evident" principle that "the earth belongs . . . to the living; that the dead have neither powers nor rights over it." He first applied this principle to property, saying that, by natural right, the portion of the earth

. . . OCCUPIED BY ANY INDIVIDUAL ceases to be his when himself ceases to be, and reverts to the society. If the society has formed no rules for the appropriation of its lands . . . it will be taken by the first occupants, and these will generally be the wife and children of the decedent. If they have formed rules of appropriation, those rules may give it to the wife and children, or to some one of them, or to the legatee of the deceased. So they may give it to his creditor. But the child, the lagatee or creditor, takes it, not by natural right, but by a law of the society of which he is a member, and to which he is subject. Then no man can, by *natural right,* oblige the lands he occupied, or the persons who succeed him in that occupation, to the payment of debts contracted by him. For if he could, he might during his own life eat up the usufruct of the lands for several generations to come; and then the lands would belong to the dead, and not to the living, which is the reverse of our principle. What is true of every member of the society, individually, is true of them all collectively; since the rights of the whole can be no more than the sum of the rights of the individuals.

He then applied the principle to the public debt by writing:

I SUPPOSE that the received opinion, that the public debts of one generation devolve on the next, has been suggested by our seeing habitually in private life that he who succeeds to lands is required to pay the debts of his ancestor or testator, without considering that this requisition is municipal only, not moral, flowing from the will of the society . . . but that between society and society, or generation and generation there is no municipal obligation, no umpire but the law of nature . . . would it not be wise and just for that nation [France] to declare in the constitution they are forming that neither the legislature nor the nation itself can validly contract more debt than they may pay within their own age?

He then went on to apply this reasoning to laws as well as debts:

. . . NO SOCIETY CAN MAKE a perpetual constitution, or even a perpetual law. The earth belongs always to the living generation. They may manage it then, and what proceeds from it, as they please, during their usufruct. They are masters too of their own persons, and consequently may govern them as they please.

This was not an idle thought of the moment with Jefferson. He returned to it repeatedly throughout the remainder of his life.

During Jefferson's second year as Secretary of State his fear of a monarchist plot had become an *idée fixe,* and he seemed to feel that "Federalist" and "Monarchist" were synonymous. He wrote to William Short, chargé in Paris, of proposals to subvert the form of government "to make way for king, lord and commons. There are high names here in favor of this doctrine." Then he added, in cipher, "Adams, Jay, Hamilton, Knox, and many of the Cincinnati. The second says nothing: the third is open. Both are dangerous. They pant after union with England, as the power which is to support their projects, and are most determined anti-Gallicans. It is prognosticated that our Republic is to end with the President's life, but I believe they will find themselves all head and no body." By inference this might even implicate Washington, who was a member of the Society of Cincinnati.

Jefferson's distrust of John Adams stemmed from a series of newspaper articles written by the latter under the title *Discourses of Davilla,* which led to an act by Jefferson which unintentionally involved both men in a public controversy that rent the executive branch and presaged the rift that ultimately developed between the friends. Thomas Paine had written *The Rights of Man* in Europe. A man named Beckley loaned a copy to Jefferson, asking him to send it on to a man named Smith after he had read it. Jefferson sent with it a covering letter in which he said that he was "extremely pleased to find it will be reprinted here and that something is at length to be publicly said against the political heresies which have sprung up among us." A Philadelphia printer used the letter, without permission, as a preface to the American edition of Paine's work. Everybody knew, or thought they knew, that the "political heresies" to which he referred were Adams *Discourses.* Accusing the Vice-President of heresy was a serious charge, and Jefferson did not deny it when he wrote to Washington:

I AM AFRAID the indiscretion of a printer had committed me with my friend, Mr. Adams, for whom, as one of the most honest and disinterested men alive, I have a cordial esteem, increased by long habits of concurrence in opinion in the days of his republicanism; and even since his apostasy to hereditary monarchy and nobility, though we differ, we differ as friends should. . . . Mr. Adams will unquestionably take to himself the charge of political heresy, as conscious of his own views of drawing the present government to the form of the English constitution, and, I fear, will consider me as meaning to injure him in the public eye. . . .

Then a new pen took up the feud. A series of newspaper articles attacking Jefferson appeared over the signature Publicola. Jefferson was sure John Adams had written them. He said, "A writer under the name of Publicola, in attacking all Paine's principles, is very desirous of involving me in the same censure with the author. I certainly merit the same, for I profess the same principles. . . . A Boston paper has declared that Mr. Adams has no more concern in the publication of the writings of Publicola than the author of the *Rights of Man* himself . . . the disavowal is not enterely credited, because not from Mr. Adams himself, and because the style and sentiments raise so strong a presumption." Publicola was *an* Adams—but not John. It was his able and outspoken twenty-four-year-old son John Quincy.

Finally, Jefferson wrote a peace overture to Adams saying, in part:

I HAVE A DOZEN TIMES taken up my pen to write to you, and as often laid it down again, suspended between opposing considerations. I determine, however, to write from a conviction that truth between candid minds can never do harm . . . that you and I differ in our ideas of the best form of government, is well known to us both; but we have differed as friends should do, respecting the purity of each other's motives, and confining our difference of opinion to private conversation. And I can declare with truth, in the presence of the Almighty, that nothing was further from my intention or expectation than to have either my own or your name brought before the public on this occasion. The friendship and confidence which has so long existed between us required this explanation from me, and I know you too well to fear any misconstruction of the motives of it.

To this Adams replied:

IF YOU SUPPOSE that I have, or ever had, a design or desire of attempting to introduce a government of King, Lords, and Commons, or in other words, a hereditary Executive, or a hereditary senate, either into the government of the United States, or that of any individual state, you are wholly mistaken. There is not such a thought expressed or intimated in any public writing or private letter, and I may safely challenge all mankind to produce such a passage, and quote the chapter and verse. If you have ever put such a construction on anything of mine, I beg you would mention it to me, and I will undertake to convince you that it has no such meaning.

In the field of foreign affairs Jefferson started, during his first months in the Cabinet, to push an interest that would ultimately lead to the Louisiana Purchase. Years before, in his *Notes on Virginia,* he had forecast the importance of the Mississippi River to western settlers. Now, with war between Spain and England brewing, he saw a chance to force Spain's hand on navigation of the river, and wrote a bellicose memorandum to the American chargé in Madrid:

YOU WILL BE ENABLED to meet the minister [of Spain] in conversations on the subject of navigation of the Mississippi, to which we wish you to lead his attention immediately. Impress him thoroughly with the necessity of an early, and even an immediate settlement of this matter . . . he must be made to understand unequivocally that a resumption of the negotiation is not desired on our part, unless he can determine, in the first opening of it, to yield the immediate and full enjoyment of that navigation. . . . You know that the navigation cannot be practiced without a port, where the sea and river vessels may meet and exchange loads. . . . The fixing on a proper port, and the degree of freedom it is to enjoy in its operations, will require negotiation, and be governed by events. There is danger, indeed, that even the unavoidable delay of sending a negotiator here, may render the mission too late for the preservation of peace. It is impossible to answer for the forbearance of our western citizens. We endeavor to quiet them with the expectation of an attainment of their rights by peacable means. But should they, in a moment of impatience, hazard others, there is no saying how far we may be led; for neither themselves nor their rights will ever be abandoned by us.

The Secretary spent much time trying to negotiate trade treaties with England and France. In this, as in all else, Jefferson was pro-France, anti-England, although the British were far and away the best customer and leading supplier. Hamilton, as usual, interfered. In fact, according to Jefferson, the Treasury Secretary gave the British envoy behind-the-scenes information on what was going on in the Cabinet and Congress. No trade treaties were concluded, but Jefferson expressed his philosophy of free trade and hinted at the retaliatory tactics which he would some day expand into the disastrous Embargo Act:

INSTEAD OF EMBARRASSING commerce under piles of regulating laws, duties and prohibitions, could it be relieved from all its shackles in all parts of the world, could every country be employed in producing that which nature has best fitted it to produce, and each be free to exchange with others mutual surpluses for mutual wants, the greatest mass possible would then be produced of those things which contribute to human life and human happiness; the numbers of mankind would be increased, and their condition bettered. . . . But should any nation, contrary to our wishes, suppose it may better find its advantages by continuing its system of prohibitions, duties and regulations, it behooves us to protect our citizens, their commerce and navigation, by counterprohibitions, duties and regulations, also.

As the end of Washington's first term approached, in the fall of 1792, fairly definite party lines had been drawn. Generally, they were based on economic interests. Those who labored to produce—farmers and artisans—were usually Republicans, and looked to Jefferson as their champion. They who benefited by commerce, finance and the carrying trade were usually Federalists, led by Hamilton. Coincidently, the division was also geographical. New England was Federalist, the agricultural South and West were Republican. The middle states were a battleground.

Jefferson and Hamilton partisans had created such a clamor in the press that the President intervened to calm his two able aides. He wrote each of them soothing letters appealing for their co-operation in terms of patriotism, saying:

HOW UNFORTUNATE, and how much to be regretted is it, then, that while we are encompassed on all sides with avowed enemies, and insidious friends, internal dissensions should be harrowing and tearing our vitals. . . . My earnest wish, and my fondest hope . . . is that instead of wounding suspicions and irritating charges, there may be liberal allowances, mutual forbearance and temporizing yieldings on all sides.

Jefferson replied:

THAT SUCH DISSENSIONS have taken place is certain, and even among those who are nearest to you in the administration. To no one have they given deeper concern than myself; to no one equal mortification at being myself a part of them. . . . That I have utterly, in my private conversations, disapproved of the system of the Secretary of the Treasury, I acknowledge and avow; and this was not merely a speculative difference. His system flowed from principles adverse to liberty, and was calculated to undermine and demolish the Republic, by creating an influence of his department over the members of the legislature.

He then proceeded to enumerate, at great length, Hamilton's iniquities. The Treasury Secretary had corrupted the legislature so that their votes were no longer those of "representatives of the people, but of deserters of the rights and interests of the people." He was trying to get all power into the executive branch of central government, "for the purpose of subverting, step by step, the principles of the Constitution." He had private relations with the British envoy which had sabotaged Jefferson's plan to induce England to "abate their severities against our commerce." Jefferson then went on to rehash, at a length that must have been boring to Washington, the newspaper mudslinging campaign that had been going on for a year, laying all the blame at Hamilton's door.

His long peroration started with an announcement of his intention to resign at the end of Washington's term:

WHEN I CAME into this office, it was with a resolution to retire from it as soon as I could with decency. It pretty early appeared to me that the proper moment would be the first of those epochs at which the Constitution seems to have contemplated a periodical change or renewal of the public servants. In this I was confirmed by your resolution respecting the same period; from which, however, I am happy in hoping you have departed. I look to that period with the longing of a wave-worn mariner, who has at length the land in view, and shall count the days and hours which still lie between me and it. In the meanwhile, my main object will be to wind up the business of my office, avoiding as much as possible all new enterprise.

But, after he was again a private citizen, he would keep up the fight if necessary in justice to his honor and the welfare of his country:

IF MY OWN JUSTIFICATION, or the interest of the Republic shall require it, I reserve to myself the right of then appealing to my country, subscribing my name to whatever I write, and using with freedom and truth the facts and names necessary to place the cause and its just form before that tribunal. To a thorough disregard of the honors and emoluments of office, I join as great a value for the esteem of my countrymen, and, conscious of having merited it by an integrity which cannot be reproached, and by an enthusiastic devotion to their rights and liberty, I will not suffer my retirement to be clouded by the slanders of a man whose history, from the moment at which history can stoop to notice him, is a tissue of machinations against the liberty of the country which has not only received and given him bread, but heaped its honors on his head.

Hamilton wrote a similar, though shorter and less violent letter to the Chief Executive in which he placed the blame on Jefferson and suggested that both he and Jefferson might be replaced in the Cabinet. He concluded by saying:

NEVERTHELESS, I pledge my honor to you, sir, that if you shall hereafter form a plan to reunite the members of your administration upon some steady principle of co-operation, I will faithfully concur in executing it during my continuance in office. And I will not directly or indirectly say or do a thing that shall endanger a feud.

These were pleasant words, even if they were not sincere.

As Washington's second inauguration neared, Jefferson changed his mind about resigning. He wrote to his daughter Martha:

I HAVE FOR SOME TIME past been under an agitation of mind which I scarcely ever experienced before, produced by a check on my purpose of returning home at the close of this session of Congress. . . . My mind was fixed on it with a fondness which was extreme, the purpose firmly declared to the President, when I became assailed from all quarters with a variety of objections. Among these it was urged that my retiring just when I had been attacked in the public papers would injure me in the eyes of the public, who would suppose I either withdrew from investigation, or because I had not tone of mind sufficient to meet slander. The only reward I ever wished on my retirement was to carry with me nothing like a disapprobation of the public. These representations have for some weeks past shaken a determination which I have thought the whole world could not have shaken. . . . I feel a possibility that I may be detained here into the summer.

A few days later he told the President, "That I should be willing, if he had taken no arrangements to the contrary, to continue somewhat longer, how long I could not say, perhaps till summer, perhaps autumn."

When the new Congress met, in March, 1793, Hamilton and the Federalists were still riding high, but Jefferson could be encouraged by a slim Republican majority in the lower house, due largely to the admission of staunchly Republican Kentucky to the Union. Although the Federalists still dominated the Senate, Jefferson wrote, "I think we may consider the tide of this government as now at the fullest, and that it will, from the commencement of the next session of Congress, retire and subside into the true principles of the Constitution."

Early in 1793 came news of a new development in the French Revolution. The King had been dethroned and then executed, an event which Jefferson calmly, and callously, commented on by writing, "We have just received here the news of the decapitation of the King of France. Should the present foment in Europe not produce republics everywhere, it will at least soften the monarchical governments by rendering monarchs amenable to punishment like other criminals." The excesses of the Jacobins did not unduly distress the Virginian. Previously he had written to Lafayette, "we are not to expect to be translated from despotism to liberty in a featherbed." Now he sought to comfort his ex-secretary William Short, still in Europe, by writing:

IN A STRUGGLE which was necessary, many guilty persons fell without the forms of trial, and with them some innocent. These I deplore as much as anybody, and shall deplore some of them to the day of my death. But I deplore them as I should have done had they fallen in battle. It was necessary to use the arm of the people, a machine not quite so blind as balls and bombs, but blind to a certain degree. A few of their cordial friends met at their hands the fate of enemies. But time and truth will rescue and embalm their memories, while their posterity will be enjoying that very liberty for which they would never have hesitated to offer up their lives. The liberty of the whole earth was depending on the issue of the contest, and was ever such a prize won with so little innocent blood? My own affections have been deeply wounded by some of the martyrs to this cause, but rather than it should have failed I would have seen half the earth desolated; were there but an Adam and Eve left in every country, and left free, it would be better than as it now is.

But the complexion of affairs in France created a practical problem for the American Secretary of State. With the end of the monarchy there was no recognized government to which to make payments on America's war debt to France. Jefferson agreed to a temporary suspension of payment. But, in several letters, he established the principle that has since guided the United States in recognizing new foreign governments. He wrote:

WE CERTAINLY CANNOT deny to other nations that principle whereon our government is founded, that every nation has a right to govern itself internally under what forms it pleases, and to change these forms at its own will; and externally to transact business with other nations through whatever organ it chooses, whether that be a king, convention, assembly, committee, president, or whatever it be. The only thing essential is the will of the nation.

A more perplexing problem soon arose. Europe flamed into war, with England and Spain against France. The treaty of 1778 between the United States and France was still in force and provided, "The two parties guarantee mutually from the present time, and forever against all other powers, to wit: The United States to his most Christian Majesty, the present possessions of the crown of France in America . . . the contracting parties declare, that in case of a rupture between France and England, the . . . guarantee declared in the said article shall have its full force and effect the moment such war shall break out." In the French view this clearly meant that the United States was bound to fight any English encroachments in the French West Indians. Washington called a Cabinet meeting which Jefferson reported in his *Ana:*

THE PRESIDENT SENDS a series of questions to be considered and calls a meeting. Although those sent me were in his own handwriting yet it was palpable from the style . . . that the language was Hamilton's, and the doubts his alone. They led to a declaration . . . that our treaty with France was void. . . . Knox subscribed at once to Hamilton's opinion that we ought to declare the treaty void, acknowledging at the same time, like a fool that he is, that he knew nothing about it. I was clear it remained valid. . . . The President told me . . . he had never had a doubt about the validity of the treaty; but that since a question had been suggested he thought it ought to be considered.

But even France's friend Jefferson had no intention of going to war. He was pragmatic about it, saying, "I hope France, England and Spain will all see it to their interest to let us make bread for them in peace and to give us a good price for it." He took a broader view when he wrote, "No country perhaps was ever so thoroughly against war as ours. These dispositions pervade every description of its citizens, whether in or out of office. They cannot perhaps suppress their affections, nor their wishes. But they will suppress the effects of them so as to preserve a fair neutrality." But he did not think that the Secretary of the Treasury wanted a "fair neutrality." "Hamilton," he said, "is panic-struck if we refuse our breech to every kick which Great Britain may choose to give it. He is for proclaiming at once the most abject principles." And on another occasion, "If anything prevents it being a mere English neutrality, it will be that the penchant of the President is not that way, and, above all, the ardent spirit of our constituents. The line is now drawn so clearly as to show on one side: [pro-English] (1) The fashionable circles of Philadelphia, New York, Boston and Charleston; natural aristocrats. (2) Merchants trading on British capital. (3) Paper [money] men. All the old Tories are found in some one of the three descriptions. On the other side are: (1) Merchants trading on their own capital. (2) Irish merchants. (3) Tradesmen, mechanics, farmers and every other possible description of our citizens."

The Cabinet agreed unanimously that a proclamation should be issued as to the position of the United States, but Jefferson was adamant that it should be a presidential statement that the country was at peace, not a neutrality proclamation. He based this on the hairsplitting distinction that, under the Constitution, the President could not proclaim neutrality any more than he could declare war —that was a congressional prerogative. Also, he wanted to keep the British Minister guessing as to the American intentions so that he could get "the broadest neutral privileges as a price." Attorney General Randolph drew a proclamation and showed it to Jefferson to convince him that it did not contain the word "neutrality."

Jefferson's efforts to gain concessions from George Hammond, the British Minister, came to naught. Behind his back, Alexander Hamilton had already assured the Britisher that the Cabinet did not interpret the French treaty as requiring America to enter the war. It was at this time that Hammond wrote his government that he would cultivate Hamilton and by-pass Jefferson, who was "blinded by his attachment to France and hatred of Great Britain."

Treading the path of fair neutrality was made no easier for Jefferson by the arrival in Philadelphia, on the day that the neutrality proclamation was issued, of a new French Minister, Edmond Charles Genêt, who carried secret instructions which called for actions far beyond the scope of a minister to a neutral country. He was to see to the fitting out of privateers in United States ports; inflame the people with "anonymous publications"; and try to seize Louisiana from Spain with a private army to be recruited in America.

France could not have chosen a worse man as a missionary to America for either proper or improper purposes. Genêt was opinionated, tactless and flew into violent rages when opposed. The United States Minister in Paris had warned Washington that he had "the manner and look of an upstart." Also, he received a complete misconception of the attitude of the American people as a result of the rousing receptions tendered him by the Republicans on the trip from the debarkation point in Charleston to Philadelphia. He was sure that the public was panting to come to the aid of France, that they were held in check only by the executive branch of the government.

Jefferson rather endorsed this view when he said that Genêt's arrival "would furnish occasion for the *people* to testify their affections without respect to the cold caution of their government." The Secretary at first received the new Minister at face value. He wrote, "It is impossible for anything to be more affectionate, magnanimous than the purport of his mission." He quoted Genêt as saying, "We know that under present circumstances we have a right to call upon you for the guaranty of our islands. But we do not desire it. We wish you to do nothing but what is for your own good, and we will do all in our power to promote it. Cherish your own peace and prosperity. . . . We see in you the only person on earth who can love us sincerely, and merit to be so loved." Jefferson concluded, "In short, he offers everything, and asks nothing."

Jefferson's honeymoon with Genêt is the shortest in diplomatic history. The Frenchman presented his credentials on May 18, 1793. On July 7 Jefferson wrote, "Never in my opinion was so calamitous an appointment made as that of the present Minister of France here. Hotheaded, all imagination, no judgment, passionate, disrespectful and even indecent towards the President in his written as well as verbal communications, talking of appeals from him to Congress, from them to the people, urging the most unreasonable and groundless propositions, and in the most dictatorial style, etc., etc., etc. . . . He renders my position immensely difficult."

In the ensuing weeks Genêt almost wrecked the pro-French Republican party. His insolence and intemperance culminated in criticisms of Washington that only the lunatic fringe of Republicans would tolerate. Jefferson said, "he will sink the Republican interest if they do not abandon him." On August 16 he wrote to Gouverneur Morris, American Minister to France, instructing him to request Genêt's recall, saying:

MR. GENÉT HAD BEEN THEN but a little time with us; and but a little more was necessary to develop in him a character and conduct so unexpected and so extraordinary as to place us in the most distressing dilemma between our regard for his nation, which is constant and sincere, and a regard for our laws. . . . When the government forbids their citizens to arm and engage in the war, he undertakes to arm and engage them. When they forbid vessels to be fitted in their ports for cruising on nations with whom they are at peace, he commissions them to fit and cruise. . . .

Not content with using our force, whether we will or not, in the military line against nations with whom we are at peace, . . . he . . . endeavors to excite discord and distrust between our citizens and those whom they have entrusted with their government, between the different branches of our government, between our nation and his.

But none of these things, we hope, will be found in his power. That friendship which dictates to us to bear with his conduct yet a while, lest the interests of his nation here should suffer injury, will hasten them to replace an agent whose dispositions are such a misrepresentation of theirs, and whose continuance here is inconsistent with order, peace, respect and that friendly correspondence which we hope will ever subsist between the two nations.

The Genêt incident was the most distressing episode in Jeffersons' term of office. It involved his deep affection for the French and belief in their revolution, his great respect for Washington; and he had to "descend daily into the arena like a gladiator" to prevent Hamilton and Knox from making political hay by exposing Genêt's worst offenses to the public and thus causing an open rift with France. Of Jefferson's handling of the matter a future great Secretary of State, John Quincy Adams, later said, "Mr. Jefferson's papers on that controversy present the most perfect model of diplomatic discussion and expostulation in modern times."

In September, after the Genêt affair, Jefferson again tendered his resignation; Washington again induced him to withdraw it. In the fall there was an epidemic of yellow fever in Philadelphia and the government moved to nearby Germantown, where Jefferson was fortunate to get a room with two beds and invited Madison and Monroe to stay with him, making this the only occasion in history when three Presidents of the United States literally slept together.

On December 31, 1793, Jefferson resigned for the third time— and this time he meant it. He wrote to Madison:

I HAVE NOW BEEN in the public service four and twenty years. . . . I have served my tour. . . . There has been a time when . . . perhaps, the esteem of the world was of higher value in my eye than everything in it. But age, experience and reflection, preserving to that only its due value, have set a higher on tranquillity. The motion of my blood no longer keeps time with the tumult of the world. It leads me to seek happiness in the lap and love of my family, in the society of my neighbors and my books, in the wholesome occupations of my farm and my affairs, in an interest or affection in every bud that opens, in every breath that blows around me, in an entire freedom of rest, of motion, of thought, owing account to myself alone of my hours and actions.

So, at the age of fifty, the great Virginian for the second time announced his permanent retirement from public life, little knowing that his most grueling years of public service lay ahead.

CHAPTER VI

THE TWO PARTY SYSTEM

❦

"I return to farming with an ardor which I scarcely knew in my youth and which has got the better entirely of my love of study. Instead of writing ten or twelve letters a day, which I have been in the habit of doing as a thing of course, I put off answering my letters now, farmerlike, till a rainy day and then find it sometimes postponed by other necessary occupations." So wrote Jefferson early in 1794, at the beginning of three years which he devoted to his family and farm. And, he added, "I think it is Montaigne who has said that ignorance is the softest pillow on which a man can rest his head. I am sure it is true as to everything political, and shall endeavor to estrange myself to everything of that character."

Jefferson tried to remain a mute bystander in political affairs, but it was not entirely possible. The balance of power in the Cabinet was destroyed when he left. His successor was the Attorney General, Edmund Randolph, a wishy-washy Republican who was no match for Hamilton. The latter virtually took over foreign affairs as well as fiscal ones. Also, shortly after Jefferson went to Monticello, James Monroe went to Paris as Minister, and forty-five-year-old James Madison married the vivacious widow Dolly Todd and, for a time, was more interested in his bride than in Congress.

None of the three great Virginia Republicans were active on the Philadelphia firing line, and Washington was dependent solely on Federalist advisers. Years later, in editing his *Ana,* Jefferson wrote:

FROM THE MOMENT . . . of my retiring from the administration, the Federalists got unchecked hold of General Washington. His memory was already sensibly impaired by age, the firm tone of mind for which he had been remarkable was beginning to relax, its energy was abated; a listlessness of labor, a desire for tranquillity had crept on him and a willingness to let others act and even think for him.

During the first year of Jefferson's retirement the "Whisky Rebellion" fanned his ire against Hamilton. Jefferson called the Treasury Secretary's excise levy on whisky an "infernal tax" because it bore solely on his people, the farmers. Whisky was an agricultural product. Western farmers could not bring bulky grain to market over the rugged Alleghenies. But if they ran it through a pot still to convert it to whisky, a year's crop could be carried on a pack mule. The farmers of western Pennsylvania—a hotbed of Republicanism —refused to pay the tax. When they rioted, drove out the tax collectors, and held a meeting to talk of secession, Washington called out twelve thousand militia who marched across the mountains, accompanied by Hamilton, to suppress the "rebellion." The army was greeted by welcoming committees rather than armed rebels, and Jefferson commented that they had been "objects of . . . laughter, not of . . . fear," but that, in the west, "a separation which was perhaps a very distant and problematical event is now near and certain."

Jefferson saw grave danger in Hamilton riding at the head of an army. He reported to Monroe that:

. . . THE SERVILE COPYIST of Mr. Pitt thought he, too, must have his alarms, his insurrections and plots against the Constitution. . . . Hence the example of employing military force for civil purposes when it has been impossible to produce a single fact of insurrection . . . But it answered the favorite purposes of strengthening government and increasing public debt; and, therefore, an insurrection was announced and proclaimed and armed against but could never be found.

The Federalists blamed the whisky insurrection on the recently formed Democratic societies, political clubs which were patterned after the Jacobin Society of France. The most famous of these became New York's Tammany Hall. They were fiercely pro-French and anti-English and criticized violently any act of government counter to their convictions. Washington, always sensitive to criticism, abhorred them. In this day, when public criticism of government is taken for granted, it is interesting to recall what the "Father of His Country" said on the subject:

CAN ANYTHING BE more absurd, more arrogant, or more pernicious to the peace of society than for self-created bodies, forming themselves into permanent censors, and under the shade of night in a conclave, . . . to declare that this act is unconstitutional, and that act is pregnant of mischief. . . . Such a stretch of arrogant presumption . . . is not to be reconciled with laudable motives.

In this Jefferson saw Washington departing from his aloof position to side with the Federalists. He wrote to Madison:

THE DENUNCIATION of the Democratic societies is one of the extraordinary acts of boldness of which we have seen so many from the faction of Monocrats. It is wonderful indeed that the President should have permitted himself to be the organ of such an attack on the freedom of discussion, the freedom of writing, printing and publishing.

He ended this letter with a veiled hint that he would like to see

Madison succeed Washington. "I do not see, in the minds of those with whom I converse, a greater affliction than the fear of your retirement; but this must not be, unless to a more splendid and a more efficacious post. There I should rejoice to see you; I hope I may say, I shall rejoice to see you." Madison replied that for reasons that were "insuperable as well as obvious" he could not consider Jefferson's suggestion. But, he told Jefferson, "You ought to be preparing yourself . . . to hear truths which no inflexibility will be able to withstand." To this frightening thought Jefferson replied:

AS TO MYSELF, the subject had been thoroughly weighed and decided on. . . . The idea being once presented to me, my own quiet required that I should face it and examine it. I did so thoroughly and had no difficulty to see that every reason which had determined me to retire from the office I then held operated more strongly against that which was insinuated to be my object. . . . The little spice of ambition which I had in my younger days has long since evaporated, and I set still less store by a posthumous than present name. The question is forever closed with me.

In this exchange of letters the Presidency was not mentioned by name. This was the beginning of the concept that it is not quite "decent" for a man to admit that he is available as a presidential candidate.

After Jefferson retired, Federalist John Jay had been appointed Ambassador to England with instructions to make a treaty to eliminate many of the abuses which rankled the Americans—trading restrictions, the incitement of Indians, the continued occupation of northern posts which the English had agreed to abandon at the end of the Revolution, impressment of seamen, and much more. Jay made a treaty—in which every article except one was favorable to the British. The Federalist Senate ratified it, and Washington, with advice from Hamilton, hesitantly signed it. When it was published the Republicans, and the public, rose in mighty wrath. In Charleston it was burned by the public executioner. In Philadelphia it was burned before the house of the British Minister. In New York, Hamilton, now retired from the Cabinet, was stoned from the platform when he spoke to defend it.

Of Jay's treaty Jefferson wrote to Monroe in France:

SO GENERAL A BURST of dissatisfaction never before appeared against any transaction. Those who understand the particular articles of it condemn these articles. Those who do not understand them minutely condemn it generally as wearing a hostile face to France. This last is the most numerous class, comprehending the whole body of the people, who have taken a greater interest in this transaction than they were ever known to do in any other. It has, in my opinion, completely demolished the monarchical party here.

When the lower house reluctantly endorsed the treaty as a bad bargain but better than war, Jefferson wrote:

THE CAMPAIGN OF CONGRESS has closed. Though the Anglomen have in the end got their treaty through, and so far have triumphed over the cause of Republicanism, yet it has been to them a dear-bought victory. It has given the most radical shock to their party which it has ever received . . . nothing can support them but the colossus of the President's merits with the people, and the moment he retires . . . his successor, if a Monocrat, will be overborne by the Republican sense of his constituents. . . . In the meantime, patience.

As the end of Washington's second term approached Jefferson wrote to former Virginia neighbor Philip Mazzei, now in Italy:

THE ASPECT OF OUR POLITICS has wonderfully changed since you left us. In place of that noble love of liberty and republican government which carried us triumphantly through the war, an Anglican monarchical and aristocratical party has sprung up, whose avowed object is to draw over us the substance, as they have already done the forms, of the British government. . . . It would give you a fever were I to name to you the apostates who have gone over to these heresies, men who were Samsons in the field and Solomons in the council, but who have had their heads shorn by the harlot England. . . . In short, we are likely to preserve the liberty we have obtained only by unremitting labors and perils. But we shall preserve it. . . . We have only to awake and snap the Lilliputian cords with which they have been entangling us during the first sleep which succeeded our labors.

Samson and Solomon obviously referred to Washington who, in Jefferson's view, was now completely controlled by the Federalists.

Mazzei permitted Jefferson's letter to be published in Italy. It was picked up by a Paris paper and finally found its way back to the Federalist press in America, where it was bitterly condemned as a slander of the great Washington. Few Americans of either political persuasion would brook criticism of the first President. Shortly after the Mazzei letter appeared in print, Washington wrote to Jefferson, "I had no conception that parties would, or even could go, the length I have been witness to," or that "every act of my administration would be tortured, and the grossest and most insidious misrepresentations of them be made . . . and that too in such exaggerated and indecent terms as could scarcely be applied to a Nero, a notorious defaulter, or even a common pickpocket." The two Founding Fathers never met nor corresponded after Washington left office.

The election of 1796 brought Jefferson back to Philadelphia as Vice-President, despite his repeated avowals that he was forever finished with public life. In truth, Jefferson had nothing to do with his selection as a candidate nor with the election. At that time the refinements of the two-party system had not yet developed. There was no formal nomination of a candidate by a convention, no caucuses, no definite party platform. Two candidates were selected by the leaders of each party, without specifying which was the presidential and which the vice-presidential candidate. The Federalists selected John Adams and Thomas Pinckney, a South Carolinian who, they hoped, could split the vote of the Republican South. The Republicans selected Jefferson and Aaron Burr of New York. The man who received the greatest number of electoral votes would be President. The one who came in second, regardless of party, would be Vice-President.

Jefferson was not consulted about being a candidate, and in the months preceding the election he calmly tilled his land, remote from the furor. He wrote none but strictly personal letters until the issue was decided. His neighbor Madison avoided him during this period, saying, "I have not seen Jefferson and have thought it best to present him no opportunity of protesting to his friends against being embarked in the contest."

It is almost certain that a large majority of the people favored Republican sentiment; yet Adams received seventy-one electoral votes to Jefferson's sixty-eight. Only a minute percentage of the people voted directly in the national election. Women, Indians and slaves could not vote; nor could five out of six white males meet the property and other requirements for the franchise. Also, the presidential electors were selected by the legislatures in about half of the states.

It was not until mid-December that Jefferson replied to a letter from Madison acquainting him with the still inconclusive trend of the electoral vote. "There is nothing I so anxiously hope as that my name come out either second or third. These would be indifferent to me; as the last would leave me at home the whole year, and the other two-thirds of it." Speculating on the possibility of a tie which would throw the decision into the House of Representatives, Jefferson continued, "In that case, I pray you and authorize you fully to solicit on my behalf that Mr. Adams may be preferred. . . . Let those come to the helm who think they can steer clear of the difficulties. I have no confidence in myself for the undertaking."

When the results were in, Jefferson again wrote to Madison, reiterating his satisfaction that he had not been elected to the Presidency:

No ARGUMENTS WERE WANTING to reconcile me to a relinquishment of the first office, or acquiescence under the second. . . . It is the only office in the world about which I am unable to decide in my own mind whether I had rather have it or not have it. Pride does not enter into the estimate; for I think with the Romans that the general of today should be a soldier tomorrow if necessary. I can particularly have no feelings which would revolt at a secondary position to Mr. Adams. I am his junior in life, was his junior in Congress, his junior in the diplomatic line, his junior lately in our civil government. Before the receipt of your letter, I had written the enclosed one to him. . . . I enclose it open for your perusal . . . if anything should render the delivery of it ineligible in your opinion, you may return it to me. If Mr. Adams can be induced to administer the government on its true principles, and to relinquish his bias to an English constitution, it is to be considered whether it would not be, on the whole, for the public good to come to a good understanding with him as to his future elections. He is, perhaps, the only sure barrier against Hamilton's getting in.

The letter to Adams which he enclosed to Madison was never forwarded. The latter, a shrewd politician, did not want to start the administration by a coalition with Adams. To his old friend Jefferson had written:

THE PUBLIC and the public papers have been much occupied lately in placing us in a point of opposition to each other. I trust with confidence that less of it has been felt by ourselves personally. . . . No one . . . will congratulate you with purer disinterestedness than myself. . . . I have no ambition to govern men. It is a painful and thankless office. . . . I devoutly wish you may be able to shun for us this war, by which our agriculture, commerce and credit will be destroyed. If you are, the glory will be all your own; and that your administration may be filled with glory and happiness to yourself and advantage to us is the sincere wish of one who . . . retains still for you the solid esteem of the moments when we were working for our independence, and sentiments of respect and affectionate attachment.

Jefferson was quite content with the only routine duty of the Vice-President, presiding over the Senate. He said, "A more tranquil and unoffending station could not have been found for me." And later, to his daughter Martha, "We are lounging our time away, doing nothing and having nothing to do." This was not quite correct. He immediately saw the need for definite rules to govern Senate procedure, "So little has the parliamentary branch of the law been attended to that I not only find no person here, but not even a book to aid me. I had at an early period of life read a good deal on the subject and commonplaced what I read. This commonplace has been my pillow."

As Vice-President, Adams had guided the Senate without formal rules—or much consistency in making decisions. Jefferson felt that the presiding officer should have "some known system of rules, that he may neither leave himself free to indulge caprice or passion, nor open to the imputation of them." With the aid of his Commonplace Book he developed a *Manual of Parliamentary Procedure* based to some extent on the rules of the English Parliament—perhaps the only case in which he willingly borrowed from the British. The *Senate Manual* of the present day still contains Jefferson's *Manual*.

He considered the rules of the Senate as necessary not only for decorous and efficient operation, but as a protection for minority groups in a legislative body. In the first section of the *Manual* he said that:

NOTHING TENDED MORE to throw power into the hands of administration and those who acted with the majority . . . than a neglect of, or departure from, the rules of proceeding; that these forms, as instituted by our ancestors, operated as a check and control on the actions of the majority; and that they were, in many instances, a shelter and protection to the minority against the attempts of power.

Relations with France deteriorated rapidly under the new administration. In French eyes the Jay treaty was a repudiation of Franco-American friendship. Monroe had held their resentment in check, but when he was recalled the French refused to receive Charles Pinckney, the new Minister, and broke off diplomatic relations by recalling their Minister to America. They also started to seize American ships.

Adams called a special session of Congress and addressed it in a warlike, anti-French speech asking for a provisional army, the addition of twelve warships to America's navy of three frigates, and authorization to arm merchant ships. Jefferson believed that there was no desire for war or warlike preparations on the part of the country as a whole. He said:

WHEN WE [THE CONGRESS] first met, our information from the members from all parts of the Union was that peace was the universal wish. Whether they will now raise their tone to that of the Executive and embark in all the measures indicative of war, and, by taking a threatening posture, provoke hostilities from the opposite party, is far from being certain. There are many who think that not to support the Executive is to abandon government. As far as we can judge as yet the changes in the late election have been unfavorable to the Republican interest; still, we hope they will neither make nor provoke war.

Jefferson was still for neutrality:

I DO SINCERELY WISH that we could take our stand on a ground perfectly neutral and independent towards all nations. It has been by constant object through my public life and with respect to the English and French particularly.

But he was still anti-English. He believed that the English-loving Federalists were trying to:

THROW DUST IN THE EYES of our own citizens, as to fix on those who wish merely to recover self-government the charge of subserving one foreign influence because they resist submission to another. . . . After plunging us in all the broils of the European nations there would remain but one act to close our tragedy, that is, to break up our Union; and even this they have ventured seriously and solemnly to propose and maintain. . . . I can scarcely withhold myself from joining the wish of Silas Deane, that there were an ocean of fire between us and the Old World.

The sensitive Virginian did not find the tranquillity he expected in his subordinate position. He wrote:

I HAVE FORMERLY SEEN warm debates and high political passions. But gentlemen of different politics would then speak to each other, and separate the business of the Senate from that of society. It is not so now. Men who have been intimate all their lives cross the streets to avoid meeting and turn their heads another way, lest they should be obliged to touch their hats. This may do for young men with whom passion is enjoyment, but it is afflicting to peaceable minds.

As a last resort short of war Adams decided to send a three-man commission to France. They were not officially received, but they were approached by a Swiss banker named Hottinguer and two associates named Bellamy and Hauteval. These worthies assured the American commissioners that they had the ear of French Foreign Minister Talleyrand and that in consideration of a sizable loan to France, plus fifty thousand pounds "under the table" for certain members of the French Directory, everything could be arranged—providing that Adams apologized for the nasty things he had said about France in his speech to the special session of Congress. The commissioners reported the incident to the administration back home. When their report was laid before Congress the letters X, Y, and Z were substituted for the names of the French agents, and thus history refers to the matter as the "XYZ Affair."

The Federalists in the Senate realized that there was political dynamite in the envoy's papers that would demolish the pro-French Republicans, and passed a bill ordering them published. Of this Jefferson wrote to Madison:

THE FIRST IMPRESSIONS from them are very disagreeable and confused. Reflection, however, and analysis resolve them into this. Mr. Adams' speech to Congress in May is deemed such a national affront that no explanation on other topics can be entered on till that, as a preliminary, is wiped away by humiliating disavowals or acknowledgments. . . . There were, interwoven with these overtures, some base propositions on the part of Talleyrand, through one of his agents, to sell his interest and influence with the Directory towards soothing difficulties with them, in consideration of a large sum (fifty thousand pounds sterling). . . . No difficulty was expressed towards an adjustment of all differences and misunderstandings, or even ultimately a payment for spoliations, if the insult from our Executive should be first wiped away. . . . The little slanderous imputation before mentioned has been the bait which hurried the opposite party into this publication. . . . It is evident, however, on reflection, that these papers do not offer one motive the more for our going to war. Yet such is their effect on the minds of wavering characters, that I fear that to wipe off the imputation of being French partisans, they will go over to the war measures so furiously pushed by the other party.

He tried to exonerate the French government from complicity in the XYZ scandal, saying, "There are . . . some swindling propositions for a sum of fifty thousand pounds from certain unofficial characters which probably were meant for themselves alone, or for themselves and Talleyrand (whose character we have always known to be very corrupt), but there is not the smallest ground to believe the Directory knew anything of them." And he believed—or hoped—that the country as a whole would pass over the affair lightly. He wrote to his son-in-law, "The fermentation excited here by the publication of the dispatches . . . is still kept up . . . by anonymous letters of French conspirators who are to burn the city. . . . But the country in general seems not moved."

In this he was wrong. Public reaction to the XYZ Affair was much more intense than he anticipated. It has been immortalized by the famous toast at a dinner tendered to John Marshall, one of the commissioners, "Millions for defense but not one cent for tribute." Party lines vanished as all Americans raged with fierce indignation at the French proposal, which was not only insulting but "infamously degrading." In Congress, moderate Republicans switched sides; others left their posts so that the "War Hawks," as Jefferson called them, had a decided majority in both houses—a good three to one in the Senate. But Jefferson, as always, was optimistic when he wrote:

PARTY PASSIONS are indeed high. Nobody has more reason to know it than myself. I receive daily bitter proofs of it from people who never saw me, nor know anything of me. . . . At this moment all the passions are boiling over, and one who keeps himself cool and clear of the contagion is so far below the point of ordinary conversation that he finds himself insulated in every society. However, the fever will not last. . . .

Reflection and . . . information are all which our countrymen need to bring themselves and their affairs to rights. They are essentially republicans. They retain unadulterated the principles of '76. . . . It is our duty still to endeavor to avoid war; but if it shall actually take place, no matter by whom brought on, we must defend ourselves. If our house be on fire, without inquiring whether it was fired from within or without, we must try to extinguish it. In that, I have no doubt, we shall act as one man.

In their extremity, some rabid southern Republicans talked of secession, to which Jefferson replied with a defense of the two-party system and the checks and balances which it represents:

IN EVERY FREE and deliberating society there must, from the nature of man, be opposite parties and violent dissensions and discords; and one of these, for the most part, must prevail over the other for a longer or shorter time. Perhaps this party division is necessary to induce each to watch and relate to the people the proceedings of the other. But if on a temporary superiority of the one party, the other is to resort to a scission of the Union, no federal government can ever exist. . . . Seeing, therefore, that an association of men who will not quarrel with one another is a thing which never yet existed, from the greatest confederacy of nations down to a town meeting or a vestry; seeing that we must have somebody to quarrel with, I had rather keep our New England associates for that purpose, than to see our bickerings transferred to others.

"Better keep together as we are, haul off from Europe as soon as we can, and from all attachments to any portions of it; and if they show their power just sufficiently to hoop us together, it will be the happiest situation in which we can exist. If the game runs sometimes against us at home we must have patience till luck turns, and then we shall have an opportunity of winning back the principles we have lost. For this a game where principles are the stake. Better luck, therefore, to us all.

By 1798 the French had captured over three hundred American merchant vessels, and an undeclared war with France was raging on the sea. At home, the Federalists took advantage of war hysteria to pass three measures that have come to be known as the Alien and Sedition Acts.

The first of these increased the period of residency required for naturalization as a citizen to fourteen years. This had little to do with the French. It was directed against the "wild Irishmen" who were emigrating in goodly numbers and whom one Federalist described as "United Irishmen, Freemasons and the most God-provoking Democrats this side of hell." The second merely provided that "dangerous aliens" could be deported. The catch in it was that the President was empowered to decide who was dangerous. In one case when Adams was asked what one particular alien was charged with he replied, "Nothing in particular, but he's too French." When the French savant Comte de Volney left to escape deportation, Jefferson said, "It suffices for a man to be a philosopher and to believe that human affairs are susceptible of improvement, and to look forward rather than back to the Gothic ages, to mark him as an anarchist, disorganizer, atheist and enemy of the government."

The third law was the Sedition Act. This made it a federal offense to "write, print, utter or publish . . . any false, scandalous and malicious writing" against the government, either house of Congress, or the President; or to oppose or resist "any law of the United States or any act of the President of the United States"; or "to excite any unlawful combination therein." Under the act a Republican editor could go to jail for criticizing the administration; or the Democratic societies could be construed as "unlawful combinations." In this violation of the freedom of speech and of the press Jefferson saw a new threat of monarchy. He wrote:

I CONSIDER THOSE LAWS as merely an experiment on the American mind to see how far it will bear an avowed violation of the Constitution. If this goes down, we shall immediately see attempted another act of Congress declaring that the President shall continue in office during life, reserving to another occasion the transfer of the succession to his heirs and the establishment of the Senate for life.

While the Senate was debating the Alien and Sedition Acts Jefferson relinquished the gavel and went home to Monticello to write a document which was, in effect, a second Declaration of Independence and a new call to revolt. This time the enemy was the strong federal government which was trampling on the Bill of Rights and usurping the powers of the state legislatures. The paper is known as the *Kentucky Resolutions*. He had to write in secrecy, for what he wrote was seditious and might have led to his impeachment for treason.

His nine resolutions attacked the validity of not only the pending laws, but all acts and laws which were based on powers not specifically granted to the central government by the Constitution, which included, in his mind, Hamilton's financial system. He started by saying, "Resolved, that the several states composing the United States of America are not united on the principle of unlimited submission to their general government; but that, by a compact under the style and title of a Constitution for the United States and of amendments thereto, they constituted a general government for special purposes—delegated to that government certain definite powers, reserving, each state to itself, the residuary mass of right to their own self-government; and that whensoever the general government assumes undelegated powers, its acts are unauthoritative, void and of no force." The first resolution continued to say that the federal government "was not . . . the exclusive or final judge of the extent of the powers delegated to itself; since that would have made its discretion, and not the Constitution, the measure of its powers." He concluded that each state had a right to judge for itself as to the extent of the central government's powers.

The next five resolutions spelled out why the Alien and Sedition Acts were unconstitutional and therefore "altogether void and of no force." The seventh resolution generally condemned the federal government for usurping "unlimited power," but added that other excesses could be revised and corrected "at a time of greater tranquillity, while those specified in the preceding resolutions call for immediate redress."

The eighth section affirmed that the state which adopted the resolutions was "determined, as it doubts not its co-states are, to submit to undelegated and consequently unlimited powers in no man, or body of men, on earth; that in cases . . . where powers are assumed which have not been delegated, a nullification of the act is the rightful remedy: that every state has a natural right . . . to nullify of their own authority all assumptions of power by others within their limits: that without this right, they would be under the dominion, absolute and unlimited, of whosoever might exercise this right of judgment for them. With such powers, continued Jefferson, "the general government may place any act they think proper on the list of crimes, and punish it themselves whether enumerated or not enumerated by the Constitution as cognizable by them: that they may transfer its cognizance to the President, or any other person, who may himself be the accuser, counsel, judge and jury; whose *suspicions* may be the evidence, his *order* the sentence, his *officer* the executioner and his breast the sole record of the transaction . . . the inhabitants of these states being by this precedent reduced, as outlaws, to the absolute dominion of one man, and the barrier of the Constitution thus swept away from us all." Further, "successive acts of the same character, unless arrested at the threshold, necessarily drive these states into revolution and blood." The ninth resolution proposed that a "committee of correspondence" seek joint action by other states, an echo of Revolutionary days.

For all practical purposes the eighth resolution, had it been widely adopted as Jefferson wrote it, would have made a union of states impossible. Under it no state would have been required to accept any law or act of the federal government which it considered unconstitutional.

With his resolutions Jefferson was carrying the fight to the state legislatures, in some of which Republican sentiment was dominant. He had in mind that they would be adopted by a bellwether state and spread by the committee of correspondence to other states. John Breckenridge, speaker of the Kentucky Assembly, agreed to introduce them in that body, but before doing so he redrafted the eighth resolution drastically. He retained the reference to certain acts being "void and of no effect," but he eliminated the concept that a state could nullify a federal law within its own borders, as well as all reference to revolution and bloodshed. As passed by Kentucky the resolutions were merely a public protest which instructed Kentucky's congressmen to seek the repeal of the "aforesaid unconstitutional and obnoxious acts." Madison drew up a similar but still milder set of resolutions which were passed by the Virginia legislature.

No other state acted on the Kentucky and Virginia resolutions. The southern states were silent. The northern and middle states returned them with generally adverse comments. Jefferson proposed to Madison that these comments be answered by a declaration which made it clear that the protesting states were "determined, were we to be disappointed in this, to sever ourselves from that union we so much value rather than give up the rights of self-government which we have reserved and in which alone we see liberty, safety and happiness." This reference to disunion was amazing, coming from Jefferson; although, at the time, the right of a state or group of states to secede was widely held and frequently proposed. Normally, Jefferson was a strong unionist, but not if the union impinged on the right of self-government. Madison hastened to Monticello and induced Jefferson to modify his extremist expression.

Jefferson's opposition to the Sedition Act went far beyond party politics. This law represented, to him, the most infamous tyranny

—a tyranny over men's minds and opinions. He had implicit faith in mankind, if man's mind were not fettered. To a young man seeking advice he wrote:

I JOIN YOU . . . in branding as cowardly the idea that the human mind is incapable of further advances. This is precisely the doctrine that the present despots of the earth are inculcating and their friends here re-echoing; and applying especially to religion and politics . . . But thank heaven the American mind is already too much opened to listen to these impostures; and while the art of printing is left to us science can never be retrograde. What is once acquired of real knowledge can never be lost. To preserve the freedom of the human mind then, and freedom of the press, every spirit should be ready to devote itself to martyrdom, for as long as we may think as we will, and speak as we think, the condition of man will proceed in improvement.

In 1799 the Federalists were riding high. There was no check to their control of all three branches of the central government. All that was needed to assure the complete collapse of the Republicans was a declared war with France, or at least a continuation of the unofficial hostilities until after next year's election. Then, out of a clear sky, Adams completely disrupted the Federalists by re-establishing diplomatic relations with France with a view to a prompt settlement of the differences between the two countries. The public support of the Federalists had been based on the French war. Now, as the 1800 election loomed, they were left without an issue.

The death of Washington in December, 1799, also deprived them of the prestige of the great man's name, for he had become an outright Federalist after he retired from office. Jefferson made no immediate comment on the first President's death but, twelve years later, he wrote this analysis of his character:

I THINK I KNEW General Washington intimately and thoroughly, and were I called on to delineate his character, it should be in terms like these.

"His mind was great and powerful, without being of the very first order. . . . It was slow in operation, being little aided by invention or imagination, but sure in conclusion. Hence the common remark of his officers of the advantage he derived from councils of war where, hearing all suggestions, he selected whatever was best; and certainly no general ever planned his battles more judiciously. But if deranged during the course of the action . . . he was slow in readjustment. The consequence was that he often failed in the field and rarely against an enemy in station, as at Boston and York. He was incapable of fear, meeting personal dangers with the calmest unconcern. Perhaps the strongest feature in his character was prudence, never acting until every circumstance, every consideration, was maturely weighed; refraining if he saw a doubt, but, when once decided, going through with his purpose whatever obstacles opposed. His integrity was most pure, his justice the most inflexible I have ever known. . . . He was, indeed, in every sense of the words, a wise, a good and a great man. His temper was naturally high toned; but reflection and resolution had obtained a firm and habitual ascendancy over it. If ever, however, it broke its bonds he was most tremendous in his wrath. . . . His heart was not warm in its affections, but he exactly calculated every man's value, and gave him a solid esteem proportioned to it. . . . Although in the circle of his friends, where he might be unreserved with safety, he took a free share in conversation, his colloquial talents were not above mediocrity, possessing neither copiousness of ideas, nor fluency of words. In public, when called on for a sudden opinion, he was unready, short and embarrassed. Yet he wrote readily, rather diffusely, in an easy and correct style. This he had acquired by conversation with the world, for his education was merely reading, writing and common arithmetic, to which he added surveying at a later day. . . . On the whole his character was, in its mass, perfect; in nothing bad; in few points indifferent; and it may truly be said that never did nature and fortune combine more perfectly to make a man great, and to place him in the same constellation with whatever worthies have merited from man an everlasting remembrance.

Jefferson wrote several of these "pen portrait" character studies of contemporaries—what would now be called "profiles." Of George IV, when Prince of Wales, he wrote:

HE HAS NOT a single element of mathematics, of natural or moral philosophy, or of any other science on earth, nor has the society he has kept been such as to supply the void of education. It has been that of the lowest, the most illiterate and profligate persons of the kingdom, without choice of rank or mind, and with whom the subjects of conversation are only horses, drinking matches, bawdy houses and the terms the most vulgar. . . . He has not a single idea of justice, morality, religion or of the rights of men, or any anxiety for the opinion of the world. He carries that indifference for fame so far that he would probably not be hurt were he to lose his throne, provided he could be assured of having always meat, drink, horses and women.

And, later, he wrote of Napoleon:

. . . WHOSE THIRST FOR BLOOD appeared unquenchable, the great oppressor of the rights and liberties of the world, shut up within the circle of a little island of the Mediterranean, and dwindled to the condition of a humble and degraded pensioner on the bounty of those he had most injured. How miserably, how meanly has he closed his inflated career! What a sample of the bathos will his history present! He should have perished on the swords of his enemies, under the walls of Paris.

Jefferson did not seek the Presidency in 1800; in his long public career he never actively ran for office. He stayed quietly at Monticello but, this time, he did not remain completely aloof. He proposed a change in the manner of naming the Virginia electors. They had been elected by popular vote by districts, which had cost the Republicans one electoral vote in 1796. Jefferson wrote Monroe suggesting that they should be appointed by the solidly Republican legislature, although he thought the old system was basically better. "All agree that an election by districts would be best, if it could be general; but while ten states choose either by their legislatures or by a general ticket, it is folly and worse than folly for the other six not to do it. In these ten states the minority is certainly unrepresented; and their majorities . . . have the weight of their whole state in their scale."

The rift in the Federal party was further widened when Adams, at long last, realized that the majority of his Cabinet was controlled by Hamilton. When he abruptly called for the resignations of the Secretaries of War and State he completely alienated the Hamiltonians. Hamilton wrote, "I will never more be responsible for him [Adams] by my direct support, even though the consequence should be the election of Jefferson." Actually, Republican victory was assured by a political blunder on the part of Hamilton of which Jefferson's running mate, Aaron Burr, took prompt advantage.

Hamilton and Burr were opposing leaders in New York, where electors were selected by the combined houses of the legislature, in which the Federalists had a majority. Jefferson wrote, "New York determines the election. In any event, we may say that if the *city* election of New York is in favor of the Republican ticket the issue will be Republican." In the spring elections of 1800 for the New York legislature Hamilton put up a slate of unknown nonentities. He was solely concerned with having legislators whom he could control. Burr shrewdly secured a group of able and prominent men as candidates, regardless of whether they were good Republicans. He also devised a means of creating more voters by buying small pieces of property under joint deeds, so that all of twenty or more Tammany Irishmen who were part owners would have the franchise. This was the genesis of the policy, long attributed to Tammany, of voting "early and often." New York City, for the first time, went Republican, giving that party a majority of a single vote in the combined houses of the state legislature and, consequently, the state's twelve electoral votes went to Jefferson and Burr. The final electoral vote was Jefferson seventy-three, Burr seventy-three, Adams sixty-five, Pinckney sixty-four.

The Republicans, too, had made a mistake. One elector from South Carolina was supposed to have thrown his vote away from Burr. When he failed to do it Jefferson and Burr ended in a tie, and the choice between them for the Presidency and the Vice-Presidency was thrown into the House of Representatives, in which each of the sixteen states cast one vote as a unit.

The Constitution made no provision for what would happen if the vote in the House was tied. The Federalists hoped that, by creating this situation, the Presidency would devolve on their President of the Senate until a new election could be held. They threw their votes in the House to Burr. Either candidate needed nine states to win. Through thirty-five ballots the vote stood eight states for Jefferson, six for Burr and two blank. Finally, on the thirty-sixth ballot, the single representative from Delaware switched, and Jefferson was elected.

While the balloting was in progress there may have been an effort on the part of the Federalists to make a "deal" with Jefferson. Jefferson claimed that he was approached by Gouverneur Morris and that Adams was a party to it. Years later he wrote:

COMING OUT of the Senate chamber one day, I found Gouverneur Morris on the steps. He stopped me, and began a conversation on the strange and portentous state of things then existing, and went on to observe that the reasons why the minority of states was so opposed to my being elected were that they apprehended that, (1) I would turn all Federalists out of office; (2) put down the navy; (3) wipe off the public debt.

That I need only to declare, or authorize my friends to declare, that I would not take these steps, and instantly the event of the election would be fixed. I told him that . . . I should certainly make no terms; should never go into the office of President by capitulation, nor with my hands tied. . . . About the same time, I called on Mr. Adams. . . . I observed to him that a very dangerous experiment was then in contemplation, to defeat the presidential election by an act of Congress declaring the right of the Senate to name a President of the Senate, to devolve on him the government during any interregnum: that such a measure would probably produce resistance by force, and incalculable consequences, which it would be in his power to prevent by negativing such an act. He seemed to think such an act justifiable, and observed it was in my power to fix the election by a word in an instant, by declaring I would not turn out the federal officers, nor put down the navy, nor sponge the national debt.

Shortly before his death Jefferson wrote, under most pathetic circumstances, an account of his public services. Of his term as Vice-President he said:

THERE IS ONE [service] the most important in its consequences, of any transaction in any portion of my life; to wit, the head I personally made against the federal principles and proceedings during the administration of Mr. Adams. Their usurpations and violations of the Constitution at that period, and their majority in both houses of Congress were so great, so decided and so daring, that after combating their aggressions, inch by inch, without being able in the least to check their career, the Republican leaders thought it would be best for them to give up their useless efforts there, go home, get into their respective legislatures, embody whatever of resistance they could be formed into, and if ineffectual, to perish there as in the last ditch. All, therefore, retired, leaving Mr. Gallatin alone in the House of Representatives, and myself in the Senate, where I then presided as Vice-President. Remaining at our posts and bidding defiance to the browbeatings and insults by which they endeavored to drive us off also, we kept the mass of Republicans in phalanx together, until the legislatures could be brought up to the charge; and nothing on earth is more certain than that if myself particularly, placed by my office of Vice-President at the head of the Republicans, had given way and withdrawn from my post, the Republicans throughout the Union would have given up in despair, and the cause would have been lost forever. . . . No person who was not a witness of the scenes of that gloomy period can form any idea of the afflicting persecutions and personal indignities we had to brook. They saved our country, however.

CHAPTER VII

THE CHIEF EXECUTIVE

ç

On the night of March 3, 1801, the candles burned low as John Adams sat up late signing appointments for a swarm of new federal officials ere his term expired at midnight. Early next morning, before the inauguration of his successor, he and wife Abigail started on their long journey to Massachusetts. Abigail was glad to leave the unfinished executive mansion in the new capital city of Washington to which the government had moved the previous June. She had written a long letter of complaint that she was surrounded by forests, but there was nobody to cut the wood for the thirteen fires that the house required, nor a single bell to summon the thirty servants that the establishment needed. Her sole consolation was "the great unfinished audience room" which she used as "a drying room to hang up the clothes in."

The Senate wing of the Capitol was finished. Pennsylvania Avenue was a causeway running through a swamp. That, plus seven or eight boardinghouses, a tavern, a washerwoman and a few shops, was Washington, D.C. Gouverneur Morris wrote, "We want nothing here but houses, cellars, kitchens, well-informed men, amiable women and other little trifles of this kind to make our city perfect."

Even before his inauguration Jefferson made it clear that there would be none of the trappings of monarchy during his administration. When he left his boardinghouse to take the oath of office, an eyewitness reported that "His dress was of plain cloth, and he rode on horseback to the Capitol without a single guard or even servant in his train, dismounted without assistance, and hitched the bridle of his horse to the palisades." He strode into the Senate chamber to deliver a short and straightforward inaugural address calling for an end to the political turmoil of the last decade and stating the principles which would govern his administration:

LET US . . . fellow citizens, unite with one heart and one mind. Let us restore to social intercourse that harmony and affection without which liberty and even life itself are but dreary things. And let us reflect that having banished from our land that religious intolerance under which mankind so long bled and suffered, we have yet gained little if we countenance a political intolerance as despotic, as wicked, and capable of as bitter and bloody persecutions. During the throes and convulsions of the ancient world, during the agonizing spasms of infuriated man, seeking through blood and slaughter his long-lost liberty, it was not wonderful that the agitation of the billows should reach even this distant and peaceful shore. . . . But every difference of opinion is not a difference of principle. We have called by different names brethren of the same principle. We are all Republicans—we are all Federalists. If there be any among us who would wish to dissolve this Union, or to change its republican form, let them stand undisturbed as monuments of the safety with which error of opinion may be tolerated where reason is left free to combat it. I know, indeed, that some honest men fear that a republican government cannot be strong, that this government is not strong enough. . . . I believe this, on the contrary, the strongest government on earth. I believe it the only one where every man . . . would meet invasions of the public order as his own personal concern. Sometimes it is said that man cannot be trusted with the government of himself. Can he then be trusted with the government of others? Or have we found angels in the forms of kings to govern him? Let history answer this question. . . .

Kindly separated by nature and a wide ocean from exterminating havoc of one-quarter of the globe . . . possessing a chosen country with room enough for our descendants to the hundredth and thousandth generation; entertaining a due sense of our equal rights . . . enlightened by a benign religion . . . with all these blessings, what more is necessary to make us a happy and prosperous people? Still one thing more, fellow citizens—a wise and frugal government, which shall restrain men from injuring one another, which shall leave them otherwise free to regulate their own pursuits of industry and improvement, and shall not take from the mouth of labor the bread it has earned. This is the sum of good government, and this is necessary to close the circle of our felicities.

About to enter, fellow citizens, on the exercise of duties which comprehend everything dear and valuable to you, it is proper that you should understand what I deem the essential principles of our government, and consequently those which ought to shape its administration. I will compress them within the narrowest compass they will bear. . . . Equal and exact justice to all men, of whatever state or persuasion, religious or political; peace, commerce and honest friendship, with all nations—entangling alliances with none; the support of the state governments in all their rights . . . the preservation of the general government in its whole constitutional vigor, as the sheet anchor of our peace at home and safety abroad; a jealous care of the right of election by the people . . . absolute acquiescence in the decisions of the majority . . . a well-disciplined militia . . . the supremacy of the civil over the military authority; economy in the public expense, that labor may be lightly burdened; the honest payment of our debts and sacred preservation of the public faith; encouragement of agriculture, and of commerce as its handmaid; the diffusion of information and the arraignment of all abuses at the bar of public reason; freedom of religion; freedom of the press; freedom of person under the protection of the habeas corpus; and trial by juries impartially selected—these principles form the bright constellation which has gone before us and guided our steps through an age of revolution and reformation. The wisdom of our sages and the blood of our heroes have been devoted to their attainment. They should be the creed of our political faith—the text of civil instruction—the touchstone by which to try the services of those we trust; and should we wander from them in moments of error or alarm, let us hasten to retrace our steps and to regain the road which alone leads to peace, liberty and safety.

The new President's first problem was purely political and had to do with the appointments that Adams had crowded into his final hours, many of them lifetime judgeships. Jefferson later said, "that one act of Mr. Adams' life, and one only, ever gave me a moment's personal displeasure. I did consider his last appointments to office as personally unkind. . . . It seems but common justice to leave a successor free to act by instruments of his own choice."

Jefferson would not practice outright party patronage. He said, "I had foreseen, years ago, that the first Republican President who should come into office after all the places in the government had become exclusively occupied by Federalists would have a dreadful operation to perform. . . . On him . . . was to devolve the office of an executioner, that of lopping off. I cannot say that it has worked harder than I expected. . . ." He was much in favor of letting bygones be bygones, except with the hard-core Hamiltonians. He wrote John Page that he was "very much in hopes we shall be able to restore union to our country. Not indeed that the Federal leaders can be brought over. They are invincibles; but I really hope their followers may. The bulk of these last were real Republicans, carried over from us by French excesses. . . . A moderate conduct throughout, which may not revolt our new friends and may give them tenets with us, must be observed." In this spirit of conciliation he made few changes in Federal appointees, "Out of many thousands of officers in the United States, nine only have been removed for political principle, and twelve for delinquencies, chiefly pecuniary. The whole herd have squealed out as if all their throats were cut."

He promptly established the rules for his "new deal":

LEVEES ARE DONE AWAY. The first communication to the next Congress will be, like all subsequent ones, by message, to which no answer will be expected. The diplomatic establishment in Europe will be reduced to three ministers. . . . The army is undergoing a chaste reformation. The navy will be reduced to the legal establishment by the last of this month. Agencies in every department will be revised. We shall push [Congress] to the uttermost in economizing.

Believing the Sedition Act "a nullity as absolute . . . as if Congress had ordered us to fall down and worship a golden calf" he considered it his duty to release all offenders under the act, "as it would have been to have rescued from the fiery furnace those who should have been cast into it for refusing to worship the image." Stringent economy was the watchword, but, in Jefferson's mind, the Bank of the United States stood in the way of complete fiscal reform. "We can pay off [Hamilton's] debt in fifteen years; but we can never get rid of his financial system. It mortifies me to be strengthening principles which I deem radically vicious, but this vice is entailed on us by the first error."

The bank and the permanent judgeships were the last vestiges of Federalism. There was nothing that Jefferson could do about either:

MY GREAT ANXIETY at present is to avail ourselves of our ascendancy to establish good principles and good practices; to fortify Republicanism behind as many barriers as possible that the outworks may give time to rally and save the citadel, should that be again in danger. On their part, they have retired into the judiciary as a stronghold. There the remains of Federalism are to be preserved and fed from the Treasury, and from that battery all the works of Republicanism are to be beaten down and erased . . . they have multiplied useless judges merely to strengthen their phalanx.

Peace was the keynote of Jefferson's first administration, a lull in Europe's wars and an end to discord in home politics. Business was good. For 1802 he could report that "the receipts of external duties have exceeded those of any other year." Eight million dollars were paid off on the national debt and there were four million left in the Treasury: proof that "merely by avoiding false objects of expense we are able, without a direct tax, without internal taxes and without borrowing, to make large and effectual payments toward the discharge of our public debt and the emancipation of our posterity from that moral canker." Economy, he said, was "among the first and most important Republican virtues," as was private enterprise. "Agriculture, manufactures, commerce and navigation, the four pillars of our prosperity, are the most thriving when left most free to individual enterprise." Among these strong pillars of prosperity he did not include "banking institutions and moneyed corporations," which he feared. But he was convinced that government should keep hands off business and agriculture: "Were we directed by Washington when to sow and when to reap, we should soon want bread."

To crown his first administration Jefferson doubled the area of the United States in one stroke by purchasing the Louisiana Territory.

There was some inconsistency between Jefferson's principles and his behavior in this transaction. In 1801 he wanted no "entangling alliances." In 1802 he said, "The day that France takes possession of New Orleans . . . we must marry ourselves to the British fleet and nation." Also, Jefferson insisted that the central government had only such powers as were specifically granted to it by the Constitution; and that document gave it no authority to acquire additional territory. To buy Louisiana, Jefferson had to adopt Hamilton's doctrine of the "implied powers" of the federal government.

The opening step in the acquisition of Louisiana was a long letter to Robert Livingston, American Minister in Paris, in which Jefferson instructed him to sound out the French government on ceding only New Orleans and "the Floridas"—meaning western Florida, not the peninsula. It said, in part:

THERE IS ON THE GLOBE one single spot the possessor of which is our natural and habitual enemy. It is New Orleans, through which the produce of three-eighths of our territory must pass to market. . . . France, placing herself in that door, assumes to us the attitude of defiance. Spain might have retained it quietly for years. Her pacific dispositions, her feeble state, would induce her to increase our facilities there, so that her possession of the place would be hardly felt by us. . . . Not so can it ever be in the hands of France . . . circumstances render it impossible that France and the United States can continue long friends when they meet in so irritable a position. . . .

We must . . . make the first cannon which shall be fired in Europe the signal for the tearing up any settlement she may have made, and for holding the two continents of America in sequestration for the common purposes of the united British and American nations. . . .

I should suppose that all these considerations might, in some proper form, be brought into view of the government of France. Though stated by us it ought not to give offense, because we do not bring them forward as a menace but as consequences not controllable by us, but inevitable from the course of things. . . . If France considers Louisiana, however, as indispensable for her views, she might perhaps be willing to look about for arrangements which might reconcile it to our interests. If anything could do this, it would be the ceding to us the island of New Orleans and the Floridas. . . . Every eye in the United States is now fixed on the affairs of Louisiana. Perhaps nothing since the Revolutionary War has produced more uneasy sensations through the body of the nation.

This letter Jefferson delivered, unsealed, to Du Pont de Nemours, who was returning to France, asking him to read it and use his influence with the French government. Jefferson said:

I TRUST THAT YOU will have it in your power to impress on that government considerations in the scale against which the possession of Louisiana is nothing. In Europe, nothing but Europe is seen, or supposed to have any right in the affairs of nations; but this little event, of France's possessing herself of Louisiana, which is thrown in as nothing, as a mere makeweight in the general settlement of accounts—this speck which now appears as an almost invisible point on the horizon, is the embryo of a tornado which will burst on the countries on both sides of the Atlantic and involve in its effects their highest destinies.

When Livingston's negotiations proved fruitless James Monroe was dispatched to Paris as a special envoy. Suddenly, on the day after Monroe arrived, the French offered the Americans not merely New Orleans but all of Louisiana for one hundred million francs. War between France and England was imminent. Napoleon needed money. And he knew that, if the Americans decided to take Louisiana as Jefferson threatened, the French would have no chance of holding it across three thousand miles of water dominated by the British fleet. Monroe and Livingston haggled the price down to sixty million francs and closed the deal—without a vestige of authority from home. The eight hundred and twenty-eight thousand square miles were purchased for fifteen million dollars, an average of about three cents an acre.

Jefferson had just cause to write:

I ACCEPT WITH PLEASURE and with pleasure reciprocate . . . congratulations on the acquisition of Louisiana, for it is a subject of mutual congratulation. . . . The territory acquired . . . includes all the waters of the Missouri and Mississippi, has more than doubled the area of the United States, and the new part is not inferior to the old in soil, climate, productions and important communications.

But Jefferson had broader horizons:

THE BOUNDARIES which I deem not admitting question are the high lands [the Rocky Mountains] on the western side of the Mississippi, enclosing all its waters. . . . We have some claims to extend on the seacoast westwardly to the Rio Norte or Bravo [Rio Grande], and better; to go eastwardly to the Rio Perdido, between Mobile and Pensacola, the ancient boundary of Louisiana. These claims will be a subject of negotiation with Spain, and if, as soon as she is at war, we push them strongly with one hand, holding out a price in the other, we shall certainly obtain the Floridas, and all in good time.

As to the legality of the purchase of Louisiana, Jefferson thought it should require a constitutional amendment; but there was not time. He said:

THE CONSTITUTION has made no provision for our holding foreign territory, still less for incorporating foreign nations into our Union. The Executive, in seizing the fugitive occurrence which so much advances the good of their country, have done an act beyond the Constitution. The legislature, in casting behind them metaphysical subtleties and risking themselves like faithful servants, must ratify and pay for it, and throw themselves on their country for doing for them unauthorized what we know they would have done for themselves had they been in a situation to do it.

It is the case of a guardian investing the money of his ward in purchasing an important adjacent territory, and saying to him when of age, I did this for your good; I pretend to no right to bind you; you may disavow me and I must get out of the scrape as I can; I thought it my duty to risk myself for you.

It is interesting to speculate what Jefferson's reaction would have been had Hamilton referred to such an assumption of power as a "metaphysical subtlety."

Jefferson also sought added territory through a new relationship with the western Indians, and addressed a special message to Congress on the subject. It was apparent that the Indians were "growing more and more uneasy at the constant diminution of the territory that they occupy." They were becoming reluctant to sell their land. So, said Jefferson:

IN ORDER PEACEABLY TO COUNTERACT this policy of theirs, and to provide an extension of territory which the rapid increase of our numbers will call for, two measures are deemed expedient. First: to encourage them to abandon hunting; to apply to the raising stock, to agriculture and domestic manufactures. . . . The extensive forests necessary in the hunting life will then become useless, and they will see advantage in exchanging them for the means of improving their farms and of increasing their domestic comforts. Secondly: to multiply trading houses among them, and place within their reach those things which will contribute more to their domestic comfort than the possession of extensive but uncultivated wilds. . . . I trust and believe we are acting for their greatest good.

But what of the private traders who would be put out of business by the government trading posts? Well, said Jefferson:

. . . IT MIGHT BE WORTHY the attention of Congress . . . to point in another direction the enterprise of these citizens, as profitably for themselves, and more usefully for the public. The river Missouri, and the Indians inhabiting it, are not as well known as is rendered desirable by their connection with the Mississippi, and consequently with us. . . . An intelligent officer, with ten or twelve chosen men, fit for the enterprise, and willing to undertake it . . . might explore the whole line, even to the western ocean; have conferences with the natives on the subject of commercial intercourse; get admission among them for our traders, as others are admitted; agree on convenient deposits for an interchange of articles; and return with the information acquired, in the course of two summers.

And so was born the greatest exploring expedition in America's history, that of Jefferson's young secretary, Meriwether Lewis, and William Clark. Upon the return of the expedition Jefferson reported to Congress:

THE EXPEDITION of Messrs. Lewis and Clark for exploring the river Missouri, and the best communication from that to the Pacific Ocean, has had all the success which could have been expected. They have traced the Missouri nearly to its source, descended the Columbia to the Pacific Ocean, ascertained with accuracy the geography of that interesting communication across our continent, learned the character of the country, of its commerce and inhabitants; and . . . have by this arduous service deserved well of their country.

As his first term ended Jefferson could list his accomplishments with pardonable pride. The administration was able, he said, "To do without a land tax, excise, stamp tax and the other internal taxes, to supply their place by economies so as still to support the government properly . . . to purchase a country as large and more fertile than the one we possessed before, yet ask neither a new tax, nor another soldier to be added . . . to preserve peace with all nations, and particularly an equal friendship with the two great rival powers, France and England, and to maintain the credit and character of the nation in as high a degree as it has ever enjoyed."

He was conscious that he was leading an experiment in government, a momentous experiment for all the world and one which the United States was uniquely equipped to make:

OUR PEOPLE IN A BODY are wise, because they are under the unrestrained and unperverted operations of their own understanding. . . . A nation composed of such materials, and free in all its members from distressing wants, furnishes hopeful implements for the interesting experiment of self-government; and we feel that we are acting under obligations not confined to the limits of our own society. It is impossible not to be sensible that we are acting for all mankind; that circumstances denied to others but indulged to us have imposed on us the duty of proving what is the degree of freedom and self-government in which a society may venture to leave its individual members.

With his usual bow to his desired retirement Jefferson accepted the candidacy for a second term:

I SINCERELY REGRET that the unbounded calumnies of the Federal party have obliged me to throw myself on the verdict of my country for trial, my great desire having been to retire at the end of the present term to a life of tranquillity; and it was my decided purpose when I entered into office. They force my continuance. If we can keep the vessel of state as steadily in her course for another four years, my earthly purposes will be accomplished.

But he added, "At the end of the next four years I shall certainly retire. Age, inclination and principle all dictate this."

His second inaugural address was principally a recapitulation of his first term's accomplishments, and a promise to keep up the good work. He announced that internal taxes had been abolished and that "The remaining revenue on the consumption of foreign articles is paid cheerfully by those who can afford to add foreign luxuries to domestic comforts." He added a boast to which today's sufferers under Form 1040 may look back longingly, "it may be the pleasure and pride of an American to ask, what farmer, what mechanic, what laborer, ever sees a taxgatherer of the United States?"

By mid-term he was able to report to Congress that there was money in the Treasury, "beyond the installments of public debt which we are permitted by contract to pay . . . therefore . . . to what other objects shall these surpluses be appropriated?" He did not think it would be well to eliminate import duties on "foreign luxuries, purchased only by those who are rich." Instead, excess revenues might be applied "to the great purposes of the public education, roads, rivers, canals and such other objects of public improvement as it may be thought proper to add to the constitutional enumeration of federal powers. By these operations new channels of communication will be opened between the states; the lines of separation will disappear, their interests will be identified, and their union cemented by new and indissoluble ties. Education is here placed among the articles of public care, not that it would be proposed to take its ordinary branches out of the hands of private enterprise, which manages so much better all the concerns to which it is equal; but a public institution can alone supply those sciences which, though rarely called for, are yet necessary to complete the circle, all the parts of which contribute to the improvement of the country, and some of them to its preservation." He added that he supposed an amendment to the constitution would be necessary to empower the federal government to spend money on public works, a supposition which his successors ignored.

The first note of discord in Jefferson's administration involved Aaron Burr. The Vice-President had left office in 1805 under indictment for murder in New York and New Jersey for the fatal shooting of Alexander Hamilton in a duel. He fled to the West.

Here he hatched an enterprise which Jefferson described as the "most extraordinary since the days of Don Quixote." In reporting on it to Congress the President said:

SOMETIME IN THE LATTER PART of September [1806] I received intimations that designs were in agitation in the western country unlawful and unfriendly to the peace of the Union, and that the prime mover in these was Aaron Burr. . . . It was not until the latter part of October that the objects of the conspiracy began to be perceived, but still so blended and involved in mystery that nothing distinct could be singled out for pursuit. . . .

It appeared that he contemplated two distinct objects, which might be carried on either jointly or separately, and either the one or the other first, as circumstances should direct. One of these was the severance of the Union of these states by the Allegheny Mountains; the other, an attack on Mexico. . . .

He found at once that the attachment of the western country to the present Union was not to be shaken; that its dissolution could not be effected with the consent of its inhabitants, and that his resources were inadequate, as yet, to effect it by force. He took his course then at once, determined to seize on New Orleans, plunder the bank there, possess himself of the military and naval stores, and proceed on his expedition to Mexico; and to this object all his means and preparations were now directed. He collected . . . all the ardent, restless, desperate, and disaffected persons who were ready for any enterprise analogous to their characters. He seduced good and well-meaning citizens, some by assurances that he possessed the confidence of the government and was acting under its secret patronage, a pretense which obtained some credit from the state of our differences with Spain. . . .

Orders were dispatched to every intersecting point on the Ohio and Mississippi, from Pittsburgh to New Orleans, for the employment of such force either of the regulars or the militia

. . . as might enable them . . . to suppress effectually the further progress of the enterprise.

Burr's enterprise was crippled in its early stages by the action of local officials and militia in Ohio and Kentucky, a development which gave Jefferson an opportunity to reiterate his favorite themes of self-government and states' rights when he congratulated the Governor of Ohio. "The hand of the people has given the mortal blow to a conspiracy which, in other countries, would have called for an appeal to armies, and has proved that government to be the strongest of which every man feels himself a part. It is a happy illustration, too, of the importance of preserving to the state authorities all that vigor which the Constitution foresaw would be necessary, not only for their own safety, but for that of the whole." Burr was captured in Alabama and returned to Richmond, Virginia, for trial.

The trial was a farce which enraged Jefferson and solidified his contention that a judiciary appointed for life was a menace to constitutional government—and the Republicans. Chief Justice John Marshall first refused to commit Burr for treason, and held him only for a misdemeanor. He then attended a dinner with the accused, given by the latter's counsel. A grand jury indicted Burr for both treason and a misdemeanor. Marshall permitted a subpoena to be served on Jefferson, and there followed a long wrangle as to whether a judge could require the presence of the President of the United States in court. Throughout the trial Marshall permitted political criticism of Jefferson and the administration and, finally, virtually directed the jury to throw out the treason charge. Burr was acquitted of the misdemeanor.

Jefferson said that the Federalists were "making Burr's cause their own, mortified only that he did not separate the Union or overturn the government, and proving that had he had a little dawn of success they would have joined him to introduce his object, their favorite monarchy." Of the trial he wrote, "The scenes which have been acted at Richmond are such as have never before been exhibited in any country where all regard to public character has not yet been thrown off. They are equivalent to a proclamation of impunity to every traitorous combination which may be formed to destroy the Union." And again, "We had supposed we possessed fixed laws to guard us equally against treason and oppression. But it now appears we have no law but the will of the judge. Never will chicanery have a more difficult task than has been now accomplished to warp the text of the law to the will of him who is to construe it."

During his years in public office Jefferson did a rightabout-face in his attitude toward the judiciary. In 1776 he had written to Wythe:

THE DIGNITY AND STABILITY of government in all its branches, the morals of the people, and every blessing of society depend so much upon an upright and skillful administration of justice that the judicial power ought to be distinct from both the legislature and executive, and independent of both, that so it may be a check upon both, as both should be a check upon that. The judges, therefore, should be men of learning and experience in the laws, of exemplary morals, great patience, calmness and attention; their minds should not be distracted with jarring interests; they should not be dependent upon any man or body of men.

But when the outgoing Federalists packed the courts with lifetime appointees of their own party, Jefferson became convinced that the federal courts with judges appointed for life were the greatest danger to the Constitution, and certainly should not be the sole arbiters of its meaning. After he retired from office he wrote extensively on the theme that "The judiciary of the United States is the subtle corps of sappers and miners constantly working underground to undermine the foundations of our confederate fabric." He summarized this view in one letter by saying:

THE NATION [in 1800] declared its will by dismissing functionaries of one principle and electing those of another in the two branches, executive and legislative. . . . Over the judiciary department the Constitution had deprived them of their control. . . . Intending to establish three departments, co-ordinate and independent, that they might check and balance one another, it has given . . . to one of them alone the right to prescribe rules for the government of the others, and to that one, too, which is unelected by and independent of the nation. For experience has already shown that the impeachment it has provided is not even a scarecrow. . . . The Constitution, on this hypothesis, is a mere thing of wax in the hands of the judiciary, which they may twist and shape into any form they please. It should be remembered as an axiom of eternal truth in politics that whatever power in any government is independent is absolute also, in theory only at first, while the spirit of the people is up, but in practice as fast as that relaxes. Independence can be trusted nowhere but with the people in the mass. They are inherently independent of all but moral law. My construction of the Constitution . . . is that each department is truly independent of the others, and has an equal right to decide for itself what is the meaning of the Constitution.

And in his autobiography he said:

I DO NOT CHARGE the judges with willful and ill-intentioned error, but honest error must be arrested where its toleration leads to public ruin. As for the safety of society we commit honest maniacs to bedlam, so judges should be withdrawn from the bench whose erroneous biases are leading us to dissolution. It may, indeed, injure them in fame or in fortune, but it saves the Republic, which is the first and supreme law.

In his seventh annual message to Congress, on October 27, 1807, Jefferson reported:

ON THE TWENTY-SECOND DAY of June last, by a formal order from the British admiral, the frigate "Chesapeake," leaving her port for distant service, was attacked by one of those vessels which had been lying in our harbors under the indulgences of hospitality, was disabled from proceeding, had several of her crew killed, and four taken away. . . . I immediately, by proclamation, interdicted our harbors and waters to all British armed vessels. . . .

To former violations of maritime rights, another is now added of very extensive effect. The government of that nation has issued an order interdicting all trade by neutrals between ports not in amity with them; and [it] being now at war with nearly every nation on the Atlantic and Mediterranean seas, our vessels are required to sacrifice their cargoes at the first port they touch, or to return home without the benefit of going to any other market. Under this new law of the ocean, our trade on the Mediterranean has been swept away by seizures and condemnations and that in other seas is threatened with the same fate.

Less than two months later he sent another message to Congress:

THE COMMUNICATIONS NOW MADE, showing the great and increasing dangers with which our vessels, our seamen and merchandise are threatened on the high seas and elsewhere, from the belligerent powers of Europe, and it being of great importance to keep in safety these essential resources, I deem it my duty to recommend the subject to the consideration of Congress, who will doubtless perceive all the advantages which may be expected from an inhibition of the departure of our vessels from the ports of the United States.

Congress responded by passing the Embargo Act which forbade all American vessels from leaving port except in coastwise voyages. Jefferson said:

THE EMBARGO keeping at home our vessels, cargoes and sea-men saves us the necessity of making their capture the cause of immediate war; for, if going to England, France had de-termined to take them, if to any other place, England was to take them. Till they return to some sense of moral duty, there-fore, we keep within ourselves. This gives time. Time may produce peace in Europe; peace in Europe removes all causes of difference till another European war; and by that time our debt may be paid, our revenues clear and our strength in-creased.

In the spring of 1808 Jefferson wrote:

THE EMBARGO APPEARS to be approved, even by the Federal-ists of every quarter except [New England]. The alternative was between that and war, and in fact it is the last card we have to play, short of war. But if peace does not take place in Europe, and if France and England will not consent to with-draw the operation of their decrees and orders from us, when Congress shall meet in December they will have to consider at what point of time the embargo, continued, becomes a greater evil than war.

The purpose of the Embargo Act was to force France and Eng-land to come to reasonable terms with the United States by eco-nomic pressure. Although some die-hard Jeffersonians claim that it would have worked had it been continued for a longer period, the fact is that it had little effect. Enforcement was imperfect. There was much smuggling, particularly to Canada. American ships that were at sea when it was passed continued to trade in foreign wa-ters. And Britain turned to Latin America for much of her needs. By mid-June of 1809, Jefferson was blaming the New England Federalists for the lack of effectiveness of the act:

THEY ARE NOW PLAYING a game of the most mischievous tendency, without perhaps being themselves aware of it. They are endeavoring to convince England that we suffer more by the embargo than they do, and if they will but hold out awhile, we must abandon it. It is true, the time will come when we must abandon it. But if this is before the repeal of the orders of council, we must abandon it only for a state of war. The day is not distant when that will be preferable to a longer continuance of the embargo. . . . I think that in two or three months we shall know what will be the issue.

In his last message to Congress, at the end of 1808, the President reported one side-line benefit of the Embargo Act that is generally ignored:

THE SUSPENSION of our foreign commerce, produced by the injustice of the belligerent powers, and the consequent losses and sacrifices of our citizens, are subjects of just concern. The situation into which we have thus been forced has impelled us to apply a portion of our industry and capital to internal manufactures and improvements. The extent of this conversion is daily increasing, and little doubt remains that the establishments formed and forming will—under the auspices of cheaper materials and subsistence, the freedom of labor from taxation with us, and of protecting duties and prohibitions— become permanent.

Spurred by deprivation of imported manufactured goods, America started on the road to industrialization.

Congress passed an Enforcing Act to plug the loopholes in the Embargo Act. This was too much for commercial New England, where the business depression had increased the influence of the Federalists. Newspapers appeared in mourning and screamed for resistance and secession: "It is better to suffer the amputation of the limb than to lose the whole body." Town meetings resolved that "resistance would become a virtue of the first magnitude," and demanded "relief against the unconstitutional measures of the general government."

A resolution was introduced in the House to repeal the act on June 1. Then, with the threatened secession of New England, Congress got panicky and voted to repeal it on March 4, the day after Jefferson went out of office. A year later Jefferson attributed the congressional collapse to one member who:

. . . BECAME PANIC-STRUCK and communicated his panic to his colleagues and they to a majority of the sound members of Congress. They believed in the alternative of repeal or civil war, and produced the fatal measure of repeal. This is the immediate parent of all our present evils and has reduced us to a low standing in the eyes of the world. I should think that even the Federalists themselves must now be made, by their feelings, sensible of their error. . . . Should the orders prove genuine, which are said to have been given against our fisheries, they, too, are gone; and if not true as yet, they will be true on the first breeze of success which England shall feel: it has now been some years that I am perfectly satisfied her intentions have been to claim the ocean as her conquest, and prohibit any vessel from navigating it but on such a tribute as may enable her to keep up such a standing navy as will maintain her dominion over it. She has hauled in, or let herself out, been bold or hesitating, according to occurrences, but has in no situation done anything which might amount to an acknowledged relinquishment of her intentions.

The final sentence in his analysis of British foreign policy might be applicable today if the word "Russia" was substituted for "England."

Jefferson believed to the end of his life that, had the Embargo Act been fully enforced and continued a few months longer, it would have prevented the War of 1812. Modern historians do not agree. It was the only act of his administration in which he was crossed by Congress.

During the final furor over the Embargo Act Jefferson was a "lame-duck" President. James Madison had been elected to succeed him. Early in his second administration he had announced that he would not be a candidate for a third term:

MY OPINION ORIGINALLY WAS that the President of the United States should have been elected for seven years, and forever ineligible afterwards. I have since become sensible that seven years is too long to be irremovable, and that there should be a peaceable way of withdrawing a man in midway who is doing wrong. The service for eight years, with a power to remove at the end of the first four, comes nearly to my principle as corrected by experience; and it is in adherence to that, that I determine to withdraw at the end of my second term. The danger is that the indulgence and attachments of the people will keep a man in the chair after he becomes a dotard, that re-election through life shall become habitual, and election for life follow that. General Washington set the example of voluntary retirement after eight years. I shall follow it. And a few more precedents will oppose the obstacle of habit to anyone after a while who shall endeavor to extend his term. Perhaps it may beget a disposition to establish it by an amendment of the Constitution.

James Monroe had some aspirations to the candidacy, and a temporary coolness developed between him and the President when it became obvious that Jefferson favored Madison. Jefferson tried to mollify him by writing:

I SEE WITH INFINITE GRIEF a contest arising between yourself and another, who have been very dear to each other, and equally so to me. I sincerely pray that these dispositions may not be affected between you; with me I confidently trust they will not. For independently of the dictates of public duty, which prescribes neutrality to me, my sincere friendship for you both will ensure its sacred observance. . . . The object of the contest is a fair and honorable one, equally open to you all; and I have no doubt the personal conduct of all will be so chaste as to offer no ground of dissatisfaction with each other. . . . I have ever viewed Mr. Madison and yourself as two principal pillars of my happiness. Were either to be withdrawn, I should consider it as among the greatest calamities which could assail my future peace of mind.

Although Jefferson believed that Monroe was so upright that "if his soul was turned inside out, not a spot would be found on it," Madison was the older and more experienced of his fellow Virginians, and had been closer to Jefferson. Monroe would have to wait his turn.

To Du Pont de Nemours in France Jefferson expressed his feelings on his final retirement from public life:

WITHIN A FEW DAYS I retire to my family, my books and farms; and having gained the harbor myself, I shall look on my friends still buffeting the storm with anxiety indeed, but not with envy. Never did a prisoner, released from his chains, feel such relief as I shall on shaking off the shackles of power. Nature intended me for the tranquil pursuits of science, by rendering them my supreme delight. But the enormities of the times in which I have lived have forced me to take a part in resisting them, and to commit myself on the boisterous ocean of political passions. I thank God for the opportunity of retiring from them without censure, and carrying with me the most consoling proofs of public approbation. I leave every thing in the hands of men so able to take care of them that if we were destined to meet misfortunes it will be because no human wisdom could avert them.

Upon his retirement the legislature of Virginia moved an address that summarized the accomplishments of his Presidency:

WE HAVE TO THANK YOU for the model of an administration conducted on the purest principles of republicanism; for pomp and state laid aside; patronage discarded; internal taxes abolished; a host of superfluous officers disbanded; the monarchic maxim that a national debt is a national blessing renounced, and more than thirty-three millions of our debt discharged; the native right to near one hundred millions of acres of our national domain extinguished; and without the guilt or calamities of conquest, a vast and fertile region added to our country, far more extensive than her original possessions, bringing along with it the Mississippi and . . . the trade of the West to the Pacific Ocean. . . . These are points in your administration which the historian will not fail to seize, to expand and to teach posterity to dwell upon with delight. Nor will he forget our peace with the civilized world, preserved through a season of uncommon difficulty and trial; the good will cultivated with the unfortunate aborigines of our country, and the civilization humanely extended among them . . . and that theme, which, above all other, the historic genius will hang upon with rapture, the liberty of speech and press preserved inviolate, without which genius and science are given to man in vain. . . .

From the first brilliant and happy moment of your resistance to foreign tyranny until the present day, we mark with pleasure and with gratitude the same uniform and consistent character—the same warm and devoted attachment to liberty and the Republic, the same Roman love of your country, her rights, her peace, her honor, her prosperity.

Perhaps Abraham Lincoln said it as well in fewer words. "The principles of Jefferson are the definitions and axioms of a free society."

CHAPTER VIII

PHILOSOPHY, MORALS AND
RELIGION

હ

Was Thomas Jefferson a philosopher? Some Jefferson scholars hold opposing views. Gilbert Chinard, a most esteemed Jeffersonian, said "Jefferson, in spite of his reputation, was not a philosopher, not even a *philosophe*." Dr. Adrienne Koch, of equal eminence, said that Jefferson "was a man so vitally interested in exploring ideas that to deny him the title of 'philosopher' is to argue adherence to a prejudiced definition of the term."

There is agreement that Jefferson does not merit membership among such great founders of philosophical systems as Plato, Aristotle, Aquinas, Spinoza, Kant, and Hegel, But Jefferson was a leader in his time among those who sought out new ideas, evaluated and interpreted them, gathered data to support or deny hypotheses, and fearlessly tested and applied them. It must be borne in mind that in Jefferson's day the word "philosopher" embraced those who are now called scientists. Jefferson explored every avenue which might advance knowledge or science and was an ardent disciple of scientific method at a time when it took courage and ingenuity to be one. His contemporaries evaluated his position in the sciences by electing him President of the American Philosophical Society.

In the classical sense of philosophy Jefferson, as a serious student and interpreter, certainly merited the title *philosophe* which Chinard would deny him. One of his most interesting "papers" is his Commonplace Book of Philosophers and Poets. This is not to be confused with what is generally called his Commonplace Book. In the latter he collected ideas on law and government. The former is a collection of quotations principally dealing with many aspects of philosophy, morals and ethics. Among the ancient Greek authors he favored Homer, with twelve quotations, in Greek, from the *Iliad* and the *Odyssey,* plus seventeen in English from Pope's translation. Euripides is also well represented. Among the Latins Cicero and Horace stand out, with added quotations from Virgil and Ovid.

Jefferson retained a respect and affection for the classical writers throughout his life. When he was nearing eighty he wrote:

WHEN THE DECAY OF AGE has enfeebled the useful energies of the mind, the classic pages fill up the vacuum of the grave into which we are all sooner or later to descend.

And of course, they should be read in the original:

I ENJOY HOMER in his own language infinitely beyond Pope's translation of him, and both beyond the dull narrative of the same event by Dares Phrygios; and it is an innocent enjoyment. I thank on my knees him who directed my early education for having put into my possession this rich source of delight: and I would not exchange it for anything which I could then have acquired.

It was from Homer that he chose the epitaph for his wife's tomb:

"In the house of Hades men forget their dead,
    Yet will I even there remember my dear companion."

Scholars have endeavored to interpret Jefferson's selections from the ancient philosophers, moralists and poets to prove that he favored this or that school of classic philosophy. They point to many quotations indicating a Stoic influence. From Homer, "Death is the worst: a Fate we must all try," and "To labor is the lot of man below: and when Jove gave us life he gave us woe." From Cicero, "All must die; if only there should be an end to misery in death," and "What is agreeable in life, when we must night and day reflect that, at some time or other, we must die?" And from Euripides, "We follow our fate here and there wherever it takes us. Whatever will happen, destiny must be overcome, by bearing it."

But late in life Jefferson wrote:

I . . . AM AN EPICUREAN. I consider the genuine (not the imputed) doctrines of Epicurus as containing everything rational in moral philosophy which Greece and Rome have left us. Epictetus indeed, has given us what was good of the Stoics, all beyond, of their dogmas, being hypocrisy and grimace. Their great crime was in their calumnies of Epicurus and misrepresentations of his doctrines.

All evidence, particularly the handwriting, indicates that almost all of the literary Commonplace Book was compiled when Jefferson was in his late teens and twenties. Although many quotations show a typically youthful, transient concern with fate and destiny, it is safe to say that Jefferson did not long remain a convert to any ancient school. The strong moral standards that young Jefferson found in Homer, Epictetus, Euripides and Cicero and later in Jesus were the basis of a moral and philosophical concept that was Jefferson's own.

Jefferson had a great aversion to the mystical concepts of Plato. He expressed it to John Adams, late in life:

I AMUSED MYSELF with reading seriously Plato's *Republic*. I am wrong, however, in calling it amusement, for it was the heaviest taskwork I ever went through. I had occasionally before taken up some of his other works, but scarcely ever had patience to go through a whole dialogue. While reading through the whimsies, the puerilities and unintelligible jargon of this work, I laid it down often to ask myself how it could have been, that the world should have consented to give reputation to such nonsense as this? How the *soi-disant* Christian world, indeed, should have done it, is a piece of historical curiosity. But how could the Roman good sense do it? And particularly, how could Cicero bestow such eulogies on Plato? Although Cicero did not wield the dense logic of Demosthenes yet he was able, learned, laborious, practiced in the business of the world and honest. He could not be the dupe of mere style, of which he was himself the first master in the world.

He had considerable respect for Cicero, but not as an orator. In one letter he blamed the Roman orator for establishing the standard of the verbose and redundant speeches in the Congress and added, "I doubt if there is a man in the world who can now read one of his orations through but as a piece of taskwork."

In a letter to John Page, written when he was twenty, he expresses his early view of life and fate:

PERFECT HAPPINESS, I believe, was never intended by the Deity to be the lot of one of his creatures in this world; but that he has very much put in our power the nearness of our approaches to it is what I have steadfastly believed.

The most fortunate of us, in our journey through life, frequently meet with calamities and misfortunes which may greatly afflict us; and, to fortify our minds against the attacks of these calamities and misfortunes should be one of the principal studies and endeavors of our lives. The only method of doing this is to assume a perfect resignation to the divine will, to consider that whatever does happen, must happen; and that by our uneasiness, we cannot prevent the blow before it does fall, but we may add to its force after it has fallen. These considerations, and others such as these, may enable us in some measure to surmount the difficulties thrown in our way; to bear up with a tolerable degree of patience under this burden of life; and to proceed with a pious and unshaken resignation, till we arrive at our journey's end, when we may deliver up our trust into the hands of him who gave it and receive such reward as to him shall seem proportioned to our merit. Such, dear Page, will be the language of the man who considers his situation in this life, and such should be the language of every man who would wish to render that situation as easy as the nature of it will admit. Few things will disturb him at all: nothing will disturb him much.

Among more modern writers represented in the literary Commonplace Book, Jefferson quoted most frequently from Milton, Shakespeare and Lord Bolingbroke. From Milton he copied numerous passages belittling women, for instance:

> "Therefore God's universal law
> Gave to man despotic power
> Over his female in due awe."

There are other antifeminine quotes from Euripides, including these from *Medea,* "Mortals should beget children from some other source and there should be no womankind; thus there would be no ill for men." And again, "O Zeus, why hast thou established women, a curse deceiving men, in the light of the sun?"

These quotes on women are further evidence that the literary Commonplace Book was compiled during Jefferson's youthful misogynist period after he was jilted by Rebecca Burwell and before he married. But he never accorded equal status to women. While he was President he tersely remarked, "The appointment of a woman to office is an innovation for which the public is not prepared, nor am I."

Jefferson's quotes from Shakespeare seem to indicate that he

revered the bard as a moralist and observer of human nature,
rather than a poet or playwright. He quotes from *Henry the Fourth,*
"But if it is a sin to covet honor, I am the most offending soul
alive." And from *Julius Caesar,* a quote that Jefferson could not
pass up:

> "This man
> Is now become a god, and Cassius is
> A wretched creature, and must bend his body
> If Caesar carelessly but nod to him."

Jefferson felt that Shakespeare and a few others justified the
reading of fiction, providing that the fiction was carefully selected
and purposefully read. In recommending a list of books he said:

A LITTLE ATTENTION . . . to the nature of the human mind
evinces that the entertainments of fiction are useful as well as
pleasant. That they are pleasant when well written every person feels who reads. But wherein is its utility asks the reverend sage, big with the notion that nothing can be useful but
the learned lumber of Greek and Roman reading with which
his head is stored?

I answer, everything is useful which contributes to fix in the
principles and practices of virtue. When any original act of
charity or of gratitude, for instance, is presented either to our
sight or imagination, we are deeply impressed with its beauty
and feel a strong desire in ourselves of doing charitable and
grateful acts also. On the contrary when we see or read of any
atrocious deed, we are disgusted with its deformity, and conceive an abhorrence of vice. . . . We never reflect whether the
story we read be truth or fiction. If the painting be lively, and
a tolerable picture of nature, we are thrown into a reverie,
from which if we awaken it is the fault of the writer. I appeal
to every reader of feeling and sentiment whether the fictitious
murder of Duncan by Macbeth in Shakespeare does not excite
in him as great a horror of villainy as the real one of Henry

IV by Ravaillac as related by Davila? . . . The field of imagination is thus laid open to our use, and lessons may be formed to illustrate and carry home to the heart every moral rule of life. Thus a lively and lasting sense of filial duty is more effectually impressed on the mind of a son or daughter by reading *King Lear* than by all the dry volumes of ethics and divinity that ever were written. This is my idea of well-written romance, of tragedy, comedy and epic poetry.

Jefferson had a rather "on the fence" attitude toward poetry. He, with the rest of the English-speaking literate world, was completely taken in by the Ossian hoax in the mid-eighteenth century and wrote to a relative of James MacPherson, who perpetrated the hoax:

OSSIAN'S POEMS . . . have been and will, I think, during my life, continue to be to me the sources of daily and exalted pleasures. The tender and sublime emotions of the mind were never before so wrought up by the human hand. I am not ashamed to own that I think this rude bard of the north the greatest poet that has ever existed. Merely for the pleasure of reading his works, I am become desirous of learning the language in which he sung, and of possessing his songs in their original [Gaelic]. . . . Manuscript copies of any which are in print, it would at any time give me the greatest happiness to receive. The glow of one warm thought is to me worth more than money.

Later in life he said:

. . . OF ALL MEN LIVING, I am the last who should undertake to decide as to the merits of poetry. In earlier life I was fond of it and easily pleased. But as age and cares advanced, the powers of fancy have declined. Every year seems to have plucked a feather from her wings, till she can no longer waft one to those sublime heights to which it is necessary to accompany the poet.

And, in an essay titled *Thoughts on English Prosody* he added:

WHAT PROVES THE EXCELLENCE of blank verse is that the taste lasts longer than for rhyme. The fondness for the jingle leaves us with that for the rattles and baubles of childhood, and if we continue to read rhymed verse at a latter period of life it is such only where the poet has had force enough to bring great beauties of thought and diction into this form. When young any composition pleases which unites a little sense, some imagination and some rhythm, in doses however small. But as we advance in life these things fall off one by one, and I suspect we are left at last with only Homer and Vergil, perhaps with Homer alone.

A concept of Jefferson's opinion on suitable reading for a young man may be gained from a letter to his fifteen-year-old favorite nephew, Peter Carr, who had been brought up in Jefferson's household. After advising the boy on the first importance of virtue and honesty, Jefferson continued:

AN HONEST HEART being the first blessing, a knowing head is the second. It is time for you now to begin to be choice in your reading; to begin to pursue a regular course in it; and not to suffer yourself to be turned to the right or left by reading anything out of that course. . . . For the present, I advise you to begin a course of ancient history, reading every thing in the original and not in translations . . . reading the following books, in the following order: Herodotus, Thucydides, Xenophontis *Hellenica,* Xenophontis *Anabasis,* Arrian, Quintus Curtius, Diodorus Siculus, Justin. . . . In Greek and Latin poetry, you have read or will read at school Vergil, Terence,

Horace, Anacreon, Theocritus, Homer, Euripides, Sophocles. Read also Milton's *Paradise Lost,* Shakespeare, Ossian, Pope's works, Swift's works, in order to form your style in your own language. In morality, read Epictetus, Xenophontis *Memorabilia,* Plato's Socratic dialogues, Cicero's philosophies, Antoninus, and Seneca.

It is interesting to speculate whether there is a single fifteen year old in the United States today who could pursue that program of reading in the languages in which it was originally written.

Another section of this same letter to young Carr has nothing to do with philosophy or morals, but it is interesting in the light of the current emphasis on physical fitness for youth. By substituting "automobile" for "horse" it might have been written in the 1960s:

IN ORDER TO ASSURE a certain progress in this reading, consider what hours you have free from the school and the exercises of the school. Give about two of them, every day, to exercise; for health must not be sacrificed to learning. A strong body makes the mind strong. As to the species of exercise, I advise the gun. While this gives a moderate exercise to the body, it gives boldness, enterprise and independence to the mind. Games played with the ball, and others of that nature, are too violent for the body, and stamp no character on the mind. Let your gun, therefore, be the constant companion of your walks. . . . Walking is the best possible exercise. Habituate yourself to walk very far. The Europeans value themselves on having subdued the horse to the uses of man, but I doubt whether we have not lost more than we have gained, by the use of this animal. No one has occasioned so much the degeneracy of the human body. An Indian goes on foot nearly as far in a day, for a long journey, as an enfeebled white does on his horse; and he will tire the best horses. There is no habit you will value so much as that of walking far without fatigue.

Jefferson's philosophical thinking was thoroughly materialistic. To Adams he wrote:

I FEEL, THEREFORE I EXIST. I feel bodies which are not myself: there are other existences, then. I call them *matter*. I feel them changing place. This gives me *motion*. Where there is an absence of matter, I call it *void*, or *nothing*, or *immaterial space*. On the basis of sensation, of matter and motion, we may erect the fabric of all the certainties we can have or need. I can conceive *thought* to be an action of a particular organization of matter, formed for that purpose by its Creator, as well as that *attraction* is an action of matter, or *magnetism* of loadstone. When he who denies to the Creator the power of endowing matter with the mode of action called *thinking* shall show how he could endow the sun with the mode of action called attraction, which reins the planets in the track of their orbits, or how an absence of matter can have a will, and by that will put matter into motion, then the materialist may be lawfully required to explain the process by which matter exercises the faculty of thinking. When once we quit the basis of sensation, all is in the wind. To talk of *immaterial* existences is to talk of *nothings*. To say that the human soul, angels, God, are immaterial, is to say, they are *nothings*, or that there is no God, no angels, no soul. I cannot reason otherwise.

This concern with the material, as opposed to the mystical, led him to seek explanations through the natural sciences. It shaped his views on religion, which he considered a subject for reason rather than faith. To Peter Carr, when his nephew was seventeen, he wrote:

RELIGION. Your reason is now mature enough to examine this object. In the first place divest yourself of all bias in favor of novelty and singularity of opinion. Indulge them in any other subject rather than that of religion. It is too important, and the consequences of error may be too serious. On the other hand shake off all the fears and servile prejudices under which weak minds are servilely crouched. Fix reason firmly in her seat, and call to her tribunal every fact, every opinion. Question with boldness even the existence of a god; because, if there be one, he must more approve of the homage of reason, than that of blindfolded fear. You will naturally examine first the religion of your own country. Read the Bible then, as you would read Livy or Tacitus. The facts which are within the ordinary course of nature you will believe on the authority of the writer, as you do those of the same kind in Livy and Tacitus. . . . But those facts in the Bible which contradict the laws of nature must be examined with more care, and under a variety of faces. Here you must recur to the pretensions of the writer to inspiration from God. Examine upon what evidence his pretentions are founded, and whether that evidence is so strong as that its falsehood would be more improbable than a change in the laws of nature in the case he relates. For example in the book of Joshua we are told the sun stood still several hours. Were we to read that fact in Livy or Tacitus we should class it with their showers of blood, speaking of statues, beasts, etc. But it is said that the writer of that book was inspired. Examine therefore candidly what evidence there is of his having been inspired. The pretension is entitled to your inquiry, because millions believe it. On the other hand you are astronomer enough to know how contrary it is to the law of nature that . . . the earth . . . should have stopped. . . .

You will next read the New Testament. It is the history of a personage called Jesus. Keep in your eye the opposite pretensions (1) of those who say he was begotten by God, born of a virgin, suspended and reversed the laws of nature at will and ascended bodily into heaven: and (2) of those who say he was a man of illegitimate birth, of a benevolent heart, enthusiastic mind, who set out without pretensions to divinity, ended in believing them, and was punished capitally for sedition. . . . Do

not be frightened from this inquiry by any fear of its consequences. . . . Your own reason is the only oracle given you by
heaven, and you are answerable not for the rightness but the
uprightness of the decision.

But, although faith was subject to reason, morality was not. In
the same letter in which he told young Carr to question the existence of God he also told him that God had given man a moral sense
that was not subject to science.

HE WHO MADE US would have been a pitiful bungler if he had
made the rules of our moral conduct a matter of science. For
one man of science, there are thousands who are not. What
would have become of them? Man was destined for society.
His morality therefore was to be formed to this object. He was
endowed with a sense of right and wrong merely relative to
this. This sense is as much a part of his nature as the sense of
hearing, seeing, feeling; it is the true foundation of morality. . . . The moral sense, or conscience, is as much a part of
man as his leg or arm. . . . It may be strengthened by exercise,
as may any particular limb of the body. This sense is submitted indeed in some degree to the guidance of reason; but it
is a small stock which is required for this, even a less one than
what we call common sense. State a moral case to a ploughman
and a professor. The former will decide it as well, and often
better than the latter, because he has not been led astray by
artificial rules . . . above all things lose no occasion of exercising your dispositions to be grateful, to be generous, to be
charitable, to be humane, to be true, just, firm, orderly, cou-
rageous, etc. Consider every act of this kind as an exercise
which will strengthen your moral faculties, and increase your
worth.

To Jefferson, religion should be synonymous with a moral and
ethical code based on the concept of "love thy neighbor." He said,

"Nature hath implanted in our breasts a love of others, a sense of duty to them, a moral instinct, in short, which prompts us irresistibly to feel and to succor their distresses." He claimed that he would not write about or talk about religion. "I not only write nothing on religion, but rarely permit myself to speak on it, and never but in a reasonable society." He frequently reiterated this reluctance to discuss religion, and then wrote enough on the subject to fill a good-sized book.

Jefferson was born an Anglican—now, Episcopalian. For many years he was an Episcopalian vestryman, but this was more of a public duty than an expression of faith. Late in life he said he was a Unitarian. He contributed money to build Episcopal, Presbyterian and Baptist churches in Virginia, but he decried sectarianism. He said that, "There is not a Quaker or a Baptist, a Presbyterian or an Episcopalian, a Catholic or a Protestant in heaven; that, on entering that gate, we leave those badges of schism behind, and find ourselves united in those principles only in which God has united us all." He despised priests, and by this he meant all clergy, not merely Roman Catholic or Episcopal priests. He said, "I am a Christian," but he was reviled as an atheist and a heretic.

He certainly believed in God the Creator when he wrote Adams:

I HOLD (without revelation) that when we take a view of the universe, in its parts, general or particular, it is impossible for the human mind not to perceive and feel a conviction of design, consummate skill and indefinite power in every atom of its composition. The movements of the heavenly bodies, so exactly held in their course by the balance of centrifugal and centripetal forces; the structure of the earth itself, with its distribution of lands, waters and atmosphere; animal and vegetable bodies, examined in all their minutest particular; insects, mere atoms of life, yet as perfectly organized as man or mammoth; the mineral substances, their generation and uses; it is impossible, I say, for the human mind not to believe that there is in all this design, cause and effect up to an ultimate cause, a Fabricator of all things from matter and motion, their Preserver and Regulator.

Jefferson's first "brush with the law" on the subject of religion came with his *Statute of Virginia for Religious Freedom,* which he considered one of the three greatest accomplishments of his life. In the preamble he said:

WELL AWARE THAT ALMIGHTY GOD hath created the mind free; that all attempts to influence it by temporal punishments or burdens, or by civil incapacitations, tend only to beget habits of hypocrisy and meanness, and are a departure from the plan of the Holy Author of our religion, who being Lord of both body and mind, yet chose not to propagate it by coercions on either, as was in his almighty power to do; that the impious presumption of legislators and rulers, civil as well as ecclesiastical, who being themselves but fallible and uninspired men have assumed dominion over the faith of others, setting up their own opinions and modes of thinking as the only true and infallible, and as such endeavoring to impose them on others, hath established and maintained false religions over the greatest part of the world and through all time; that to compel a man to furnish contributions of money for the propagation of opinions which he disbelieves, is sinful and tyrannical . . . that our civil rights have no dependence on our religious opinions, more than our opinions in physics or geometry . . .

To Jefferson state control of religion was "tyranny over the mind of man" in its most pernicious form. In his *Notes on Virginia* he wrote:

THE RIGHTS OF CONSCIENCE we never submitted, we could not submit. We are answerable for them to our God. The legitimate powers of government extend to such acts only as are injurious to others. But it does me no injury for my neighbor to say there are twenty gods, or no God. It neither picks my pocket nor breaks my leg. If it be said his testimony in a court of justice cannot be relied on, reject it then, and be the stigma on him. Constraint may make him worse by making him a hypocrite, but it will never make him a truer man. It may fix him obstinately in his errors but will not cure them. Reason and free inqury are the only effectual agents against error. Give a loose to them, they will support the true religion by bringing every false one to their tribunal, to the test of their investigation. They are the natural enemies of error, and of error only. Had not the Roman government permitted free inquiry, Christianity could never have been introduced. Had not free inquiry been indulged at the era of the Reformation, the corruptions of Christianity could not have been purged away. If it be restrained now, the present corruptions will be protected, and new ones encouraged. . . . It is error alone which needs the support of government. Truth can stand by itself. . . . What has been the effect of coercion? To make one half the world fools, and the other half hypocrites.

During his sojourn in France, Jefferson's antipathy toward the clergy took firm root. Throughout the rest of his life he continued to castigate "priests" as foes of liberty and true religion. "In every country and every age, the priest has been hostile to liberty," he wrote; "he is always in alliance with the despot, abetting his abuses in return for protection to his own." And it was the clergy who were the real foes of Christianity as preached by Jesus.

HIS PRINCIPLES WERE DEPARTED FROM by those who professed to be his special servants, and perverted into an engine for enslaving their oppressors in church and state. . . . The purest system of morals ever before preached to man has been adulterated and sophisticated by artificial constructions into a mere contrivance to filch wealth and power to themselves. . . . Rational men, not being able to swallow their impious heresies, in order to force them down their throats, they raise the hue and cry of infidelity, while themselves are the greatest obstacles to the advancement of the real doctrines of Jesus, and do, in fact, constitute the real Antichrist.

He added:

I ABUSE THE PRIESTS, indeed, who have so much abused the pure and holy doctrines of their master, and who have laid me under no obligations of reticence as to the tricks of their trade.

The clergy replied in kind, particularly the New England Congregationalists, who were, for the most part, ardent Federalists. During the campaign of 1800 the most vicious attacks against Jefferson came from the pulpits of Connecticut. Dr. Timothy Dwight, a Congregational clergyman and president of Yale, thundered:

FOR WHAT END shall we be connected with men of whom this is the character and the conduct? . . . Is it that we may change our holy worship into a dance of Jacobin frenzy, and that we may behold a strumpet personating a goddess on the altars of Jehovah? Is it that we may see the Bible cast into a bonfire, the vessels of the sacramental supper borne by an ass in public procession, and our children, either wheedled or terrified, uniting in chanting mockeries against God? . . . Is it that we may see our wives and daughters the victims of legal prostitution; soberly dishonored; speciously polluted; the outcasts of delicacy and virtue, the loathing of God and man?

Jefferson said that the priests "wished him to be thought atheist, deist or devil, who could advocate freedom from their religious dictations, but I have ever thought religion a concern purely between God and our consciences, for which we were accountable to Him, and not to the priests."

By the time he became President, Jefferson had come to believe that Jesus' "system of morality was the most benevolent and sublime that has been ever taught, and consequently more perfect than those of any of the ancient philosophers." And he wrote extensively on this theme. In fact, he proposed a book on the subject of which he sent an outline to Dr. Benjamin Rush in 1803 with a letter in which he said that his views were "the result of a life of inquiry and reflection, and very different from that anti-Christian system imputed to me by those who know nothing of my opinions. To the corruptions of Christianity I am, indeed, opposed; but not to the genuine precepts of Jesus himself. I am a Christian in the only sense in which he wished any one to be; sincerely attached to his doctrines in preference to all others; ascribing to himself every *human* excellence; and believing he never claimed any other. The outline for the book, which he "wished to see executed by someone of more leisure and information" than himself, was titled

SYLLABUS OF AN ESTIMATE OF THE MERIT OF THE DOCTRINES OF JESUS, COMPARED WITH THOSE OF OTHERS

In a comparative view of the ethics of the enlightened nations of antiquity, of the Jews and of Jesus, no notice should be taken of the corruptions of reason among the ancients, to wit, the idolatry and superstition of the vulgar, nor of the corruptions of Christianity by the learned among its professors.

Let a just view be taken of the moral principles inculcated by the most esteemed of the sects of ancient philosophy, or of their individuals; particularly Pythagoras, Socrates, Epicurus, Cicero, Epictetus, Seneca, Antoninus.

Philosophers. 1. Their precepts related chiefly to ourselves, and the government of those passions which, unrestrained, would disturb the tranquillity of mind. In this branch of philosophy they were really great.

2. In developing our duties to others, they were short and defective. They embraced, indeed, the circles of kindred and friends, and inculcated patriotism, or the love of our country in the aggregate, as a primary obligation: towards our neigh-

bors and countrymen they taught justice, but scarcely viewed them as within the circle of benevolence. Still less have they inculcated peace, charity and love to our fellow men, or embraced with benevolence the whole family of mankind.

Jews. 1. Their system was deism; that is, the belief in one only God. But their ideas of him and of his attributes were degrading and injurious.

2. Their ethics were not only imperfect, but often irreconcilable with the sound dictates of reason and morality, as they respect intercourse with those around us; and repulsive and antisocial, as respecting other nations. They needed reformation, therefore, in an eminent degree.

Jesus. In this state of things among the Jews, Jesus appeared. His parentage was obscure; his condition poor; his education null; his natural endowments great; his life correct and innocent: he was meek, benevolent, patient, firm, disinterested and of the sublimest eloquence.

The disadvantages under which his doctrines appear are remarkable.

1. Like Socrates and Epictetus, he wrote nothing himself.

2. But he had not, like them, a Xenophon or an Arrian to write for him. .... On the contrary, all the learned of his country, entrenched in its power and riches, were opposed to him, lest his labors should undermine their advantages; and the committing to writing his life and doctrines fell on unlettered and ignorant men; who wrote, too, from memory, and not till long after the transactions had passed.

3. According to the ordinary fate of those who attempt to enlighten and reform mankind, he fell an early victim to the jealousy and combination of the altar and the throne, at about thirty-three years of age, his reason having not yet attained the *maximum* of its energy, nor the course of his preaching, which was not of three years at most, presented occasions for developing a complete system of morals.

4. Hence the doctrines which he really delivered were de-

fective as a whole, and fragments only of what he did deliver have come to us mutilated, misstated and often unintelligible.

5. They have been still more disfigured by the corruptions of schismatizing followers, who have found an interest in sophisticating and perverting the simple doctrines he taught, by engrafting on them the mysticisms of a Grecian sophist, frittering them into subtleties and obscuring them with jargon, until they have caused good men to reject the whole in disgust, and to view Jesus himself as an impostor.

Notwithstanding these disadvantages, a system of morals is presented to us, which, if filled up in the style and spirit of the rich fragments he left us, would be the most perfect and sublime that has ever been taught by man.

The question of his being a member of the Godhead, or in direct communication with it, claimed for him by some of his followers and denied by others, is foreign to the present view, which is merely an estimate of the intrinsic merits of his doctrines. . . .

The precepts of philosophy, and of the Hebrew code, laid hold of actions only. He pushed his scrutinies into the heart of man, erected his tribunal in the region of his thoughts, and purified the waters at the fountainhead.

Later, in commenting on the *Syllabus,* Jefferson said, "It is not to be understood that I am with him in all his doctrines. I am a materialist; he takes the side of spiritualism; he preaches the efficacy of repentance towards forgiveness of sin; I require a counterpoise of good works to redeem it." He also wrote a more terse comment on the teachings of Jesus and their alleged corruptions by the clergy.

THE DOCTRINES OF JESUS are simple, and tend all to the happiness of man.

1. That there is only one God, and He all-perfect.
2. That there is a future state of rewards and punishments.

3. That to love God with all thy heart and thy neighbor as thyself is the sum of religion. These are the great points on which he endeavored to reform the religion of the Jews. But compare with these the demoralizing dogmas of Calvin.

1. That there are three Gods.

2. That good works, or the love of our neighbor, are nothing.

3. That faith is everything, and the more incomprehensible the proposition, the more merit in its faith.

4. That reason in religion is of unlawful use. . . .

Now which of these is the true and charitable Christian? He who believes and acts on the simple doctrines of Jesus? Or the impious dogmatists? . . . Their blasphemies have driven thinking men into infidelity, who have too hastily rejected the supposed author himself, with the horrors so falsely imputed to him. Had the doctrines of Jesus been preached always as pure as they came from his lips, the whole civilized world would now have been Christian.

Ten years after writing the *Syllabus* Jefferson wrote to Adams about the need for a book on religion, philosophy and morality, still protesting that he was not the one to write it. But he had taken another step. He said:

WE MUST REDUCE OUR VOLUME to the simple evangelists, select, even from them, the very words only of Jesus. . . . I have performed this operation for my own use by cutting verse by verse out of the printed book [the Bible], and arranging the matter which is evidently his, and which is as easily distinguishable as diamonds in a dunghill. The result is an octavo of forty-six pages, of pure and unsophisticated doctrines, such as were professed and acted on by the *unlettered* apostles, the apostolic fathers, and the Christians of the first century.

Elsewhere he referred to his compilation from the Gospels as "a wee little book . . . which I call the Philosophy of Jesus . . . made by cutting the texts out of the book, and arranging them on the pages of a blank book, in a certain order of time or subject. . . . If I had time I would add to my little book the Greek, Latin and French texts, in columns side by side."

Jefferson made his "wee little book" in two nights, sitting by candle light in the executive mansion after the cares of the presidential day were behind him. Much later he added the Latin, French and Greek versions, a concordance giving the chapter and verse of his selections, and titled the volume *The Life and Morals of Jesus of Nazareth Extracted Textually from the Gospels in Greek, Latin and English*. It is generally called, improperly, *The Jefferson Bible*. The finished book contained eighty-five pages, with the Greek and Latin texts in double column on the left-hand pages and the French and English on the right. He had it bound in red morocco with maps of Palestine and Asia Minor pasted in. At the time the book was considered heretical by all good churchmen, but in 1904 Congress passed an act to reproduce nine thousand copies of it for distribution among its members.

Life and Morals is a fascinating book, and a frustrating one for a reader who is familiar with the King James or Revised Standard versions of the Gospels. Jefferson eliminated all material relating to the supernatural or mystical—the miracles, angels, the Transfiguration, the Resurrection and the Nativity—of which he said, "The day will come when the account of the birth of Christ as accepted in the Trinitarian churches will be classed with the fable of Minerva springing from the brain of Jupiter."

The book starts with the second chapter of Luke, "And it came to pass in those days," and the familiar words continue through the seventh verse, "and there was no room for them at the inn." Then, to one familiar with the conventional Nativity story, there is something sadly missing. The "shepherds abiding in the field" are not there, nor is the angel of the Lord and the heavenly host saying, "Glory to God in the highest, and on earth peace, good will toward men." Jefferson did not believe in angels.

Much of the Jefferson correspondence with Adams, late in life after the political wounds had healed, dealt with religion, philosophy and speculations on man's soul and the hereafter. He summarized his religious views by writing to Adams:

THE RESULT OF YOUR fifty or sixty years of religious reading, in the four words, "Be just and good," is that in which all our inquiries must end. . . . What all agree in, is probably right. What no two agree in, most probably wrong. One of our fancoloring biographers, who paints small men as very great, inquired of me lately, with real affection, too, whether he might consider as authentic the change in my religion much spoken of in some circles. . . . My answer was, "Say nothing of my religion. It is known to my God and myself alone. Its evidence before the world is to be sought in my life; if that has been *honest and dutiful* to society, the religion which has regulated it cannot be a bad one!"

And in another letter to Adams, he expressed a philosophy of life that had come a long way from his youthful Stoicism:

YOU ASK IF I WOULD agree to live my seventy or rather seventy-three years over again? To which I say, yea. I think with you that it is a good world, on the whole; that it has been framed on a principle of benevolence, and more pleasure than pain dealt out to us. There are, indeed . . . gloomy and hypochondriac minds, inhabitants of diseased bodies, disgusted with the present and despairing of the future, always counting that the worst will happen. To these I say, how much pain have cost us the evils which have never happened! My temperament is sanguine. I steer my bark with hope in the head, leaving fear astern. My hopes, indeed, sometimes fail; but not oftener than the forebodings of the gloomy.

CHAPTER IX

SCIENCE AND THE ARTS

On January 27, 1780, an inconspicuous item appeared in the *Pennsylvania Packet* announcing that twenty-one new members had been appointed to the American Philosophical Society. The impressive list included George Washington, John Adams, Thomas Jefferson, John Jay and Alexander Hamilton. A strange thing about the item is that Washington indicated, in a later letter, that he did not know he had been elected, and Jay, Adams and Hamilton were later admitted at different times.

But there is no doubt that Jefferson was elected to the premier scientific society of America, which fellow founding Father Benjamin Franklin had started. He was a member for forty-seven years and president for seventeen. In his letter of acceptance he said that the presidency of "a body which comprehends whatever the American world has of distinction in philosophy and science in general, is the most flattering incident of my life. . . . I feel no qualification for this distinguished post, but a sincere zeal for all the objects of our institution, and an ardent desire to see knowledge so disseminated through the mass of mankind, that it may at length reach the extremes of society, beggars and kings."

The first two presidents of the society, Franklin and Rittenhouse, were practicing scientists. Jefferson was rather a dedicated amateur who was described by a contemporary as having an "enlightened love and extensive knowledge" of the sciences. A modern scientist has said, "Like all daring thinkers and workers in the pioneer days of so many of the sciences, Jefferson went off the deep end a few times. . . . He had . . . caution and daring, inquisitiveness and a willingness to change his mind in the light of new facts or as a result of further thought. What we would now call proper scientific methods appeared to be instinctive with him." Jefferson described scientific method by saying "A patient pursuit of facts, and cautious combination and comparison of them, is the drudgery to which man is subjected by his Maker, if he wishes to obtain sure knowledge." He said that he was "an empiric in natural philosophy, suffering my faith to go no further than my facts."

When, in 1807, a shower of meteorites was reported in Connecticut Jefferson at first doubted the story, but added:

WE CERTAINLY ARE NOT to deny whatever we cannot account for. A thousand phenomena present themselves daily which we cannot explain, but where facts are suggested, bearing no analogy with the laws of nature as yet known to us . . . a cautious mind will weigh well the opposition of the phenomenon to everything hitherto observed, the strength of the testimony by which it is supported, and the errors and misconceptions to which even our senses are liable.

Scores of books credit Jefferson with attainments in many fields of physical science. Such lists include meteorology, paleontology, ethnology, archaeology, zoology, astronomy, chemistry, agriculture, navigation, geology, exploration, botany, anatomy, medicine, philology, civil engineering, mechanics and natural history. It would be more precise to say that Jefferson's almost limitless interests embraced all of these things; he did not make significant contributions in most of them. In astronomy, for instance, he did observe and record an eclipse; but he used his telescope more frequently in later life to keep tabs on the workmen who were building the University of Virginia below his mountaintop home.

He said that medical science was "the most important of all others," and lent the weight of his office as President to encourage smallpox vaccination. But, on the whole, he distrusted doctors and their "visionary theories," and said that "The patient, treated on the fashionable theory, sometimes gets well in spite of the medicine." He had some rather strange medical theories. When James Madison had a case of typhus in the family Jefferson wrote to tell him how his daughters had been treated for the same disease in Paris, "The youngest took a pint of Madeira a day without feeling it." Maria was ten years old at the time. He continued, "I have . . . carried between twenty and thirty patients through it without losing a single one. . . . Instead of Madeira I have used toddy of French brandy about as strong as Madeira."

Over all, Jefferson's greatest contribution to science was his general encouragement of it. He said, "The main objects of all science are the freedom and happiness of man," and "I am for encouraging the program of science in all its branches; and not for raising a hue and cry against the sacred name of philosophy." And to the president of Harvard he wrote:

WHAT A FIELD HAVE WE at our doors to signalize ourselves in! The botany of America is far from being exhausted, its mineralogy is untouched, and its natural history or zoology totally mistaken and misrepresented. . . . It is the work to which the young men whom you are forming should lay their hands. We have spent the prime of our lives in procuring them the precious blessing of liberty. Let them spend theirs in showing that it is the great parent of science and of virtue, and that a nation will be great in both always in proportion as it is free.

Throughout his life Jefferson recorded, reported and speculated on all areas of science as it was then known. Typical is a letter to the President of William and Mary college, written from Paris:

As you seem willing to accept of the crumbs of science on which we are subsisting here, it is with pleasure I continue to hand them on. . . . Herschel's volcano in the moon you have doubtless heard of, and placed among the other vagaries of a head which seems not organized for sound induction. . . . Dr. Ingenhousz had discovered, as he supposed, from experiment, that vegetation might be promoted by occasioning streams of electrical fluid to pass through a plant. . . . Speaking one day with Monsieur de Buffon on the present ardor of chemical inquiry, he affected to consider chemistry but as cookery, and to place the toils of the laboratory on a footing with those of the kitchen. I think it, on the contrary, among the most useful of sciences, and big with future discoveries for the utility and safety of the human race.

The words "useful" and "utility" loomed large in Jefferson's concept of science. Although he said that "no discovery is barren; it always serves as a step to something else," he had little patience with what is now called pure research. "The business of life," he said, "is with matter that gives us tangible results. Handling that, we arrive at the knowledge of the ax, the plow, the steamboat and everything useful in life. But, from metaphysical speculations, I have never seen one useful result." Although he criticized the Comte de Buffon for considering "chemistry but as cookery," he also emphasized the importance of turning a knowledge of chemistry to household purposes. . . . The common herd of philosophers [i.e., scientists] seem to write only for one another. The chemists have filled volumes on the composition of a thousand substances of no sort of importance to the purposes of life." Chemists, he said, should apply their science "to domestic objects, to malting, for instance, brewing, making cider, to fermentation and distillation generally, to the making of bread, butter, cheese, soap, to the incubation of eggs, etc."

He down-graded geology except in relation to mineralogy. He believed that "The dreams about the modes of creation, inquiring whether our globe has been formed by the agency of fire or water, how many years it may have cost Vulcan or Neptune to produce what the fiat of the Creator would affect by a single act of will, is too idle to be worth a single hour of any man's life." Studying the strata of the earth "from the skin-deep scratches which we can make or find on the surface" was a waste of time "if they contain no coal or iron or other useful metal."

Botany, on the other hand, was a most essential science—as was, in Jefferson's mind, anything relating to agriculture. Botany, he said, "I rank with the most valuable sciences, whether we consider its subjects as furnishing the principal subsistence of life to man and beast, delicious varieties for our tables, refreshments from our orchards, the adornments of our flower borders, shade and perfume of our groves, materials for our buildings or medicaments for our bodies."

Jefferson had a passionate interest in the weather and climate—again, it related to agriculture. He kept a Weather Memorandum Book from 1776 to 1820 in which he recorded the temperature twice a day and encouraged others at different places to do likewise. Before the Revolution he planned a weather service which, had he carried it out, would have started the Weather Bureau many years before it came into being. He wrote:

I AM SORRY you have received so little information on the subject of our winds. I had once (before our Revolutionary War) a project on the same subject. As I had then an extensive acquaintance over this state, I meant to have engaged some person in every county of it, giving them each a thermometer, to observe that and the winds twice a day, for one year, to wit, at sunrise and at four P.M. (the coldest and the warmest point of the twenty-four hours), and to communicate their observations to me at the end of the year. I should then . . . have made a map of them, and seen how far they had analogy with the temperature of the air. I meant this to be merely a specimen to be communicated to the Philosophical Society at Philadelphia, in order to engage them, by means of their correspondents, to have the same thing done in every state, and through a series of years. . . . We might, in time, have come to some of the causes which determine the direction of the winds, which I suspect to be very various. But this long-winded project was prevented by the war which came upon us, and since that I have been far otherwise engaged.

Jefferson hoped to make an important contribution to knowledge in philology, the study of language. In 1816 he wrote:

DURING THE COURSE of my public life, and from a very early period of it, I omitted no opportunity of procuring vocabularies of the Indian languages, and for that purpose formed a model expressing such objects in nature as must be familiar to every people, savage or civilized. This being made the standard to which all were brought would exhibit readily whatever affinities of language there be between the several tribes. It was my intention, on retiring from public business, to have digested these into some order, so as to show not only what relations of language existed among our own aborigines, but by a collation with the great Russian vocabulary of the languages of Europe and Asia, whether there were any between them and the other nations of the continent. On my removal from Washington, the package in which this collection was coming by water was stolen and destroyed. It consisted of between thirty and forty vocabularies, of which I can, from memory, say nothing particular, but that I am certain more than half of them differed as radically, each from every other, as the Greek, the Latin and Icelandic.

The trunk containing his Indian vocabularies had been rifled by a thief who, when he discovered that it contained nothing of value to him, threw the unintelligible papers overboard.

Jefferson's most important specific scientific contribution was

Notes on Virginia. Almost a century after its publication a secretary of the Smithsonian Institution described it as "the first comprehensive treatise upon the topography, natural history and natural resources of one of the United States . . . if measured by its influence it is the most important scientific work as yet published in America."

Over a quarter of *Notes* was devoted to natural history. In the area of botany Jefferson started by saying, "A complete catalogue of the trees, plants, fruits, etc., is probably not desired," then continued with several pages of plants that were "medicinal . . . esculent . . . ornamental or . . . useful for fabrication." This included everything from "Arsmart. Polygonum Sagittatum" to "squashes. Cucurbita melopepo."

In connection with North American animals he devoted most of his attention to refuting the Comte de Buffon's theory that animal life in America was inferior in size to that in Europe because the New World was cooler and more moist. As to the theory, Jefferson merely said, "Nature has hidden from us her *modus agendi.* Our only appeal on such questions is to experience; and I think that experience is against the supposition." He then went on to wave the flag by comparing, in parallel columns, the weights of animals from both worlds. Europe scored only with the red deer. They had nothing to compare with America's 1,800-pound buffalo; their bears were puny 153-pounders against American monsters of 410 pounds; even the American flying squirrel was a hefty 4 ounces compared to the 2.2-ounce mite of the Old World. Everything in the land of the free was bigger and better.

To top it off there was the mammoth. Of the bones which had been found in Ohio he said:

IT IS REMARKABLE that the tusks and skeletons have been ascribed by the naturalists of Europe to the elephant, while the grinders have been given to the hippopotamus, or river horse. Yet it is acknowledged that the tusks and skeletons are much larger than those of the elephant, and the grinders many times greater than those of the hippopotamus and essentially different in form. Wherever these grinders are found, there also we find the tusks and skeleton; but no skeleton of the hippopotamus nor grinders of the elephant. It will not be said that the hippopotamus and elephant came always to the same spot, the former to deposit his grinders, and the latter his tusks and skeleton. For what became of the parts not deposited there? . . . The skeleton of the mammoth (for so the incognitom has been called) bespeaks an animal of five or six times the cubic volume of the elephant, as Monsieur de Buffon has admitted.

And what happened to this gigantic animal? Jefferson was not sure, although he did not believe that any species of animal became extinct. Instead, he reported the Indian belief:

THAT IN ANCIENT TIMES a herd of these tremendous animals came to the Bigbone licks, and began a universal destruction of the bear, deer, elks, buffaloes and other animals which had been created for the use of the Indians; that the Great Man above, looking down at this, was so enraged that he seized his lightning, descended on the earth, seated himself on a neighboring mountain, on a rock of which his seat and the print of his feet are still to be seen, and hurled his bolts among them till the whole were slaughtered, except the big bull, who presenting his forehead to the shafts, shook them off as they fell; but missing one at length, it wounded him in the side; whereon, springing round, he bounded over the Ohio, over the Wabash, the Illinois, and finally over the Great Lakes, where he is living at this day.

When Jefferson went to France he brought Buffon a panther skin for which he had paid sixteen dollars in Philadelphia, "and it presented to him a new species." Later, when Buffon insisted that the gigantic moose that Jefferson described was merely a species of deer, Jefferson asked Governor Sullivan of New Hampshire to send him the horns, bones and skin of a moose. Sullivan mounted a natural history expedition of which Jefferson wrote:

HE HAD MADE THE ACQUISITION the object of a regular campaign, and that, too, of a winter one. The troops he employed sallied forth, as he writes me, in the month of March—much snow—a herd attacked—one killed—in the wilderness—a road to be cut twenty miles—to be drawn by hand from the frontiers to his house—bones to be cleaned, etc., etc., etc.

The Governor of New Hampshire sent the ex-Governor of Virginia a bill for sixty pounds which Jefferson ruefully paid and, perhaps, got his money's worth when Buffon told him, "I should have consulted you before publishing my natural history, and then I should have been sure of my facts."

Buffon also claimed that the American Indian was far inferior to European man; that he had "neither hair or beard, and no passion for his female," and that he was "much less sensitive and yet more fearful and cowardly." This led Jefferson to a spirited defense of the original Americans.

I AM ABLE TO SAY, in contradiction to this representation, that he is neither more defective in ardor, nor more impotent with his female, than the white reduced to the same diet and exercise; that he is brave, when an enterprise depends on bravery . . . he will defend himself against a host of enemies, always choosing to be killed, rather than to surrender . . . that his friendships are strong and faithful to the uttermost extremity; that his sensibility is keen, even the warriors weeping most bitterly on the loss of their children, though in general they endeavor to appear superior to human events; that his vivacity and activity of mind is equal to ours in the same situation; hence his eagerness for hunting, and for games of chance. . . . It had been said that Indians have less hair than the whites, except on the head. . . . But this is a fact of which fair proof can scarcely be had. With them it is disgraceful to be hairy on the body. They say it likens them to hogs.

Jefferson did not realize the scientific value of the extensive observations which he recorded in *Notes*. He wrote, "I have sometimes thought of sending my *Notes* to the Philosophical Society as a tribute to them, but this would seem as if I considered them worth something, which I am conscious that they are not. . . . I shall therefore refer it to further thought." The later thoughts caused him to send the book.

One of Jefferson's most avid scientific interests was paleontology. This was somewhat inconsistent with his statements that science should be useful—but he was fascinated with old bones. His most memorable contribution in this field was the *Megalonyx jeffersonii*. This started when a man named John Stuart sent him some bones unearthed in Kentucky with a note saying, "Observing by your *Notes* your very curious desire for examining into the antiquity of our country, I thought the bones of a tremendous animal of the clawed kind lately found . . . by some saltpeter manufacturers about five miles from my house might afford you some amusement, have therefore procured you such as were saved." Stuart did not know what kind of an animal it might have been, but he had an idea. His letter continued "I do not remember to have seen any account in the history of our country, or any other, of such an animal, which was probably of the lion kind. I am induced to think so from a perfect figure of that animal carved upon a rock near the confluence of the Great Kenawha, which appears to have been done many centuries ago." Jefferson eagerly asked Stuart to search for more bones. The latter found a few and also wrote of a story which he had heard many years before of some hunters who, while camped near the site of the find, had heard an "astonishing roaring . . . as loud as thunder."

Jefferson jumped to the conclusion that he was on the track of a gigantic American lion which would convince European scientists for all time of the superiority of American animals. He wrote to Rittenhouse, then president of the Philosophical Society:

SOME MAKERS OF SALTPETER, in digging up the floor of one of those caves beyond the Blue Ridge . . . found some of the bones of an animal of the family of the lion, tiger, panther, etc., but as pre-eminent over the lion in size as the mammoth is over the elephant. I have now in my possession the principal bones of a leg, the claws and other phalanges, and hope soon to receive some others, as I have taken measures for obtaining what are not already lost or may still be found. One of the claw bones in my possession, without its horny fang, measures seven inches long, and a larger one was found and has been lost. This phalange in the lion is under two inches in length. Its bulk entitles it to give to our animal the name of the Great Claw, or *Megalonyx*. The leg bone does not indicate so vast an excess of size over that of the lion, perhaps not more than a double or treble mass. But of this we shall be better able to judge when a fuller collection of the bones shall be made. The whole of them shall be deposited with the society.

He did not question that the animal was a gigantic member of the cat family and hastened to so describe his *Megalonyx* in a paper for the Philosophical Society, speculating that it still roamed the western wilds:

IN THE PRESENT INTERIOR of our continent there is surely space enough . . . for mammoths and *Megalonyxs* who may exist there. . . . Our entire ignorance of the immense country to the west and northwest . . . does not authorize us to say what it does not contain. . . . In fine, the bones exist; therefore the animal has existed. The movements of nature are in a never-ending circle. The animal species which has once been put into a train of motions is still probably moving in that train. For, if one link in nature's chain might be lost, another

and another might be lost till this whole system of things
should vanish by piecemeal.

He set off for Philadelphia to deliver the paper, the bones, and
to take office as president of the society and vice-president of the
United States. Fortunately, before doing any of these, he dropped
into a Philadelphia bookstore and bought a copy of the London
Monthly Magazine. It contained an article and a picture of which
Jefferson later wrote to Stuart:

ON MY ARRIVAL at Philadelphia, I met with an account published in Spain of the skeleton of an enormous animal from
Paraguay, of the clawed kind, but not of the lion class at all;
indeed, it is classed with the sloth, anteater, etc., which are not
of the carnivorous kinds. . . . The skeleton is now mounted at
Madrid, is twelve feet long and six feet high. There are several
circumstances which lead to a supposition that our *Megalonyx*
may have been the same animal with this.

By a remarkable coincidence news of the centuries-old bones
from two continents had come together in Philadelphia—and on
the day before Jefferson was to deliver his paper. He hastily edited
references to lions, tigers or panthers from his paper and added a
footnote mentioning the Spanish paleontologist's *Megatherium,* or
giant sloth. Jefferson's bones were actually from this extinct giant
sloth and they are still on display in the Academy of Natural Sciences in Philadelphia, labeled *"Megalonyx jeffersonii."*

In 1807 the Philosophical Society was anxious to complete a
skeleton of a mammoth. Jefferson sent William Clark, ex-compan-
ion of Meriwether Lewis, to "stop at the lick, employ laborers and
superintend the search at my expense . . . and send me the specific
bones wanted." Soon he could exultantly write to Dr. Caspar Wistar, eminent paleontologist of the Society, that General Clark had
found over three hundred bones which he had "shipped . . . in
three large boxes down the Ohio, via New Orleans, for this place

where they are daily expected." When they arrived he invited Wistar to study them at the White House, saying, "The bones are spread in a large room where you can work at your leisure, undisturbed by any mortal from morning till night, taking your breakfast and dinner with us. It is a precious collection." Like Abigail Adams, who used it to dry clothes, Jefferson had found a practical use for the East Room of the White House.

Jefferson's preoccupation with old bones while the Embargo Act was pinching their pocketbooks did not escape his New England critics. One poem, entitled *The Embargo,* advised him to:

> Go, WRETCH, resign thy presidential chair,
> Disclose thy secret measures, foul or fair,
> Go, search with curious eyes for horned frogs,
> 'Mid the wild wastes of Louisianian bogs;
> Or where the Ohio rolls his turbid stream
> Dig for huge bones, thy glory and thy theme.

This doggerel probably would have been long forgotten had it not been the first published work of William Cullen Bryant, written at the age of thirteen. To such criticism Jefferson replied:

OF ALL THE CHARGES brought against me by my political adversaries, that of possessing some science has probably done them the least credit. Our countrymen are too enlightened themselves to believe that ignorance is the best qualification for their service.

In any profile of Jefferson the scientist, Jefferson the inventor is always mentioned. Here, too, although he created a few inventions of his own and improved on the work of others, his greatest contribution was his encouragement of the development of ideas. After thanking Robert Livingston for a description of a simple steam engine and permission to communicate it to the Philosophical Society, he continued to suggest a novel use for such a machine:

THERE IS ONE OBJECT to which I have often wished a steam engine could be adopted. You know how desirable it is both in town and country to be able to have large reservoirs of water on the top of our houses, not only for use (by pipes) in the apartments, but as a resource against fire. . . . We might indeed have water carried from time to time in buckets to cisterns on the top of the house, but this is troublesome. . . . Could any agent be employed which would be little or no additional expense or trouble except the first purchase, it would be done. Every family has such an agent, its kitchen fire. It is small indeed, but if its small but constant action could be accumulated so as to give a stroke from time to time which might throw ever so small a quantity of water from the bottom of a well to the top of the house (say one hundred feet) it would furnish more than would waste by evaporation, or be used by the family. I know nobody who must better know the value of such a machine than yourself, nor more equal to the invention of it.

Like Benjamin Franklin, Jefferson "never . . . thought of monopolizing by patent any useful idea which happens to offer itself." When he invented a hemp beater, for example, he said, "As soon as I can speak of its effect with certainty I shall probably describe it anonymously in the public papers, in order to forestall the prevention of its use by some interloping patentee." However, he felt that "an inventor ought to be allowed a right to the benefit of his invention for some certain time," and, in 1791, he drafted a bill To Promote the Progress of the Useful Arts from which the present patent laws grew.

But he had somewhat mixed feelings about how much protection an inventor deserved. He said, "That one new idea leads to another, that to a third, and so on through a course of time until someone, with whom no one of these ideas was original, combines all together, and produces what is justly called a new invention."

He wrote a more lengthy discourse on ideas as applied to inventions long after he ceased to be responsible for patents.

IF NATURE HAS MADE any one thing less susceptible than all others of exclusive property, it is the action of the thinking power called an idea, which an individual may exclusively possess as long as he keeps it to himself; but the moment it is divulged, it forces itself into the possession of every one, and the receiver cannot dispossess himself of it. Its peculiar character, too, is that no one possesses the less, because every other possesses the whole of it. He who receives an idea from me, receives instruction himself without lessening mine; as he who lights his taper at mine, receives light without darkening me. That ideas should freely spread from one to another over the globe, for the moral and mutual instruction of man, and improvement of his condition, seems to have been peculiarly and benevolently designed by nature. . . . Inventions then cannot, in nature, be a subject of property. Society may give an exclusive right to the profits arising from them, as an encouragement to men to pursue ideas which may produce utility, but this may or may not be done according to the will and convenience of the society, without claim or complaint from anybody.

Many of Jefferson's inventions were in the nature of "gadgets", such as a violin musicstand that folded into a table; or the clock over the front door of Monticello with cannon balls as weights which indicated the day of the week as they dropped down the wall. His most substantial invention was the moldboard for a plow. He thought much about plows, which he considered "the most useful instrument known to man," and he said, "The plow is to the farmer what the wand is to the sorcerer. Its effect is really like sorcery." He started thinking about improving the plow when he watched peasants work while traveling through France. His notes on the trip said, "The awkward figure of their moldboard leads one to consider what should be its form. The offices of the moldboard are to receive the sod after the share has cut under it, to raise it gradually, and to reverse it. The fore end of it, then, should be horizontal to enter under the sod, and the hind end perpendicular to throw it over, the intermediate surface changing gradually from the horizontal to the perpendicular. It should be as wide as the furrow, and of a length suited to the construction of the plow." The notes continued to describe, with sketches in the margin, how such a moldboard could be carved from a block of wood with saw and adz. While he was Secretary of State he made, or had made, a model based on his first description and, through the years, improved upon it and broadcast models and descriptions in America, France and England.

Praise for what amounted to the first constructive improvement since ancient times on the most basic implement of husbandry was widespread and, although Jefferson deprecated his contribution, he was plainly pleased when he acknowledged honors from France:

I HAVE RECEIVED . . . the medal of gold by which the Society of Agriculture at Paris have been pleased to make their approbation of the form of moldboard which I had proposed; also . . . the information that they had honored me with the title of foreign associate in their society. I receive with great thankfulness these testaments of their favor, and should be happy to merit them by greater services. . . . I fear . . . I shall be to them but an unprofitable member, and shall have little to offer of myself worthy their acceptance.

A most common comment on Jefferson is that he was a "universal man." He, like Franklin, is often compared to the titans of the Renaissance. His universality was great, but he was not alone among the Founding Fathers in this. The age of specialization had not yet dawned, and it was usual for a well-educated man to function, or at least dabble, in many fields. But Jefferson was unique among the Founding Fathers in one respect, his devotion to the arts—as an amateur, patron, collector, performer and creator.

Jefferson believed that appreciation of the beautiful was an inborn sense, like morality, but distinct from it:

. . . FOUNDED IN A DIFFERENT FACULTY, that of taste, which is not even a branch of morality. We have indeed an innate sense of what we call beautiful, but that is exercised chiefly on subjects addressed to the fancy, whether through the eye in visible forms, as landscape, animal figure, dress, drapery, architecture, the composition of colors, etc., or to the imagination directly, as imagery, style or measure in prose or poetry, or whatever else constitutes the domain of criticism or taste, a faculty entirely distinct from the moral one.

And of this inborn sense he said tersely, "Taste cannot be controlled by law."

He was not always entirely consistent in his views on painting and sculpture. In 1785 he wrote to Madison, "I am an enthusiast on the subject of the arts . . . but it is an enthusiasm of which I am not ashamed, as its object is to improve the taste of my countrymen, to increase their reputation, to reconcile to them the respect of the world and to procure them its praise." A year later he said that painting and sculpture were "too expensive for the state of wealth of our country. It would be useless, therefore, and preposterous, for us to make ourselves connoisseurs in those arts. They are worth seeing but not studying." Much later, when he was made a member of the Society of Artists of the United States, he said that art could contribute to America; by "embellishing with taste a country already overflowing with the useful productions, it may be able to give an innocent and pleasing direction to accumulations of wealth, which would otherwise be employed in the nourishment of coarse and vicious habits." This is an interesting prophecy of the great private art collections and endowments on which America's present cultural eminence is based.

As with much else, Jefferson formed his first ideas about art from books. When he was young there was literally no sculpture in Virginia, and painting was represented by but a few crude portraits. But the earliest records of his library indicate at least nine books on painting and six on sculpture. From the latter he listed in his building notebook, before he went to Europe, thirteen classic statues with which he hoped to grace his home, and paintings that he hoped to acquire, with the note, "Bellini tells me that historical paintings on canvas six feet by twelve feet will cost fifteen pounds sterling if copied by a good hand."

Jefferson's personal contact with the plastic arts started with his arrival in Paris at the age of forty-one. He was immediately exposed to a group of intellectuals who represented the best taste in Europe's capital. He started buying inexpensive casts and copies for his hilltop home. Soon he would write of the French:

WERE I TO PROCEED to tell you how much I enjoy their architecture, sculpture, painting, music, I should want words. . . . I am almost ready to say it is the only thing which from my heart I envy them, and which, in spite of all the authority of the Decalogue, I do covet.

He developed warm personal relationships with many artists. American artist John Trumbull sought his help in securing life portraits for his series of paintings on the Revolution—and introduced him to Maria Cosway, with whom he absorbed so much beauty. He later offered Trumbull a post as his secretary so that he might continue "his great pursuit . . . and further his improvement." He was thus the first American statesman to propose the European practice of subsidizing an artist. Trumbull declined the offer.

Among the European painters he was impressed with the work of Jacques Louis David, saying, at one time, "I do not feel an interest in any pencil but that of David." This was probably because David's canvases reflected ancient republican virtue with a classical quality. Generally, Jefferson preferred works of art with a purpose or message. Although he loved beauty for beauty's sake, he favored a picture or statue which symbolized some worthy idea or ideal, or inspired to virtue or morality, or commemorated some great man or event of history. At Monticello, he had paintings of his triumvirate of greats, Newton, Bacon and Locke, and busts of Washington, Franklin, John Paul Jones, Lafayette, Turgot and Voltaire.

He went to great length to get commemorative pictures on American history, hoping to make them widely available. "On the subject of the portraits of Columbus and Americus Vespucius. . . . While I resided at Paris, knowing that these portraits and those of some other of the early American worthies were in the gallery of Medicis at Florence, I took measures for engaging a good artist to take and send me copies of them. I Considered it as . . . of some public concern that our country should not be without the portraits of its first discoverers. . . . I wish them to be multiplied for safe preservation, and consider them as worthy a place in every collection." And to John Trumbull he wrote, when forwarding his subscription for a print of the Declaration of Independence painting, "What discourages our citizens in the purchase of prints is the tawdry taste prevailing for gewgaw gilt frames . . . [that] cost as much, and often more than the print itself. While it is right to indulge the luxury of the rich with copies of exquisite and perfect execution, would it not be worth your while to have one of mere outline engraved which could be sold for a dollar apiece? Were such to be had, scarcely a hovel in the U.S. would be without one." Jefferson was not looking for personal aggrandizement. He merely wanted every home in the land to have a picture commemorating the glorious birth of "life, liberty, and the pursuit of happiness."

Although he never tried his own hand at painting, he did buy, in France, a set of engraving tools—a current craze with many famous amateurs of the period, including such diverse ones as Marie Antoinette and Goethe. He rather felt that amateur dabbling was for the girls and wrote, in connection with the kind of education that was desirable for women:

THE ORNAMENTS, TOO, and the amusements of life, are entitled
to their portion of attention . . . drawing is thought less of in
this country than in Europe. It is an innocent and engaging
amusement, often useful, and a qualification not to be neglected in one who is to become a mother and an instructor.

Jefferson was, for a time, the unofficial art commissioner of the
United States in France, and it might be said that he contributed
something to the birth of Franco-American cultural relations. When
the Virginia legislature passed a resolution "for procuring a statue
of General Washington to be of the finest marble, the best work-
manship," the assignment of getting it executed fell on Jefferson.
Two portraits of Washington had been sent to France for the purpose, but this method did not please Jefferson. He wrote to Virginia:

THERE COULD BE NO QUESTION raised as to the sculptor who
should be employed, the reputation of Monsieur Houdon, of
this city, being unrivaled in Europe. . . . Of course no statue
of General Washington which might be a true evidence of his
figure to posterity could be made from his picture. Statues are
made every day from portraits, but if the person be living they
are always condemned by those who know him for want of
resemblance.

Getting Washington to sit for the sculptor might be a problem.
To induce him Jefferson wrote:

I FIND THAT a Monsieur Houdon, of this place, possesses the
reputation of being the first statuary in the world. I sent for
him and had some conversation with him on the subject. He
thinks it cannot be perfectly done from a picture, and is so
enthusiastically fond of being the executor of this work that
he offers to go to America for the purpose of forming your

bust from the life, leaving all his business here in the meantime.

He then added, rather coyly:

MONSIEUR HOUDON is at present engaged in making a statue of the King of France. A bust of Voltaire executed by him is said to be the finest in the world.

Another question was how Washington should be garbed. There were those who favored a classic Roman toga. Jefferson opposed, and when Washington agreed with his view he replied, "I am happy to find, that the modern dress for your statue would meet your approbation. . . . I think a modern in antique dress as just an object of ridicule as a Hercules or Marius with a periwig and a *chapeau bras."* Nineteen years later he would reverse himself on this. In connection with another projected Washington statue he reverted to the classical, saying, "As to style or costume, I am sure the artist and every person of taste in Europe would be for the Roman, the effect of which is undoubtedly of a different order. Our boots and regimentals have a very puny effect."

The size of the statue must also be decided. Jefferson insisted it be life-size, although he conceded that statutes:

. . . AS THEY ARE GENERALLY a little elevated, they appear smaller, but we think it important that some one monument should be preserved of the true size as well as figure, from which all other countries, and our own, at any future day when they shall desire it, may take copies, varying them in their dimensions as may suit the particular situation in which they wish to place them."

Jefferson was himself the subject of much portraiture. His first portrait was not painted until he was forty-three—ten years after he had written the Declaration of Independence. But during the last half of his life he sat for thirteen painters and sculptors for portraits and busts, not including silhouettes, sketches, pastels, etc. In sitting for the most famous portraitists of the day—Stuart, West, Trumbull, Otis, Sully, both Peales, and others—Jefferson possibly had a slight vanity, although he considered the chore of posing as part of his duty as a public figure. In his last years, when Sully wanted him to sit for a portrait for West Point, he wrote a rather amusing letter of acquiescence:

MR. SULLY, I fear, however, will consider the trouble of his journey, and the employment of his fine pencil, as illy bestowed on an ottamy of seventy-eight. Voltaire, when requested by a female friend to sit for his bust by the sculptor Pigalle, answered [Voltaire's words were in French in the original], "I'm seventy-six years old, and Monsieur Pigalle, I am told, has come to model my face. But Madame, it would be necessary that I have a face. One will hardly find its place: my eyes are buried in three pouches, my jaws are of old parchment badly stretched over bones which hold on to nothing; the few teeth I had are gone." I will conclude, however, with him, that what remains is at your service, and that of the pencil of Mr. Sully.

Shortly before he died Jefferson posed for a life mask—an unhappy experience which he described to James Madison:

I WAS TAKEN IN by Mr. Browere. He said his operation would be of about twenty minutes, and less unpleasant than Houdon's method. I submitted without inquiry. But it was a bold experiment on his part on the health of an octogenary worn down by sickness as well as age. Successive coats of grout plastered on the naked head and kept there an hour would have been a severe trial of a young and hale man. He suffered the plaster also to get so dry that separation became difficult and even dangerous. He was obliged to use freely the mallet and chisel to break it into pieces and get off a piece at a time. These strokes of the mallet would have been sensible almost to a loggerhead. The family became alarmed, and he confused, till I was quite exhausted, and there became real danger that the ears would tear from the head sooner than from the plaster. I now bid adieu forever to busts and even portraits.

There is no complete catalogue of Jefferson's private art collection, but among his papers is a memorandum that he owned, "forty-six portraits in oil; eleven portraits in crayon; fourteen pictures, prints and engravings with frames more than twelve inches; thirty-nine pictures under twelve inches with gilt frames." One contemporary described the drawing room at Monticello as "a noble salon . . . hung thick with the finest reproductions of the pencil—historical paintings of the most striking subjects from all countries and all ages; the portraits of distinguished men and patriots, both of Europe and America, and medallions and engravings in endless profusion."

Other more detailed contemporary descriptions of Jefferson's home convey the impression of a combination art gallery and natural history museum. One, in 1816, says:

MR. JEFFERSON HAS a large collection of mathematical, philosophical and optical instruments and Indian curiosities. Among the latter are busts of a male and female, sitting in Indian position. . . . There is also in the hall a representation of a battle between the Panis and Osages, also a map of the Missouri and its tributary streams, both executed by Indians on dressed buffalo hides; bows, arrows, poisoned lances, pipes of peace, wampum belts, moccasins, etc., several dresses and cooking utensils of the Mandan and other nations of the Missouri.

The statuary in the hall consists of a colossal bust of Mr. Jefferson . . . on the pedestal of which are represented the twelve tribes of Israel, and the twelve signs of the zodiac. A full-length figure of Cleopatra, in a reclining position, after she had applied the asp; and the busts of Voltaire and Turgot, in plaster; there is likewise a model of one of the pyramids of Egypt.

In the parlor are busts of the Emperors Alexander of Russia and Napoleon of France sitting on columns, and a sleeping Venus.

In the bow of the dining room are busts of General Washington, Dr. Franklin, Marquis de Lafayette and Paul Jones in plaster.

The collection of paintings is considered by connoisseurs to be of the first rate; among them is the "Ascension," by Poussin; the "Holy Family," by Raphael; "Scourging of Christ," by Rubens; "Crucifixion," by Guido; and a great many other scriptural and historical pieces, by the first masters; portraits, prints, medallions, medals, etc., of celebrated characters and events.

The collection of natural curiosities is tolerably extensive, and consists of mammoth and other bones, horns of different kinds, a head of the mountain ram, petrifactions, crystalizations, minerals, shells, etc. In short it is supposed there is no private gentleman in the world in possession of so perfect and complete a scientific, useful and ornamental collection.

From this description, Monticello would have been a nightmare to a modern decorator, but it certainly must have looked "lived in."

CHAPTER X

ARCHITECT AND FARMER

❦

THE PRIVATE BUILDINGS are very rarely constructed of stone or brick, much the greatest portion being of scantling and boards, plastered with lime. It is impossible to devise things more ugly, uncomfortable, and happily, more perishable. . . . The only public buildings worthy of mention are the capitol, the palace, the college, and the hospital for lunatics, all of them in Williamsburg. . . .

"There are no other public buildings but churches and courthouses, in which no attempts are made at elegance. . . . The genius of architecture seems to have shed its maledictions over this land. . . . Perhaps a spark may fall on some young subjects of natural taste, kindle up their genius, and produce a reformation in this elegant and useful art.

Jefferson so described the architecture of Virginia in 1792. That same year, the Chevalier de Chastellux, after visiting Monticello, said that Jefferson was the "first American who has consulted the fine arts to know how he should shelter himself from the weather." In the other arts Jefferson was an "interested bystander." In architecture he was a participant and, in America, a pioneer.

As with all else, Jefferson was first exposed to architecture through books. His bibles were the published works of Andrea Palladio, sixteenth-century Italian architect, of which he had six editions in his library. Palladio was the prophet of Roman classic architecture, and Jefferson became his devoted disciple; for Jefferson's taste in architecture was far from catholic. He was strictly a classicist. In condemning American architecture he ignored the Georgian style and the influence of Christopher Wren. To him, "The Gothic idea . . . is worthy of those bigots in religion and government by whom it has been recommended." In Europe he completely ignored the great Gothic cathedrals. But he became whimsically lyrical in describing examples of classical structures to a female cousin of Lafayette's:

HERE I AM, Madam, gazing whole hours at the Maison Carrée like a lover at his mistress. The stocking weavers and silk spinners around it consider me a hypochondriac Englishman about to write with a pistol the last chapter of his history. This is the second time I have been in love since I left Paris. The first was with a Diana at the Château de Laye-Épinaye in Beaujolais, a delicious morsel of sculpture by M. A. Slodtz. This, you will say, was in rule, to fall in love with a female beauty—but with a house! It is out of all precedent. No, Madam, it is not without a precedent in my own history. While in Paris I was violently smitten with the Hôtel de Salm, and used to go to the Tuileries almost daily to look at it. The *loueuse de chaises,* inattentive to my passion, never had the complaisance to place a chair there, so that, sitting on the parapet and twisting my neck round to see the object of my admiration, I generally left it with a *torti-colli*.

From Lyons to Nismes I have been nourished with the remains of Roman grandeur . . . from a correspondent at Nismes you will not expect news. . . . I am immersed in antiquities from morning to night. For me the city of Rome is actually existing in all the splendor of its empire. I am filled with alarms for the event of the eruptions daily making on us by the Goths, the Visigoths, Ostrogoths and Vandals, lest they should reconquer us to our original barbarism.

At a time when residential architecture was virtually ignored in America, Jefferson stated the need quite simply:

ARCHITECTURE IS WORTH great attention. As we double our number every twenty years we must double our houses. . . . It is, then, among the most important arts; and it is desirable to introduce taste into an art which shows so much.

He started to make architectural drawings in 1796 when there were no professional architects in America, and his early fine and elaborate drawings represent the best collection of papers in this area prior to the plans for the national Capitol and executive mansion. To him, architecture was a study in mathematics:

A PORTICO MAY BE from five to ten diameters of the column deep, or projected from the building. If of more than five diameters, there must be a column in the middle of each flank, since it must never be more than five diameters from center to center of column.

In other fields Jefferson's mind forged ahead into the new and untried. In architecture he looked backward to precedent and tradition, adopting classical models to current needs. If he was not the father of the post-Revolutionary classic revival in American architecture, his enthusiasm for the designs of ancient Rome gave wide impetus to it. Certainly the Capitol building which he designed for Virginia in 1785 was the first reproduction of a classic temple for modern utilitarian purposes—in either America or Europe— and established the character of the public buildings of most of the new states.

Of the Virginia capitol Jefferson wrote in his autobiography:

I WAS WRITTEN TO in 1785 (being then in Paris) by directors appointed to superintend the building of a capitol in Richmond, to advise them as to a plan . . . Thinking it a favorable opportunity of introducing into the state an example of architecture in the classic style of antiquity, and the Maison Carrée of Nismes, an ancient Roman temple, being considered as the most perfect model existing of what may be called cubic architecture, I applied to M. Clerissault, who had published drawings of the antiquities of Nismes, to have me a model of the building made in stucco, only changing the order from Corinthian to Ionic, on account of the difficulty of the Corinthian capitals. . . . To adapt the exterior to our use, I drew a plan for the interior, with the apartments necessary for legislative, executive and judiciary purposes; and accommodated in their size and distribution to the form and dimensions of the building.

To James Madison he wrote:

I SHALL SEND THEM a plan taken from the best morsel of ancient architecture now remaining. It has obtained the approbation of fifteen or sixteen centuries and is therefore preferable to any design which might be newly contrived. It will give more room, be more convenient and cost less than the plan they sent me. Pray encourage them to wait for it and to execute it. It will be superior in beauty to anything in America, and not inferior to anything in the world. It is very simple.

After he sent his designs he was appalled to learn that work had been started on the capitol building before they were received. He bombarded Madison with letters of which this is typical:

DO . . . EXERT YOURSELF to get the plan begun on set aside and that adopted which was drawn here. It was taken from a model which has been the admiration of sixteen centuries;

which has been the object of as many pilgrimages as the tomb of Mahomet; which will give unrivaled honor to our state, and furnish a model whereon to form the taste of our young men. It will cost much less, too, than the one begun because it does not cover one-half the area.

The building was finally conformed to his designs and is still in use, although flanking wings have been added.

Jefferson was Secretary of State when work was started on the nation's capital city on the banks of the Potomac. Although Washington was the prime mover, selecting the site and making final decisions, Jefferson took the first definite steps toward designing the new community. The Residence Act for the new seat of government empowered the President "to purchase or accept such quantity of land . . . as the President shall deem proper for the United States" and to "provide suitable buildings for the accommodation of Congress and for the President and for the public buildings of the United States." Jefferson's proposal went farther than this. He said:

THE EXPRESSION "such quantity of land as the President shall deem proper for the United States" is vague. It may therefore be extended to the acceptance or purchase of land enough for the town; and I have no doubt it is the wish and perhaps expectation [of Congress]. In that case, it will . . . be laid out in lots and streets. I should propose these to be at right angles, as in Philadelphia, and that no streets be narrower than one hundred feet, with footways of fifteen feet. Where a street is long and level, it might be one hundred and twenty feet wide. I should prefer squares of at least two hundred yards every way, which will be about eight acres each. . . .

I doubt much whether the obligation to build the houses at a given distance from the street contributes to its beauty. It produces a disgusting monotony; all persons make this complaint against Philadelphia. The contrary practice varies the appearance, and is much more convenient to the inhabitants.

In Paris it is forbidden to build a house beyond a given height; and it is admitted to be a good restriction. It keeps down the price of ground, keeps the houses low and convenient, and the streets light and airy. Fires are much more manageable when houses are low.

After the land was acquired Jefferson drew a sketch plan of the community which he proposed, a town rather than a city—Jefferson did not like cities. When this was transmitted to Major Pierre Charles L'Enfant, planner of the capital, the Frenchman asked Jefferson if he had any plans of other cities and Jefferson replied, "I have examined my papers and found the plans of Frankfurt on the Main, Karlsruhe, Amsterdam, Strasbourg, Paris, Orléans, Bordeaux, Lyons, Montpellier, Marseilles, Turin and Milan, which I send in a roll by the post. They are on large and accurate scales, having been procured by me while in those respective cities myself." At least three of these plans were of cities with the radial or fan-shaped feature that L'Enfant superimposed on Jefferson's rectangular plan.

Jefferson also suggested to L'Enfant:

WHENEVER IT IS PROPOSED to prepare plans for the Capitol I should prefer the adoption of some one of the models of antiquity which have had the approbation of thousands of years; and for the President's house I should prefer the celebrated fronts of modern buildings which have already received the approbation of all good judges. Such are the Galerie du Louvre, the Gardes Meubles, and two fronts of the Hôtel de Salm.

When the city planner did not come forward with designs for public buildings, Jefferson prepared the specifications for a competition of designs for the Capitol and White House, anonymously submitting a design of his own for the latter, based on Palladio's

Villa Rotunda. The design of James Hoban, a young Irish architect from South Carolina, was preferred over Jefferson's.

None of the initial designs for the Capitol building, for which Jefferson did not make a sketch, were entirely acceptable. Most promising was that of Stephen Hallet, a French architect. Working with him, Jefferson proposed a building based on the Pantheon in Paris, and made a small sketch to show how it might be adapted. Then Dr. William Thornton, an amateur, submitted the design for the present building of which Jefferson said:

DR. THORNTON'S PLAN of a Capitol has been produced, and has so captivated the eyes and judgment of all as to leave no doubt . . . of its preference over all which have been produced. . . . It is simple, noble, beautiful, excellently distributed, and moderate in size.

Jefferson's most ambitious architectural creation was the University of Virginia. He described his basic architectural concept of a university as follows:

I CONSIDER THE COMMON PLAN followed in this country, but not in others, of making one large and expensive building, as unfortunately erroneous. It is infinitely better to erect a small and separate lodge for each separate professorship, with only a hall below for his class, and two chambers above for himself; joining these lodges by barracks for a certain portion of the students, opening into a covered way to give a dry communication between all the schools. The whole of these arranged around an open square of grass and trees would make it what it should be in fact, an academical village instead of a large and common den of noise, of filth and of fetid air. It would afford that quiet retirement so friendly to study, and lessen the dangers of fire, infection and tumult.

As finally constructed the university consisted of ten pavilions, each different, based on such classic structures as the Theater of Marcellus, the Fortuna Virilis, the Baths of Diocletian and the Temple of Trajan. The two rows of pavilions are joined, at one end, by the rotunda-topped library, adapted from the Pantheon in Rome.

Jefferson designed courthouses, at least one church, and perhaps a dozen residences for friends in Virginia. He spent thirty-five years building his most widely known architectural creation—his own home—but, strangely, he wrote little concerning it. He started it in 1771 or 1772 as a two-story house. This, apparently, was not quite finished as he envisioned it when he went to Europe. In 1796 he began such extensive alterations that the remodeled structure was an entirely different house of one story, with three levels. The Duc de la Rochefoucauld-Liancourt visited him that year and said, of his home:

MONTICELLO, according to its first plan, was infinitely superior to all other houses in America, in point of taste and convenience; but at that time Mr. Jefferson had studied taste and the fine arts in books only. His travels in Europe have supplied him with models; he has appropriated them to his design; and his new plan, the execution of which is already much advanced, will be accomplished before the end of next year, and then his house will certainly deserve to be ranked with the most pleasant mansions in France and England.

The alterations at Monticello were not finished "next year"— or for many years. Late in life Jefferson wrote, "Architecture is my delight and putting up and pulling down one of my favorite amusements." But if building Monticello as a residence was an amusement, running Monticello and its adjacent acreage was not. The land was Jefferson's living. First and last he was a farmer. He loved the land and of those who tilled it he said:

THOSE WHO LABOR in the earth are the chosen people of God, if ever he had a chosen people, whose breasts he has made his peculiar deposit for substantial and genuine virtue. It is the focus in which he keeps alive that sacred fire, which otherwise might escape from the face of the earth. Corruption of morals in the mass of cultivators is a phenomenon of which no age nor nation has furnished an example. . . . Generally speaking, the proportion which the aggregate of the other classes of citizens bears in any state to that of its husbandmen is the proportion of its unsound to its healthy parts. . . . While we have land to labor, then, let us never wish to see our citizens occupied at a workbench or twirling a distaff. Carpenters, masons, smiths are wanting in husbandry; but, for the general operations of manufacture, let our workshops remain in Europe. . . . The mobs of great cities add just so much to the support of pure government as sores do to the strength of the human body.

Jefferson owned about eleven thousand acres in several parcels in Albemarle and adjacent counties. Most of it was uncultivated woodland; Virginia land was cheap, but labor to farm it was dear and scarce. He described the basic farming practice of the area in a letter to Washington:

THE HIGHLANDS, where I live, have been cultivated about sixty years. The culture was tobacco and Indian corn as long as they would bring enough to pay the labor. Then they were turned out. After four or five years rest they would bring good corn again, and in double that time perhaps good tobacco. Then they would be exhausted by a second series of tobacco and corn.

That these were happy years is evident from the recollections of one of Jefferson's slaves, recorded many years after the master's death:

MR. JEFFERSON always singing when ridin' or walkin'; hardly

see him anywhar out doors but what he was a singin'; had a
fine clear voice, sung minnits [minuets] and sich . . .

Except for the years between 1793 and 1796 and during the last
seventeen years of his life, his lands were, of necessity, managed
by overseers, a fact which he bemoaned to Washington when he
left the Cabinet:

I FIND, on a more minute examination of my lands that the
short visits heretofore made to them permitted, that a ten years'
abandonment of them to the ravages of overseers has brought
on them a degree of degradation far beyond what I had expected. . . . Time, patience and perseverance must be the
remedy.

Jefferson undertook to restore his land with a program of crop
rotation, fertilization and soil conservation unusual in his time. Of
the first two practices he wrote:

IT IS NOT TO BE believed that spontaneous herbage is the only
or best covering during rest, so may we expect that a substitute
for it may be found which will yield profitable crops. Such perhaps are clover, peas, vetches, etc. A rotation then may be
found, which by giving time for the slow influence of the atmosphere, will keep the soil in a constant and equal state of
fertility. But the advantage of manuring is that it will do more
in one than the atmosphere would require several years to do,
and consequently enables you so much the oftener to take ex-
hausting crops from the soil.

His son-in-law, Thomas Mann Randolph—"a man of science,
sense, virtue and competence"—convinced him of the merit of
contour plowing. To artist Charles Peale he wrote:

OUR COUNTRY IS HILLY and we have been in the habit of plowing it straight rows whether up- and downhill, in oblique lines, or however they lead; and our soil was all rapidly running into the rivers. We now plow horizontally, following the curvatures of the hills and hollows, on the dead level, however crooked the lines may be. Every furrow thus acts as a reservoir to receive and retain the waters, all of which go to the benefit of the growing plant, instead of running off into the streams.

Jefferson did not create these modern practices, but his example did much to exploit them. He felt that agriculture had much to learn from the sciences and that agriculture itself:

. . . IS A SCIENCE of the very first order. It counts among its handmaids the most respectable sciences, such as chemistry, natural philosophy, mechanics, mathematics generally, natural history, botany. In every college and university a professorship of agriculture, and the class of its students, might be honored as the first.

After his final retirement from public life he was active in the formation of the Albemarle County Agricultural Society, and endeavored to spread the idea by writing a *Scheme for a System of Agricultural Societies*. This proposed:

WERE PRACTICAL AND OBSERVING husbandmen in each county to form themselves into a society, commit to writing themselves, or state in conversations at their meetings to be written down by others, their practices and observations, their experiences and ideas, selections from these might be made from time to time . . . for more general purposes. By an interchange of these selections among the societies of the different counties, each might thus become possessed of the useful ideas and processes of the whole; and every one adopt such of them as he should deem suitable to his own situation. . . .

Every one must have seen farms otherwise equal, the one

producing the double of the other by the superior culture and management of its possessor; and every one must have under his eye numerous examples of persons setting out in life with no other possession than skill in agriculture, and speedily, by its sole exercise, acquire wealth and independence. To promote, therefore, the diffusion of this skill and thereby to procure, with the same labor now employed, greater means of subsistence and of happiness to our fellow citizens, is the ultimate object of this association.

The scheme continued to propose that information should be exchanged on market crops, "wheat, tobacco and hemp"; "the care and services of useful animals . . . the destruction of noxious quadrupeds, fowls, insects and reptiles"; "rotation of crops"; "implements of husbandry"; "manures, plasters, green dressings, fallows and other means of ameliorating the soil"; and "a succinct report of the different practices of husbandry in the county, including the bad as well as the good, that those who follow the former may read and see their own condemnation in the same page which offers better examples for their adoption . . . the choicest processes, culled from every farm, would compose a course probably near perfection."

This sounds like the forebear of the Department of Agriculture, but Jefferson was opposed to it becoming a government activity. He wrote:

YOU KNOW SOME HAVE proposed to Congress to incorporate such a society. I am against that because I think Congress cannot find in all the enumerated powers any one which authorizes the act, much less the giving the public money to that use. I believe, too, if they had the power, it would soon be used for no other purpose than to buy with sinecures useful partisans. I believe it will thrive best if left to itself, as the philosophical societies are.

During his years in Europe Jefferson sought out any plant or seed which he thought might be useful to American agriculture. He wrote, "We are probably far from possessing, as yet, all the articles of culture for which nature has fitted our country. To find out these will require abundance of unsuccessful experiments." He exported several types of rice seed which he thought might thrive in the Carolinas. Of one from Lombardy he said, "The exportation of it in the husk being prohibited, I could not bring with me but as much as my pockets would hold. . . . It may serve to raise seed from." To his own horticultural smuggling he added bribery, saying, "Poggio, a muleteer who passes every week between Vercelli and Genoa, will smuggle a sack of rough rice for me to Genoa, it being death to export it in this form."

He made something of a fetish of trying to introduce the olive tree to America because "The olive tree is assuredly the richest gift of heaven. I can scarcely except bread." He shipped hundreds of trees to America, to no avail. Later he wrote, "It is now twenty-five years since I sent my southern fellow citizens two shipments . . . of the olive tree of Aix, the finest olives in the world. If any of them still exist, it is merely as a curiosity in their gardens; not a single orchard of them has been planted." He persevered because he felt that "One service of this kind rendered to a nation is worth more to them than all the victories of the most splendid pages of their history, and becomes a source of exalted pleasure to those who have been instrumental to it."

With James Madison he imported some purebred Merino sheep, and then wrote to his successor in the White House:

WHAT SHALL WE DO with them? I have been so disgusted with the scandalous extortions lately practiced in the sale of these animals, and with the description of patriotism and praise to the sellers, . . . that I am disposed to consider as right whatever is the reverse of what they have done. . . . The few who can afford it should incur the risk and expense of all new improvements, and . . . I will throw out a first idea. . . . Give all the full-blooded males we can raise to the different counties of our state, one to each, as fast as we can furnish them. . . . Our whole state may thus . . . be filled in a very few years with this valuable race, and more satisfaction result to ourselves than money ever administered to the bosom of a shaver. There will be danger that what is here proposed, though but an act of ordinary duty, may be perverted into one of ostentation, but malice will always find bad motives for good actions. Shall we therefore never do good?

Throughout much of his life Jefferson was firmly convinced that "The United States . . . will be more virtuous, more free and more happy employed in agriculture than as carriers or manufacturers. It is a truth, and a precious one for them, if they could be per-suaded of it." But after the failure of the Embargo Act he started to change. By 1809 he would write, "An equilibrium of agriculture, manufactures and commerce is certainly become essential to our independence." And by 1816 he was convinced that:

WE MUST NOW PLACE the manufacturer by the side of the agriculturist. Shall we make our own comforts, or go without them, at the will of a foreign nation? He, therefore, who is now against domestic manufacture, must be for reducing us either to dependence on that foreign nation, or to be clothed in skins, and to live like wild beasts in dens and caverns. I am not one of these; experience has taught me that manufactures are now as necessary to our independence as to our comfort . . . in so complicated a science as political economy, no one axiom can be laid down as an expedient for all times and circumstances, and for their contraries.

By manufacturing Jefferson had in mind the expansion of the type of home industry which Monticello represented. He wrote to Thaddeus Kosciusko, Polish patriot of Revolutionary days:

WE HAVE REDUCED the large and expensive machinery for most things to the compass of a private family, and every family of any size is now getting machines on a small scale for their household purposes. Quoting myself as an example, and I am much behind many others in this business, my household manufactures are just getting into operation on the scale of a carding machine costing sixty dollars only, which may be worked by a girl of twelve years old, a spinning machine, which may be made for ten dollars, carrying six spindles for wool, to be worked by a girl also, another which can be made for twenty-five dollars, carrying twelve spindles for cotton, and a loom, with a flying shuttle, weaving its twenty yards a day. I need two thousand yards of linen, cotton and woolen yearly to clothe my family [including slaves], which this machinery, costing one hundred and fifty dollars only, and worked by two women and two girls, will more than furnish. For fine goods there are numerous establishments at work in the large cities, and many more daily growing up . . . so that nothing is more certain than that come peace when it will, we shall never again go to England for a shilling where we have gone for a dollar's worth. Instead of applying to her manufacturers there, they must starve or come here to be employed.

Jefferson's principal excursion into manufacturing was a nailery, which he started in 1794. A year later he wrote, "I am myself a nail maker . . . my new trade of nail making is to me in this country what an additional title of nobility or the ensigns of a new order are in Europe." The nail business went well, for a while, but Jefferson's later letters regarding it are mostly plaintive efforts to collect from those to whom he had extended credit and, in the end, embarrassed requests for longer credit on nail stock that he purchased. It finally petered out—Thomas Jefferson, who was nearly everything else, was no businessman. But some of his nails are still holding houses together in Virginia.

A description of Jefferson the farmer, in 1796, was left by the Duc de la Rochefoucauld-Liancourt:

... AT PRESENT HE IS employed with activity and perseverance in the management of his farms and buildings, and he orders, directs and pursues in the minutest detail every branch of business relative to them. I found him in the midst of the harvest, from which the scorching heat of the sun does not prevent his attendance. His Negroes are nourished, clothed and treated as well as white servants could be. As he cannot expect any assistance from the two small neighboring towns, every article is made on his farm; his Negroes are cabinetmakers, carpenters, masons, bricklayers, smiths, etc. The children he employs in a nail factory, which yields already a considerable profit. The young and old Negresses spin for the clothing of the rest. He animates them by rewards and distinctions: in fine, his superior mind directs the management of his domestic concerns with the same abilities, activity and regularity which he evinced in the conduct of public affairs, and which he is calculated to display in every situation of life.

The cultivation of his farms, and most of his construction work, was carried on entirely by slave labor. After his marriage Jefferson usually had about two hundred slaves, whom he called "servants" or his "people." All records show Jefferson as a humane and considerate master. Isaac Jefferson, the slave who left his "Recollections," said, "old master very kind to servants," and one Monticello overseer, in his memoirs, complained at the rarity of whipping. Jefferson's account books contain frequent entries showing that he borrowed small sums of money from his coachman, Jupiter.

He freed a few of his slaves, after they had been trained to take care of themselves. One of his house servants learned to cook in Paris. When Jefferson later left Philadelphia the Negro wished to remain there and Jefferson made this unusual agreement with him:

HAVING BEEN AT GREAT EXPENSE in having James Hemings taught the art of cookery, desiring to befriend him, and to require from him as little in return as possible, I do hereby promise and declare, that if the said James shall go with me to Monticello in the course of the ensuing winter, when I go to reside there myself, and shall there continue until he shall have taught such person as I shall place under him for the purpose to be a good cook, this previous condition being performed, he shall be thereupon made free, and I will thereupon execute all proper instruments to make him free.

Still, Jefferson remained a slaveholder throughout his life; and this seems a great contradiction for the man who wrote "all men are created equal." The answer was in the times. To Jefferson the institution of slavery was a great evil to which he was wholly opposed. But, in the economy of Virginia, it was a "necessary evil." He was against general emancipation if it meant abandoning the slaves to take care of themselves. He favored gradual emancipation, preferably combined with colonization, after the Negroes had been prepared for it. In his autobiography, written at the end of his life, he wrote:

NOTHING IS MORE CERTAINLY written in the book of fate than that these people are to be free. Nor is it less certain that the two races, equally free, cannot live in the same government.

He gave as his reasons why the races could not live together:

DEEP-ROOTED PREJUDICES entertained by the whites; ten thousand recollectons, by the blacks, of the injuries they have sustained; new provocations; the real distinction which nature has made; and many other circumstances will divide us into parties, and produce convulsions, which will probably never end but in the extermination of one or the other race.

Some detractors of Jefferson have made much of a section of *Notes on Virginia* in which he compared the black and white races to the disadvantage of the former. His generalized description of Negroes suggested the comic, shiftless "darky." This is one of the cases, where, as a scientific observer, he "went off the deep end." However, he did conclude:

IT WILL BE RIGHT to make great allowances for the difference of condition, of education, of conversation, of the sphere in which they move. . . . I advance it therefore, as a suspicion only that the blacks, whether originally a distinct race, or made distinct by time and circumstances, are inferior to the whites in the endowments both of body and mind. . . . This unfortunate difference in color, and perhaps of faculty, is a powerful obstacle to the emancipation of these people. . . . Among the Romans emancipation required but one effort. The slave, when made free, might mix with, without staining, the blood of his master. But with us a second is necessary, unknown to history. When freed, he is to be removed beyond the reach of mixture.

Some years later when Benjamin Banneker, a Negro mathematician, sent Jefferson an almanac he had compiled, the Virginian wrote him:

NOBODY WISHES MORE than I do to see such proofs as you exhibit, that nature has given to our black brethren talents equal to those of the other colors of man, and that the appearance of a want of them is owing merely to the degraded condition of their existence both in Africa and America. I can add with truth that nobody wishes more ardently to see a good system commenced for raising the condition both of their body and mind to what it ought to be, as fast as the imbecility of their present existence, and other circumstances which cannot be neglected, will admit.

Jefferson's earliest diatribe against slavery was also contained in *Notes:*

THERE MUST DOUBTLESS BE an unhappy influence on the manners of our people produced by the existence of slavery among us. The whole commerce between master and slave is a perpetual exercise of the most boisterous passions, the most unremitting despotism on the one part, and degrading submissions on the other. Our children see this, and learn to imitate it; for man is an imitative animal. . . . If a parent could find no motive either in his philanthropy or his self-love for restraining the intemperance of passion towards his slave, it should always be a sufficient one that his child is present. But generally it is not sufficient. The parent storms, the child looks on, catches the lineaments of wrath, puts on the same airs in the circle of smaller slaves, gives a loose to the worst of passions, and thus nursed, educated and daily exercised in tyranny, cannot but be stamped by it with odious peculiarities. The man must be a prodigy who can retain his manners and morals undepraved by such circumstances.

And with what execrations should the statesman be loaded who, permitting one-half the citizens thus to trample on the rights of the others, transforms those into despots, and these into enemies. Destroys the morals of the one part, and the *amor patriae* of the other. . . . With the morals of the people, their industry also is destroyed. For in a warm climate, no man will labor for himself who can make another labor for him. This is so true, that of the proprietors of slaves a very small proportion indeed are ever seen to labor.

And can the liberties of a nation be thought secure when we have removed their only firm basis, a conviction in the minds of the people that these liberties are of the gift of God? That they are not to be violated but with his wrath? Indeed I tremble for my country when I reflect that God is just: that his justice cannot sleep forever; that considering numbers, nature and natural means only, a revolution of the wheel of fortune, an exchange of situation, is among possible events, that it may become probable by supernatural interference! The Almighty has no attribute which can take side with us in such a contest.

During his public career Jefferson made several efforts toward improving the slavery situation. In the first session of the Virginia Assembly of which he was a member he sought a change in the laws to make it permissable to manumit a slave; and in 1778, his autobiography says, "I brought in a bill to prevent their further importation. This passed without opposition, and stopped the increase of the evil by importation, leaving to future efforts its final eradication." In his suggested revisions of the laws of Virginia, which included the *Statute for Religious Freedom,* he also proposed a bill which, he said in *Notes,* was:

To EMANCIPATE ALL SLAVES born after passing the act . . . and further directing that they should continue with their parents to a certain age, then be brought up, at the public expense, to tillage, arts or sciences, according to their geniuses, till the females should be eighteen, and the males twenty-one years of age, when they should be colonized to such place as the circumstances of the time should render most proper, sending them out with arms, implements of household and of handicraft arts, seeds, pairs of the useful domestic animals, etc., to declare them a free and independent people, and extend to them our alliance and protection till they shall have acquired strength.

He also proposed to eliminate slavery from the Northwest Territory after 1800.

But in 1820 the congressional fight over the admission of Missouri as a slave state and its settlement by the compromise which drew a geographical line between slave and free territory filled him with alarm. He wrote:

THIS MOMENTOUS QUESTION, like a fire bell in the night, awakened and filled me with terror; I considered it at once as the knell of the Union. It is hushed, indeed, for the moment. But this is a reprieve only, not a final sentence. A geographical line . . . once conceived and held up to the angry passions of men will never be obliterated; and every new irritation will mark it deeper and deeper. I can say, with conscious truth, that there is not a man on earth who would sacrifice more than I would to relieve us from this heavy reproach [slavery] in any *practicable* way. The cession of that kind of property, for so it is misnamed, is a bagatelle which would not cost me a second thought, if, in that way, a general emancipation and expatriation could be affected; and gradually with due sacrifices, I think it might be. But as it is, we have the wolf by the ears, and we can neither hold him, nor safely let him go. Justice is in one scale, and self-preservation in the other. Of one thing I am certain, that as the passage of slaves from one state to another would not make a slave of a single human being who would not be so without it, so their diffusion over a greater surface would make them individually happier, and proportionally facilitate the accomplishment of their emancipation. . . .

To another correspondent he said:

I HAVE BEEN among the most sanguine in believing that our Union would be of long duration. I now doubt it much, and see the event at no great distance, and the direct consequence of this question; not by the line which has been so confidently counted on—the laws of nature control this; but by the Potomac, Ohio and Missouri, or more probably, the Mississippi upwards to our northern boundary."

And to John Adams he wrote:

ARE OUR SLAVES to be presented with freedom and a dagger?
For if Congress has the power to regulate the conditions of the
inhabitants of the states within the states, it will be but another
exercise of that power to declare that all shall be free.

This he wrote forty years before the first gun was fired at Fort
Sumter.

Jefferson's best exposition of his feelings on slavery was expressed in a letter to fellow-Virginian Edward Coles in 1814. He
said that his sentiments on slavery:

. . . HAVE LONG SINCE BEEN in possession of the public, and
time has only served to give them stronger root. The love of
justice and the love of country plead equally the cause of the
people, and it is a mortal reproach to us that they should have
pleaded it so long in vain and should have produced not a
single effort, nay, I fear not much serious willingness, to relieve
them and ourselves from our present condition. From those of
the former generation who were in the fullness of age when I
came into public life, which was while our controversy with
England was on paper only, I soon saw that nothing was to be
hoped. Nursed and educated in the daily habit of seeing the
degraded condition, both bodily and mental, of those unfortunate beings, not reflecting that that degradation was very much
the work of themselves and their fathers, few minds had yet
doubted but that they were as legitimate subjects of property
as their horses or cattle. The quiet and monotonous course of
colonial life had been disturbed by no alarm, and little reflection on the value of liberty. And when alarm was taken at
an enterprise on their own, it was not easy to carry them the
whole length of the principles which they invoked for themselves. . . .

I had always hoped that the younger generation, receiving
their early impressions after the flame of liberty had been
kindled in every breast . . . would have sympathized with

oppression wherever found, and proved their love of liberty beyond their own share of it. But intercourse with them, since my
return, has not been sufficient to ascertain that they had made
towards this point the progress I had hoped, . . . and I have
considered the general silence which prevails on this subject as
indicating an apathy unfavorable to every hope. Yet the hour
of emancipation is advancing in the march of time. It will
come. . . .

As to the method by which this difficult work is to be effected. . . . I have seen no proposition so expedient, on the
whole, as that of emancipation of those born after a given day,
and of their education and expatriation at a proper age. This
would give time for a gradual extinction of that species of
labor and substitution of another, and lessen the severity of
the shock which an operation so fundamental cannot fail to
produce. The idea of emancipating the whole at once, the old
as well as the young, and retaining them here, is of those only
who have not the guide of either knowledge or experience of
the subject. For man, probably of any color, but of this color
we know, brought up from their infancy without necessity for
thought or forecast, are by their habits rendered as incapable
as children of taking care of themselves. . . .

I am sensible of the partialities with which you have looked
towards me as the person who should undertake this salutary
but arduous work. . . . But this, my dear sir, is like bidding old
Priam to buckle the armor of Hector. . . . This enterprise is for
the young; for those who can follow it up, and bear it through
to its consummation. It shall have all my prayers, and these
are the only weapons of an old man . . . my opinion has ever
been that, until more can be done for them, we should endeavor, with those whom fortune has thrown on our hands, to
feed and clothe them well, protect them from ill usage, require
such reasonable labor only as is performed voluntarily by free-
men, and be led by no repugnancies to abdicate them, and
our duties to them. The laws do not permit us to turn them

loose, if that were for their good; and to commute them for other property is to commit them to those whose usage of them we cannot control.

I hope then, my dear sir, you will . . . become the missionary of this doctrine truly Christian, insinuate and inculcate it softly but steadily through the medium of writing and conversation, associate others in your labors, and when the phalanx is formed, bring on and press the proposition perseveringly untill its accomplishment. It is an encouraging observation that no good measure was ever proposed which, if duly pursued, failed to prevail in the end. . . . And you will be supported by the religious precept "be not wearied in well-doing."

CHAPTER XI

THE OLD MAN ON THE MOUNTAIN

֍

MY MORNINGS ARE DEVOTED to correspondence. From break-fast to dinner I am in my shops, my garden, or on horseback among my farms; from dinner to dark I give to society and recreation with my neighbors and friends; and from candle-light to early bedtime I read. My health is perfect, and my strength considerably reinforced by the activity of the course I pursue; perhaps it is as great as usually falls to the lot of near sixty-seven years of age. I talk of plows and harrows, of seeding and harvesting with my neighbors, and of politics too, if they choose, with as little reserve as the rest of my fellow citizens, and feel, at length, the blessing of being free to say and do what I please, without being responsible for it to any mortal. A part of my occupation, and by no means the least pleasing, is the direction of the studies of such young men as ask it. They place themselves in the neighboring village, and have the use of my library and counsel, and make a part of my society. In advising the course of their reading, I endeavor to keep their attention fixed on the main objects of all science, the freedom and happi-ness of man.

So Jefferson described the routine of his life after he retired from the Presidency. This was the life for which he had waited during the long years of public service. Now it was almost—but not quite —perfect. He ended his letter by saying:

INSTEAD OF the unalloyed happiness of retiring unembarrassed and independent to the enjoyment of my estate, which is ample for my limited views, I have to pass such a length of time in a thralldom of mind never known to me. Except for this, my happiness would have been perfect.

Jefferson's "thralldom of mind" was caused by a lack of money. When he retired as President he said, "I have the consolation . . . of having added nothing to my private fortune during my public service, and of retiring with hands as clean as they are empty."

His hands were really less than empty. He had to borrow money to settle his accounts in Washington before going home. Jefferson was neither careless nor extravagant, but he was generous and hospitable to a fault—and there was his passion for building. One year's accounts show an income from tobacco and nails of three thousand five hundred dollars and expenses at Monticello of seven thousand dollars. His twenty-five thousand dollar salary was substantial, but so were the costs of running the White House and entertaining America's official guests—for which he received no allowance. Each year he ran a little farther into the red.

He hoped by living "like a plain country gentleman"—with thirty-seven house servants—to get back on his financial feet, but he never did. Visitors compounded his expenses. The great and the small flocked to see the sage of Monticello, and Virginia hospitality would turn none away. Twenty to thirty house guests were not uncommon. Jefferson's biographer, Henry Randall, recounts a conversation with an old house servant shortly after the master's death. Standing before the carriage houses at Monticello Randall said,

"Wormley, how often were these filled during Mr. Jefferson's time?"

"Every night, sir, in summer, and we commonly had two or three carriages under that tree."

"It took all hands to take care of your visitors?"

"Yes, sir, and the whole farm to feed them."

And in addition to visitors, there were letters.

EVERY MAIL BRINGS a fresh load. They are letters of inquiry, for the most part, always of good will, sometimes from friends whom I esteem, but much oftener from persons whose names are unknown to me, but written kindly and civilly, and to which, therefore, civility requires answers. . . . I happened to turn my letter list some time ago, and a curiosity was excited to count those received in a single year. . . . I found the number to be 1,267, many of them requiring answers of elaborate research, and all to be answered with due attention and consideration. . . . Is this life? At best it is but the life of a mill horse, who sees no end to his circle but in death. To such a life, that of a cabbage is paradise.

Although Jefferson grumbled, there is no other evidence that he did not relish much of his voluminous correspondence. Certainly "civility" did not require him to write letters such as a typical one of ten pages on crops, farm prices, land costs, weather and much more which he sent to an unknown Frenchman who asked his advice on emigrating to Virginia.

One correspondent whom he warmly welcomed was John Adams. The two old patriots had been estranged since Adams signed all those appointments in 1801. In 1810 fellow Declaration-signer Dr. Benjamin Rush undertook the role of peacemaker between the two ex-Presidents. For a year Jefferson stubbornly resisted. Then, in the fall of 1811, he wrote to Rush:

I RECUR . . . to the subject of your kind letters relating to Mr.

Adams and myself, which a late occurrence has again presented to me. . . . Two of . . . my neighbors and friends . . . during the last summer . . . fell into company with Mr. Adams, and by his invitation passed a day with him at Braintree. He spoke out to them everything which came uppermost . . . to his mind. . . . Among many other topics he adverted to the unprincipled licentiousness of the press against myself, adding, "I always loved Jefferson, and still love him."

This is enough for me. I only needed this knowledge to revive towards him all the affections of the most cordial moment of our lives. . . . I knew him to be always an honest man, often a great one, but sometimes incorrect and precipitate in his judgments.

I wish, therefore, but for an opposite occasion to express to Mr. Adams my unchanged affections for him. There is an awkwardness which hangs over the resuming a correspondence so long discontinued, unless something could arise which should call for a letter.

He asked Rush to suggest to Adams that *he* start the correspondence. Adams took quill in hand on New Year's Day, 1812, and started an exchange of some of the most memorable letters in American history. Jefferson answered his first letter by writing:

A LETTER FROM YOU calls up recollections very dear to my mind. It carries me back to the times when, beset with difficulties and dangers, we were fellow laborers in the same cause, struggling for what is most valuable to man, his right of self-government. Laboring always at the same oar, with some wave ever ahead threatening to overwhelm us, and yet passing harmless under our bark, we knew not how we rode through the storm with heart and hand and made a happy port. Still we did not expect to be without rubs and difficulties; and we have had them. . . . In your day, French depredations; in mine, English . . . And so we have gone on, and so we shall all go on, puzzled and prospering beyond example in the history of men. And I do believe we shall continue to grow, to multiply and prosper until we exhibit an association powerful, wise and happy beyond what has yet been seen by men. . . .

But whither is senile garrulity leading me? Into politics, which I have taken final leave. I think little of them and say less. I have given up newspapers in exchange for Tacitus and Thucydides, for Newton and Euclid, and I find myself much the happier. Sometimes, indeed, I look back to former occurrences, in remembrance of our old friends and fellow laborers who have fallen before us. Of the signers of the Declaration of Independence I see now living not more than half a dozen on your side of the Potomac, and on this side, myself alone.

The references in the first paragraph of the above letter to "oar," "wave" and "bark" evidence a rather unusual quirk of Jefferson's. In hundreds of his letters he used nautical allusions and similes— yet he was never aboard a ship except for his trip to France and actually disliked the sea.

Jefferson continued to believe that war should and could be avoided. He wrote to Kosciusko:

WE HAVE . . . remained in peace, suffering frequent injuries but, on the whole, multiplying, improving, prospering beyond all example. . . . When these gladiators shall have worried each other into ruin or reason, instead of lying among the dead on the bloody arena we shall have acquired a growth and strength which will place us *hors d'insulte*. Peace then has been our principle, peace is our interest, and peace has saved to the world this only plant of free and rational government now existing in it.

If it can still be preserved we shall soon see the final extinction of our national debt, and liberation of our revenues for the defense and improvement of our country. . . . The farmer will see his government supported, his children educated, and the face of his country made a paradise by the contributions of the rich alone, without his being called on to spend a cent from his earnings.

But when war came, Jefferson bowed gracefully to the inevitable:

WE ARE TO HAVE war, then? I believe so, and that it is necessary. Every hope from time, patience and the love of peace is exhausted, and war or abject submission are the only alternatives left us. I am forced from my hobby, peace.

And he advanced his ideas on how the war should be fought, saying that Great Britain:

. . . WOULD HAVE THE SEA to herself, while we should be equally predominant at land, and should strip her of all her possessions on this continent. . . . I hope we shall confine ourselves to the conquest of their possessions and defense of our harbors, leaving the war on the ocean to our privateers. . . . We have nothing to fear from their armies, and shall put nothing in prize to their fleets. Upon the whole, I have known no war entered into under more favorable auspices.

When, counter to his expectations, America's only victories were at sea, Jefferson blamed the generals, rather than his beloved militia, for the debacle on land:

THE CREATOR HAS NOT thought proper to mark those in the forehead who are of stuff to make good generals. We are first, therefore, to seek them blindfold, and then let them learn the trade at the expense of great losses. But our turn of success will come by and by.

Jefferson was confident that America would triumph, but, due

to the pernicious banking system, only at great cost to the farmers.
He wrote:

I WISH I COULD SEE . . . a better train of finance . . . banking
projects are like dosing dropsy with more water. . . . To me
this state of things brings a sacrifice of all tranquillity and comfort through the residue of life. For although the debility of
age disables me from the services and sufferings of the field,
yet, by the total annihilation in value of the produce which was
to give me subsistence and independence, I shall be like Tanta-
lus, up to the shoulders in water yet dying with thirst. We can
make indeed enough to eat, drink and clothe ourselves, but
nothing for our salt, iron, groceries and taxes, which must be
paid in money. For what can we raise for the market? Wheat?
We can only give it to our horses, as we have been doing ever
since harvest. Tobacco? It is not worth the pipe it is smoked
in. Some say whisky; but all mankind must become drunkards
to consume it. But although we feel, we shall not flinch. We
must consider now, as in the Revolutionary War, that although
the evils of resistance are great, those of submission would be
greater.

When peace came Jefferson foresaw the possibility, at long last,
of permanent amity with Great Britain. "There is not a nation on
the globe with whom I have more earnestly wished a friendly intercourse on equal conditions," he wrote, and in another letter, "Were
they once under a government which should treat us with justice
and equity, I should myself feel with great strength the ties which
bind us together, of origin, language, laws and manners; and I am
persuaded the two peoples would become in future . . . natural
friends and brethren."

When there was talk of revising the Virginia Constitution, Jefferson, at seventy-three, was still as progressive as the young man
who had labored for that enlightened document forty years before
—and he still believed that the earth belonged to the living:

ONLY LAY DOWN true principles, and adhere to them inflexibly. Do not be frightened into their surrender by the alarms of the timid, or the croakings of wealth against the ascendancy of the people. . . . The true foundation of republican government is the equal right of every citizen in his person and property, and in their management. Try by this, as a tally, every provision of our Constitution, and see if it hangs directly on the will of the people. . . .

Some men look at constitutions with sanctimonious reverence, and deem them like the ark of the covenant, too sacred to be touched. They ascribe to the men of the preceding age a wisdom more than human, and suppose what they did to be beyond amendment. I knew that age well; I belonged to it and labored with it. It deserved well of its country. It was very like the present, but without the experience of the present, and forty years of experience in government is worth a century of book-reading. . . . I am certainly not an advocate for frequent and untried changes in laws and constitutions. . . . But I know also that laws and institutions must go hand in hand with the progress of the human mind. As that becomes more developed, more enlightened, as new discoveries are made, new truths disclosed, and manners and opinions change with the change of circumstances, institutions must advance also, and keep pace with the times. We might as well require a man to wear still the coat which fitted him when a boy, as civilized society to remain ever under the regimen of their barbarous ancestors.

Early in his retirement Jefferson wrote:

I HAVE INDEED two great measures at heart, without which no republic can maintain itself in strength. (1) That of general education, to enable every man to judge for himself what will secure or endanger his freedom. (2) To divide every county into hundreds, of such size that all children of each will be within reach of a central school in it. But this division looks to many other fundamental provisions. Every hundred, besides a school, should have a justice of the peace, a constable and a captain of militia. These officers, or some others within the hundred, should be a corporation to manage all its concerns, to take care of its roads, its poor and its police by patrols, etc. . . . These little republics would be the main strength of the great one.

These "hundreds," patterned on the idea of the New England town meeting, were in line with Jefferson's basic premise of keeping government as near as possible to the grass roots—of placing in central government only those functions which local government could not perform. But his main interest in these political subdivisions was in relation to an educational program which he described to Peter Carr as follows:

ELEMENTARY SCHOOLS:

It is highly interesting to our country, and it is the duty of its functionaries, to provide that every citizen in it should receive an education proportioned to the condition and pursuits of his life. The mass of our citizens may be divided into two classes—the laboring and the learned. The laboring will need the first grade of education to qualify them for their pursuits and duties; the learned will need it as a foundation for further acquirements. A plan was formely proposed to the legislature of this state for laying off every county into hundreds or wards of five or six miles square, within each of which should be a school for the education of the children of the ward, wherein they should receive three years' instruction gratis, in reading, writing, arithmetic as far as fractions, the roots and ratios, and geography. . . .

GENERAL SCHOOLS:

At the discharging of the pupils from the elementary schools, the two classes separate—those destined for labor will engage in the business of agriculture, or enter into apprenticeships to such handicraft art as may be their choice; their companions, destined to the pursuits of science, will proceed to the college, which will consist, first, of general schools, and, second, of professional schools. The general schools will constitute the second grade of education. . . .

All the branches . . . of useful science ought to be taught in the general schools. . . . These sciences may be arranged into three departments, not rigorously scientific, indeed, but sufficiently so for our purposes. These are, (1) Language; (2) Mathematics; (3) Philosophy.

Jefferson continued to outline a specific curriculum for the general schools. The language department would teach history, belles-lettres, rhetoric and oratory and embrace a school for the deaf, dumb and blind. The mathematics department would include, in addition to pure mathematics, the subjects of physics, chemistry, botany, zoology, anatomy, the theory of medicine. Philosophy would embrace ideology, ethics, government, political economy and the law of nature and nations. After the general schools would come:

PROFESSIONAL SCHOOLS:

At the close of this course the students separate; the wealthy retiring, with a sufficient stock of knowledge to improve themselves to any degree to which their views may lead them, and the professional section to the professional schools, constituting the third grade of education, and teaching the particular sciences which the individuals of this section mean to pursue with more minuteness and detail. . . . In these professional schools each science is to be taught in the highest degree it has yet attained.

There was also to be a fourth type of school, that of "technical philosophy" to which:

. . . WILL COME THE MARINER, carpenter, shipwright, pump-maker, clockmaker, machinist, optician, metallurgist, founder, cutler, druggist, brewer, vintner, distiller, dyer, painter, bleacher, soapmaker, tanner, powder maker, saltmaker, glass-maker, to learn as much as shall be necessary to pursue their art understandingly. . . .

Through the whole of the collegiate course, at the hours of recreation on certain days, all the students should be taught the manual exercise; military evolutions and maneuvers should be under a standing organization as a military corps, and with proper officers to train and command them.

Jefferson's outline of an educational system was written when there was no program of general education in the United States. He accurately forecast the system of elementary, liberal arts, professional and vocational schools that would ultimately develop— even to an embryonic ROTC.

Although Jefferson referred to "children" in his educational plan, he really meant boys. Women could not vote, so girls needed no such preparation for self-government. Of their education he said:

A PLAN OF FEMALE EDUCATION has never been a subject of systematic contemplation with me. It has occupied my attention so far only as the education of my own daughters occasionally required. . . . A great obstacle to good education is the inordinate passion prevalent for novels, and the time lost in that reading which should be instructively employed. When this poison infects the mind, it destroys its tone and revolts it against wholesome reading. Reason and fact, plain and unadorned, are rejected. Nothing can engage attention unless dressed in all the figments of fancy, and nothing so bedecked comes amiss. The result is a bloated imagination, sickly judgment, and disgust towards all the real businesses of life. . . .

The French language, become that of the general intercourse

of nations . . . is an indispensable part of education for both sexes. . . . The ornaments, too, and the amusements of life, are entitled to their portion of attention. These, for a female, are dancing, drawing and music. The first is a healthy exercise, elegant, and very attractive for young people. Every affectionate parent would be pleased to see his daughter qualified to participate with her companions and without awkwardness, at least, in the circles of festivity of which she occasionally becomes a part. It is a necessary accomplishment, therefore, although of short use; for the French rule is wise, that no lady dances after marriage. This is founded in solid physical reasons, gestation and nursing leaving little time to a married lady when this exercise can be either safe or innocent. . . . Music is invaluable where a person has an ear; where they have not, it should not be attempted. . . .

I need say nothing of household economy, in which the mothers of our country are generally skilled, and generally careful to instruct their daughters. We all know its value, and that diligence and dexterity in all its processes are inestimable treasures.

So much for the education of women whose place, Jefferson averred to his dying day, was in the home.

When Jefferson interpreted his educational program into a legislative bill it failed to pass the Virginia Assembly. Cost was a factor, as was his provision that the "three discreet and well-informed persons" who were to be appointed as visitors to the elementary schools in each county must not include "ministers of the Gospel of any denomination"; and the further stipulation that, "no religious reading, instruction or exercise shall be prescribed or practiced inconsistent with the tenets of any religious sect or denomination." But the bill did not totally fail. From it came an appropriation of fifteen thousand dollars a year for a university.

Jefferson devoted the final eight years of his life to creating and building the University of Virginia. It was not easy. "Our university labors hard to come into existence," he wrote, and "If our legislature does not heartily push our university, we must send our children for education to Kentucky or Cambridge. The latter will return them to us fanatics and Tories, the former will keep them to add to their population. . . . All the states but our own are sensible that knowledge is power . . . while we are sinking into the barbarism of our Indian aborigines."

Central College had been incorporated at Charlottesville, within sight of Monticello, in 1816, with Jefferson, Madison and Monroe on the board. In 1818 Jefferson, against strong opposition, convinced the legislature that this still nonexistent institution should become the university. Then he wrote a report to the legislature outlining in detail its purposes and program:

SOME GOOD MEN, and even of respectable information, consider the learned sciences as useless acquirements; some think they do not better the condition of man. . . . This would leave us . . . without those callings which depend on education, or send us to other countries to seek the instruction they require. . . . Indeed, we need look back half a century, to times which many now living remember well, and see the wonderful advances in the sciences and arts which have been made within that period. Some of these have rendered the elements themselves subservient to the purposes of man, have harnessed them to the yoke of his labors. . . .

And how much more encouraging to the achievement of science and improvement is this than the desponding view that the condition of man cannot be ameliorated, that what has been must ever be, and that to secure ourselves where we are, we must tread with awful reverence in the footsteps of our fathers. This doctrine is the genuine fruit of the alliance between church and state; the tenants of which, finding themselves but too well in their present condition, oppose all advances which might unmask their usurpations and monopolies of honors, wealth and power, and fear every change, as endangering the comforts they now hold.

The report continued with a proposed program of studies and suggestions for tuition, diet, lodging and discipline. Of the last Jefferson said, "The best mode of government for youth, in large collections, is certainly a desideratum not yet attained with us. It may be well questioned whether *fear,* after a certain age, is a motive to which we should have ordinary recourse. . . . Hardening them to disgrace, to corporal punishments and servile humiliations cannot be the best process for producing erect character." He hoped to "devise and perfect a proper system of government . . . founded in reason and comity . . . to nourish in the minds of our youth the combined spirit of order and self-respect."

Designing and building the physical plant of the university was the least of Jefferson's problems. When the time came to recruit professors he wrote to England, saying, "We have determined to receive no one who is not of the first order of science in his line; and as such in every branch cannot be obtained with us, we propose to seek some of them at least in the countries ahead of us in science, and preferably in Great Britain, the land of our own language, habits and manners." Jefferson was widely censured for sending abroad for professors, but the worst storm broke when he sought to appoint free-thinking Dr. Thomas Cooper to the faculty. "An opposition has been got up," he wrote. "The serious enemies are the priests of the different religious sects. . . . Their pulpits are now resounding with denunciations against the appointment of Dr. Cooper. . . . But in despite of their fulminations against endeavors to enlighten the general mind, to improve the reason of the people and encourage them in the use of it, the liberality of this state will support this institution, . . . this beautiful and hopeful institution *in ovo.*" He even wondered, "Would it promote the success of the institution most for me to be in or out of it? Out of it, I believe."

It was March 7, 1895, little more than a year before Jefferson's death, when the university finally opened, after a fashion. Four professors from England, who had been delayed by storms at sea, arrived at the last minute and, although less than sixty students had braved the spring mud, the number increased to ninety by June, whom Jefferson described as "a very fine parcel of young men, but so defectively prepared that we have been obliged for the present year to relax our laws of reception."

Jefferson saw, in his last months, the fulfillment of a half century's interest and effort. A few months after the university opened he wrote:

I VERILY BELIEVE that as high a degree of education can now be obtained here as in [England]. And a finer set of youths I never saw assembled for instruction. . . . A great proportion of them are severely devoted to study, and I fear not to say that . . . they will exhibit their country in a degree of sound respectability it has never known, either in our days, or those of our forefathers. I cannot live to see it. My joy must only be that of anticipation.

In 1814, the Library of Congress was destroyed when the British burned the Capitol. Jefferson promptly wrote to congressman Samuel Smith:

I LEARN from the newspapers that the vandalism of our enemy has triumphed at Washington over science as well as the arts, by the destruction of the public library with the noble edifice in which it was deposited. . . . I presume it will be among the early objects of Congress to recommence their collection. . . . You know my collection, its condition and extent. I have been fifty years making it, and have spared no pains, opportunity or expense, to make it what it is . . . which I suppose is of between nine and ten thousand volumes. . . . It is long since I have been sensible it ought not to continue private property, and had provided that at my death, Congress should have the refusal of it at their own price.

But the loss they have now incurred makes the present the proper moment for their accommodation, without regard to the small remnant of time and the barren use of my enjoying it. I tender . . . it to the Library Committee of Congress . . . [it] may be valued by persons named by themselves, and the payment made convenient to the public . . . so as to spare the present calls of our country, and await its days of peace and prosperity. They may enter, nevertheless, into immediate use of it, as eighteen or twenty wagons would place it in Washington in a single trip of a fortnight.

It would seem that this generous and public-spirited offer should receive universal acclaim. It did not. The Senate unanimously passed a resolution to acquire the library, but it ran into trouble in the House. Some congressmen had heard that it contained books that were too "philosophical" in their character; Voltaire's works came under particular question. An amendment was offered instructing the Library Committee, "as soon as said library should be received at Washington, to select therefrom all books of an atheistical, irreligious and immoral tendency, if any such there were, and send the same back to Mr. Jefferson, without any expense to him."

Finally, it was decided to buy all the books for $23,950—probably less than half their value—to start a new Library of Congress. This income helped Jefferson's financial situation temporarily, but he immediately started to build a new library, saying, "I cannot live without books."

Two types of books that Jefferson could live without were grammars and dictionaries. He said that he was "not an adept at the metaphysical speculations of grammar." When asked for an opinion on a textbook on the subject he answered that his free time had been:

. . . DEVOTED TO MORE ATTRACTIVE studies, that of grammar having never been a favorite with me. The scanty foundation, laid in at school, has carried me through a life of much hasty writing, more indebted for style to reading and memory than to rules of grammar. I have been pleased to see that in all cases you appeal to usage as the arbiter of language; and justly consider that as giving law to grammar, and not grammar to usage. I concur entirely with you in opposition to purists, who would destroy all strength and beauty of style, by subjecting it to a rigorous compliance with their rules.

As an example of how slavish attention to grammar could weaken writing Jefferson quoted his own motto, " 'Rebellion *to* tyrants is obedience to God.' Correct its syntax, 'Rebellion *against* tyrants is obedience to God'; it has lost all the strength and beauty of the antithesis." Some advertising copy writer can take heart; Thomas Jefferson, at least, would have approved of "like a cigarette should."

He said that dictionaries:

. . . ARE BUT THE DEPOSITORIES of words already legitimated by usage. Society is the workshop in which new ones are elaborated. When an individual uses a new word, if ill-formed, it is rejected in society; if well-formed, adopted, and after due time, laid up in the depository of dictionaries. And if, in this process . . . our transatlantic brethren shall not choose to accompany us, we may furnish, after the Ionians, a second example of a colonial dialect improving on its primitive.

He had little respect for Samuel Johnson's dictionary. He wanted an American language to develop, and this would happen "not indeed by holding fast to *Johnson's Dictionary;* not by raising a hue and cry against every word he has not licensed; but by encouraging and welcoming new compositions of its elements." And Noah Webster, he said, was "a mere pedagogue of very limited understanding and very strong prejudices."

Jefferson had laid the groundwork for America's most important foreign policy while he was still President. In 1808, he wrote of the revolutionists in Spain:

IF THEY SUCCEED, we shall be well satisfied to see Cuba and Mexico remain in their present dependence, but unwilling to see them in that of either France or England, politically or commercially. We consider their interests and ours as the same, and that the object of both must be to exclude all European influence from this hemisphere.

When Spain's colonies in the New World revolted he was dubious of the ability of a people so long oppressed to achieve free and stable government. He wrote to Lafayette:

I WISH I COULD give better hopes of our southern brethren. The achievement of their independence of Spain is no longer a question. But it is a very serious one, what will then become of them? Ignorance and bigotry, like other insanities, are incapable of self-government. They will fall under military despotism, and become the murderous tools of the ambition of their respective Bonapartes. . . . No one, I hope, can doubt my wish to see them and all mankind exercising self-government, and capable of exercising it. But the question is not what we wish, but what is practicable.

He added:

BUT, in whatever governments they end, they will be *American* governments, no longer to be involved in the never-ceasing broils of Europe. . . . America has a hemisphere to itself. It must have its separate system of interests, which must not be subordinated to those of Europe. The insulated state in which nature has placed the American continent should so far avail it that no spark of war kindled in the other quarters of the globe should be wafted across the wide oceans which separate us from them. And it will be so.

In 1823, when Europe's Holy Alliance talked of reconquering Spain's Latin American colonies, England's Foreign Minister George Canning proposed that the United States and Great Britain join in resisting this threat. President James Monroe asked Jefferson's advice, and the old Virginian surprisingly endorsed an alliance with his ancient enemy. When Monroe sent the Canning correspondence to Monticello, Jefferson replied with a long letter which encouraged Monroe to deliver the message to Congress which has become known as the Monroe Doctrine:

THE QUESTION PRESENTED by the letters you have sent me is the most momentous which has ever been offered to my contemplation since that of independence. That made us a nation, this sets our compass and points the course which we are to steer through the ocean of time opening on us. And never could we embark on it under circumstances more auspicious. Our first and fundamental maxim should be, never to entangle ourselves in the broils of Europe. Our second—never to suffer Europe to intermeddle with cisatlantic affairs. America, North and South, has a set of interests distinct from those of Europe, and peculiarly her own. She should therefore have a system of her own, separate and apart from that of Europe. While the last is laboring to become the domicile of despotism, our endeavor should surely be to make our hemisphere that of freedom. One nation, most of all, could disturb us in this pursuit; she now offers to lead, aid and accompany us in it. By acceding to her proposition, we detach her from the band of despots, bring her mighty weight into the scale of free government and emancipate a continent at one stroke, which might otherwise linger long in doubt and difficulty. Great Britain is the nation which can do us the most harm of any one, or all on earth; and with her on our side, we need not fear the whole world.

With her, then, we should most sedulously cherish a cordial friendship; and nothing would tend more to knit our affections than to be fighting once more, side by side, in the same cause.

Not that I would purchase even her amity at the price of taking part in her wars. But the war in which the present proposition might engage us, should that be its consequence, is not her war, but ours. Its object is to introduce and establish the American system of keeping out of our land all foreign powers, of never permitting those of Europe to intermeddle with the affairs of our nations. It is to maintain our own principle, not to depart from it. . . . But I am clearly of Mr. Canning's opinion, that it will prevent instead of provoking war. With Great Britain withdrawn from their scale and shifted into that of our two continents, all Europe combined would not undertake such a war. . . .

But we have first to ask ourselves a question. Do we wish to acquire to our own confederacy any one or more of the Spanish provinces? I candidly confess that I have ever looked on Cuba as the most interesting addition which could ever be made to our system of states. The control which, with Florida point, this island would give us over the Gulf of Mexico, and the countries and isthmus bordering on it, as well as all those whose waters flow into it, would fill up the measure of our political well-being. Yet, as I am sensible that this can never be obtained, even with her own consent, but by war, and its independence, which is our second interest (and especially its independence of England) can be secured without it, I have no hesitation in abandoning my first wish to future chances. . . .

I could honestly, therefore, join in the declaration proposed, that we aim not at the acquisition of any of those possessions, that we will not stand in the way of any amicable arrangement between them and the mother country, but that we will oppose, with all our means, the forcible interposition of any other power, as auxiliary, stipendiary, or under any other form or pretext, and most especially, their transfer to any power by conquest, cession, or acquisition in any other way. I should think it, therefore, advisable that the Executive should encourage the British government to a continuance in the dispositions expressed in these letters, by an assurance of his concurrence with them as far as his authority goes; and that as it may lead to war, the declaration of which requires an act of Congress, the case shall be laid before them for consideration at their first meeting, and under the reasonable aspect in which it is seen by himself.

Monroe went a step farther, on the advice of his Secretary of State John Quincy Adams, and enunciated the principle of "America for the Americans" independently of Great Britain.

As the early years of the 1820s passed, time was running out for Jefferson. The thought of death frequently crept into his correspondence with John Adams, whom he asked, in one of the last letters to his old friend:

IS THIS LIFE?

> With lab'ring step
> To tread our former footsteps? pace the round
> Eternal?—to beat and beat
> The beaten track? to see what we have seen,
> To taste the tasted? o'er our palates to decant
> Another vintage?

It is at most but the life of a cabbage; surely not worth a wish. . . . When friends of our youth are all gone, and a generation is risen around us whom we know not, is death an evil?

> When one by one our ties are torn,
> And friend from friend is snatched forlorn,
> When man is left alone to mourn,
> Oh! then how sweet it is to die!

When trembling limbs refuse their weight,
And films slow gathering dim the sight,
When clouds obscure the mental light,
    'Tis nature's kindest boon to die!

I really think so. I have ever dreaded a doting old age, and
my health has been generally so good, and is now so good, that
I dread it still. The rapid decline of my strength during the
last winter has made me hope sometimes that I see land. During summer I enjoy its temperature, but I shudder at the ap-
proach of winter, and wish I could sleep through it with the
dormouse, and only wake with him in the spring, if ever.

Sadly, money was running out even faster than time. The depression that followed the war further depleted Jefferson's fortunes.
He was sure that most of the financial ills were traceable to the
hated bank, and expressed himself strongly on inflated currency
and deficit financing:

WE ARE NOW TAUGHT to believe that legerdemain tricks upon
paper can produce as solid wealth as hard labor in the earth.
It is vain for common sense to urge that *nothing* can produce
but *nothing:* that it is an idle dream to believe in a philosopher's stone which is to turn everything into gold, and to
redeem man from the original sentence of his Maker, "in the
sweat of his brow shall he eat his bread."

When the banks suspended specie payment he cried, "The paper
bubble is then burst," and added:

MY VOICE WAS RAISED against the establishment of banks in
the beginning. But like that of Cassandra it was not listened
to. I was set down as a madman by those who have since been
victims to them. I little thought then how much I was to suffer
by them myself, for I too am taken in by endorsements for a

friend to the amount of twenty thousand dollars, for payment of which I shall have to make sale of that much of my property.

He had endorsed a twenty thousand-dollar note for friend and neighbor Wilson Cary Nicholas. When the latter went bankrupt Jefferson wrote Madison of his sad plight:

MY OWN DEBTS had become considerable . . . when our friend Nicholas gave me the *coup de grâce*. Ever since that I have been paying twelve hundred dollars a year interest on his debt, which, with my own, was . . . making deep and rapid inroads on my capital. . . . The long succession of years of stunted crops, of reduced prices, the general prostration of the farming business . . . have . . . glutted the land market. . . . The practice occurred to me of selling on fair valuation and by way of lottery. . . . If it is permitted in my case, my lands here alone, with the mills, etc., will pay everything and leave me Monticello and a farm free. If refused, I must sell everything here, perhaps considerably in Bedford, move thither with my family, where I have not even a log hut to put my head into.

Land values were so low that his only chance of getting a fair price for his property was to sell it by lottery. For this he needed permission of the legislature. A bill was introduced for the purpose, and Jefferson wrote a lengthy disquisition, entitled *Thoughts on Lotteries,* apparently to support the measure:

IT IS A COMMON IDEA that games of chance are immoral. But what is chance? . . . If we consider games of chance immoral, then every pursuit of human industry is immoral; for there is not a single one that is not subject to chance, not one wherein you do not risk a loss for the chance of some gain. The navigator, for example, risks his ship in the hope (if she is not lost in the voyage) of gaining an advantageous freight. The merchant risks his cargo to gain a better price for it. A land-holder builds a house on the risk of indemnifying himself by a rent. The hunter hazards his time and trouble in the hope of killing game. In all these pursuits, you stake some one thing against another which you hope to win. But the greatest of all gamblers is the farmer. . . . These, then, are games of chance. Yet so far from being immoral, they are indispensable to the existence of man. . . .

There are some other games of chance, useful on certain occasions, and injurious only when carried beyond their use-ful bounds. Such are insurances, lotteries, raffles, etc. . . . The insurance of ships on voyages is a vocation of chance, yet use-ful, and the right to exercise it therefore is left free. So of houses against fire, doubtful debts, the continuance of a par-ticular life, and similar cases. Money is wanting for a useful undertaking, as a school, etc., for which a direct tax would be disapproved. It is raised therefore by a lottery, wherein the tax is laid on the willing only, that is to say, on those who can risk the price of a ticket without sensible injury for the possibility of a higher prize. An article of property, insusceptible of di-vision at all, or not without great diminution of its worth, is sometimes of so large value as that no purchaser can be found while the owner owes debts, has no other means of payment, and his creditors no other chance of obtaining it but by its sale at a full and fair price. The lottery is here a salutary in-strument for disposing of it, where many run small risks for the chance of obtaining a high prize.

The paper went on to say that Jefferson was making the appli-cation because "a fair price cannot be obtained in the ordinary way"; the market was glutted with farm land. He added:

. . . WHETHER THE APPLICANT has any particular claim to this protection is the present question. Here the answer must be left to others. It is not for me to give it. I may, however, more readily than others, suggest the offices in which I have served. I came of age in 1764, and was soon put into the nomination of justice of the county in which I live, and at the first election following I became one of its representatives in the legislature.

I was thence sent to the old Congress.

Then employed two years . . . on the revisal and reduction to a single code of the whole body of the British statutes, the acts of our Assembly, and certain parts of the common law;

Then elected Governor.

Next to the legislature, and to Congress again.

Sent to Europe as Minister Plenipotentiary.

Appointed Secretary of State to the new government.

Elected Vice-President, and

President.

And lastly, a Visitor and Rector of the University.

In these different offices, with scarcely any interval between them, I have been in the public service now sixty-nine years . . .

After reminding the Assembly of his services and accomplishments, Jefferson's plea concluded:

AND WHAT REMUNERATION do I ask? Money from the treasury? Not a cent. I ask nothing from the earnings or labors of my fellow citizens. I wish no man's comforts to be abridged for the enlargement of mine. For the services rendered on all occasions, I have been always paid to my full satisfaction. I never wished a dollar more than what the law had fixed on. My request is only to be permitted to sell my own property freely to pay my own debts. To *sell* it, I say, and not to *sacrifice* it; not to have it gobbled up by speculators to make fortunes for themselves, leaving unpaid those who have trusted to my good faith, and myself without resource in the last and most helpless stage of life.

Despite this pathetic paper the Assembly haggled over the request. "It is a part of my mortification," wrote Jefferson, "to perceive that I had so far overvalued myself as to have counted on it with too much confidence. I see in the failure of this hope a deadly blast of all my peace of mind, during my remaining days." Finally the lottery bill was passed by a slim margin, but the shares did not sell. Jefferson's grandson went north to seek relief. The mayor of New York collected eight thousand, five hundred dollars. Baltimore contributed three thousand dollars, Philadelphia five thousand dollars. There were glowing promises of more to come, and Jefferson died thinking that his home had been saved. He was wrong. The promises never materialized, and his daughter and her family were forced to leave their home shortly after Jefferson's death. Monticello, for almost a century, was in the hands of strangers or deserted and dilapidated. Incredibly, Congress never saw fit to make it a national monument. Not until 1923 did a group of prominent Americans form the Thomas Jefferson Memorial Association and raise funds to purchase and refurbish the house.

Death came quietly for Thomas Jefferson. His family was scarcely aware of his increasing debility. He continued to write a few letters. When asked by the father of a young namesake for a letter of advice to the boy, he penned these words:

THIS LETTER WILL, to you, be as one from the dead. The writer will be in the grave before you can weigh its counsels. Your affectionate and excellent father has requested that I would address to you something which might possibly have a favorable influence on the course of life you have to run, and I, too, as a namesake, feel an interest in that course. Few words will be necessary, with good dispositions on your part. Adore God. Reverence and cherish your parents. Love your neighbor as yourself, and your country more than yourself. Be just. Be true. Murmur not at the ways of Providence. So shall the life into which you have entered be the portal to one of eternal and ineffable bliss. And if to the dead it is permitted to care for the things of this world, every action of your life will be under my regard. Farewell.

To this he added a list of homilies reminiscent of his friend Franklin's *Poor Richard*:

A DECALOGUE OF CANONS FOR OBSERVATION IN PRACTICAL LIFE

1. Never put off till tomorrow what you can do today.
2. Never trouble another for what you can do yourself.
3. Never spend your money before you have it.
4. Never buy what you do not want, because it is cheap; it will be dear to you.
5. Pride costs us more than hunger, thirst and cold.
6. We never repent of having eaten too little.
7. Nothing is troublesome that we do willingly.
8. How much pain have cost us the evils which have never happened.
9. Take things always by their smooth handle.
10. When angry, count ten before you speak; if very angry, a hundred.

His last piece of writing was, according to his great-granddaughter, a poem which he wrote to his daughter Martha Randolph, titled "A Deathbed Adieu from Th. J. to M. R.":

Life's visions are vanished, its dreams are no more;
Dear friends of my bosom, why bathed in tears?
I go to my fathers, I welcome the shore
Which crowns all my hopes or which buries my cares.
Then farewell, my dear, my lov'd daughter, adieu!
The last pang of life is in parting from you!
Two seraphs await me long shrouded in death;
I will bear them your love on my last parting breath.

The two seraphs referred to are his wife and his younger daughter Maria, who had died in 1804.

The end came on the fiftieth anniversary of the adoption of his famous Declaration and two hours before his fellow signer, John Adams, passed away in Massachusetts. His oldest grandson described his death to biographer Henry Randall:

ON MONDAY, the third of July, his slumbers were evidently those of approaching dissolution; he slept until evening, when upon awaking he seemed to imagine it was morning, and remarked that he had slept all night without being disturbed— "This is the Fourth of July." He soon sunk again into sleep, and on being aroused at nine to take his medicine, he remarked in a clear distinct voice, "No, Doctor, nothing more." The omission of the dose of laudanum administered every night during his illness caused his slumbers to be disturbed and dreamy; he sat up in his sleep and went through all the forms of writing, spoke of the Committee of Safety, saying it ought to be warned. As twelve o'clock at night approached, we anxiously desired that his death should be hallowed by the anniversary of independence. At fifteen minutes before twelve we stood noting the minute hand of the watch, hoping a few minutes of prolonged life. At four A.M. he called the servants in attendance, with a strong and clear voice, perfectly conscious of his wants. He did not speak again. . . . He ceased to breathe, without a struggle, fifty minutes past meridian—July 4, 1826. I closed his eyes with my own hands. He was at all times, during his illness, perfectly assured of his approaching end, his mind ever clear, and at no moment did he evince the least solicitude about the result; he was as calm and composed as when in health. He died a pure and good man. It is for others to speak of his greatness.

Jefferson was buried, quietly, by his family and neighbors, in the burial ground on the mountainside at Monticello. This was as he wished it. His wishes were also followed for the monument and epitaph which he had drawn and described:

ON THE GRAVE, a plain die or cube of three ft. without any moldings, surmounted by an obelisk of six-ft. height, each of a single stone: on the faces of the obelisk the following inscription, and not a word more:

Here was buried
Thomas Jefferson
Author of the Declaration of American Independence,
Of the Statute of Virginia for Religious Freedom,
And Father of the University of Virginia.

Born Apr. 1, 1743 O.S.
Died July 4, 1826

INDEX

☙

Academy of Natural Sciences, 231
Adams, Abigail, 94, 174, 232
Adams, Henry, 31
Adams, John, 2, 4, 5, 9, 12n., 27,
    28, 35, 72, 74, 76, 88, 89, 90,
    112, 114, 121, 124, 126, 134,
    135, 155, 156, 157, 158, 159,
    160, 167, 170, 171, 172, 174,
    177, 201, 207, 210, 217, 219,
    264, 270, 271, 288, 295
  appointed to Court of St. James,
    91
  letter to Thomas Jefferson, 136
Adams, John Quincy, 135, 147, 288
Adams, Sam, 6, 7, 22
Africa, 11, 261
Alabama, 188
Albemarle, 252
Albemarle County, 35
Albermarle County Agricultural So-
    ciety, 254
Alien and Sedition Acts, 163, 164,
    165
Allegheny Mountains, 187
American Philosophical Society, 199
Amherst, 81
Amsterdam, 114
Ana, 127, 128, 143, 150
Anabasis, 205
Anacreon, 205
Anglicans, 77
Antifederalists, 119, 123, 126
Antoninus, 206, 214

d'Anville, Duchesse, 96
Argos, 63
Aristotle, 23, 198
Arnold, Benedict, 80, 83
Arrian, 205
Articles of Confederation, 32, 110
Attica, 63

Bacon, Francis, 127
Bailis, 47
Bank of the United States, 132, 178
Banneker, Benjamin, 261
de Barbe-Marbois, Marquis, 97, 99,
    100
Bastille, the, 116
Baths of Diocletian, 251
Bellamy, 160
Bill of Rights, 24, 164
Blackstone, 64
Blenheim, 50, 79
Blue Ridge Mountains, 33
Bolingbroke, Lord, 202
Boston, 8, 21, 22, 69, 88, 144
Boston Port Bill, 65
Boston Tea Party, 69
Botetourt, Lord, 59
Bowyer, T., 48
Bramer, 47
Breckenridge, John, 166
British Parliament, 57, 74
Browere, Mr., 241
Bryant, William Cullen, 232
de Buffon, Comte, 223, 226, 227